SONS OF THE BRAVE

SONS OF THE BRAVE
The Story of Boy Soldiers

A. W. COCKERILL

LEO COOPER IN ASSOCIATION WITH
SECKER & WARBURG

First published in Great Britain in 1984 by Leo Cooper
in association with Martin Secker & Warburg Ltd.,
54 Poland St, London W1V 3DF

ISBN 0-436-10294-3

Photoset by Rowland Phototypesetting Ltd
Bury St Edmunds, Suffolk
Printed in Great Britain by St Edmundsbury Press
Bury St Edmunds, Suffolk

CONTENTS

LIST OF ILLUSTRATIONS

1. The Royal Hibernian Military School, Phoenix Park, Dublin. Muster Parade (c. 1898). (The Military History Society of Ireland)

2. Royal Hibernian 'old sweat' with pensioner of the Royal Irish Pensioners' Hospital, Dublin (c. 1898). (The Military History Society of Ireland)

3. Two brothers in the Duke of York's Royal Military School, Dover—1940.

4. Brothers in Arms, England 1943. Ages 18, 17, 14 and 13 years.

5. Duke of York's Dover, 1981. Trooping the colour. (Dover Express and East Kent News)

6. Army Technical School, Arborfield, 1946. Passing out Parade. The Inspecting Officer is Field-Marshal Lord Montgomery. (British Army)

7. Army apprentices at lunch (c. 1947). The gentleman in the trilby is Emanuel Shinwell, MP, who was a conscientious objector and Minister of War, 1945. (British Army)

8. Pay parade at Army Technical College, Arborfield, 1980. (British Army)

9. Boys' Troop, Mounted Squadron, Corps of Royal Engineers, 1936. (Mr. Don Luckett)

10. Boy Bob Kennelly, second from right, with companions of RAOC in walking out dress (c. 1965). (Mr. R. Kennelly)

11. Boy Robt. C. Thompson, Canadian Army, enlisted aged 13 during World War 1. He was a Sgt Major when armistice was signed. (Alan R. Capan collection)

12. Trumpeters J. J. Dobbs and Greenhow, RA, on arrival in Quetta, India, April 1930. (Major J. J. Dobbs)

13. Trumpeters of the Royal Artillery Depot, Woolwich, 1929. (Major J. J. Dobbs)

14. Pte Walter Beck, aged 15, of the Nova Scotia Regiment, 1918. (Walter Beck)

15. Sample of the Army First-Class Certificate of Education awarded to soldiers in the 1920s.

16. Boy Kennelly, far left, with companions of RAOC 'junior soldiers' in fatigue dress (c. 1965). (Mr R. Kennelly)

17. Recruit Apprentice Tradesman during room inspection by Sgt K. S. Edwards, RE.

18. Boy recruits of the 5th Batt. Rifle Brigade during the 1914–18 war. (Frank Ebdon)

AUTHOR'S NOTE

There are well over a quarter million ex-boy soldiers scattered around the world; a good many of them are still in uniform. There are also many thousands of boy soldiers in training (certainly in the British and Australian armies), although they are known by any name but that of 'boy soldiers'. This is an exceedingly high number which, if anywhere near accurate, as I believe it to be, makes them a large identifiable body of soldiers and ex-soldiers.

One is therefore moved to ask why were, and are, boy soldiers so numerous in the British Army? What was their purpose? Of what benefit were they to the army? Why did the Canadian Army enlist so many in the recent past, but does so no longer? And why the Australian Army so few? Why the New Zealand Army almost none at all? What about General George Washington's Continental Army of 1776? (After all, the underage soldiers of the Continental Army were at one time subjects of King George III.) These questions, and many more they raise, are reason enough to enquire into the history of that most junior and lowly of all soldiers.

The adult recruit is for weeks, and often months, disorientated by the experience of military life. He has to accept a lifestyle, a code of discipline and an existence entirely different from any previous experience in civilian life. It is reasonable to conclude that this has been the common experience throughout history, whether he was being drafted for the War of the Spanish Succession, for Wellington's Peninsular Campaign or for service in distant India. How much more so this was for the young boys who accompanied men on active service is something we confidently leave to the imagination.

To my knowledge this is the first attempt to write a history entirely devoted to boy soldiers. There have been some autobiographical accounts of boy soldiering: John Shipp's *Memoirs of the Military Career of John Shipp* (London, 1843) and Captain R. Blakeney's *A Boy in the Peninsular War* (edited by J. Sturgis, London 1899). John Laffin's more recent *Boys in Battle* was, as the title implies, a record of underage soldiers on active service and no more.

In writing this history from the boy soldier's viewpoint I have felt it necessary to refer to conditions already much explained in regimental histories, to refer to battles and wars re-fought many times in history books, but here always with the boy soldier in mind. Background sketches are frequently necessary, to put into perspective time, place and a sense of national or personal desperation.

In this history which I present for the general reader, as well as for ex-boy soldiers themselves and anyone else who has had anything to do with them, I have set out in chronological order all that I have been able to discover. In this task I have been helped by many people. The great difficulty with which one has to contend is the utter lack of organised records treating with boy soldiers. Apart from regimental muster rolls, orderly books and the occasional AGO (Adjutant General Order) dealing specifically with young soldiers, no systematic record of their service appears to have been kept. I say appears because such records may exist, but neither I nor my researchers have come across any during three years of research and enquiry.

The bibliography and list of sources listed at the end of the book indicates the extent of this research. To Robert Kennelly (himself an ex-boy soldier) of Tonteg, Gwent, and Terry Spaeth of Saratoga Springs, New York State, I am indebted for many hours of diligent research.

By advertising the project internationally, some hundreds of letters from ex-boy soldiers came from many parts of the world; from Britain, Canada, Australia, New Zealand, the Republic of Ireland, East, Central and South Africa, the USA, Germany, Belgium, Spain and The Netherlands. To each was sent a questionnaire (see Appendix C). Most replied, though some did not.

To the editors of the following military journals and ex-service publications I express my thanks for publishing my letters of enquiry: *Soldier* (UK), DYRMS OBA Newsletter, QVS OBA Newsletter, *Sentinel* (Canada), *Sitrep* (Canada), *Army* (Australia), *Reveille* (New Zealand), *Legion Magazine* (Canada), *United Services Newsletter* (Canada), and numerous corps and regimental journals.

In 1980, Major-General A. J. Trythall, Director of Army Education, and Brigadier J. R. Smith, OBE, Chief Education Officer, UKLF, arranged for me to tour a number of junior training regiments and army apprentice colleges to interview the training staff. They placed no restrictions on my enquiries, nor did they limit the extent of the tour. To these gentlemen, the officers, warrant officers and NCOs with whom I met, my thanks are due.

In no particular order, the following officers, officials and organisations provided immense help in providing material, references and expert opinion on various aspects of the work. Brigadier H. T. Shean, OBE, Curator, RAEC Museum, Beaconsfield; Lieutenant-Colonel H. C. S. Gregory, OBE, Ghurkha Welfare Trusts; Colonel P. de la Haye, Headmaster, Duke of York's Royal Military School, Dover; Captain H. Corke, Corps of Royal Engineers; Major J. J. Dobbs, Royal Regiment of Artillery; Mr I. D. D. Eaves, Keeper of Armour, HM Tower of London; Mr D. Luckett, Australian Army Public Relations; Mr H. Shaw, Lecturer, Army Apprentices College, Arborfield; Dr W. A. B. Douglas and Professor N. Hillmer, Department of National Defence, Ottawa; Mr E. Dillan, Honorable Secretary, Royal Hibernian Military School OBA; Lieutenant-Colonel F. W. Hann, OBE, and Mr Aubrey Sadler, Duke of York's Royal Military School OBA; Mrs Rose E. B. Coombs, MBE, Imperial

War Museum; Lieutenant-Colonel W. Heard (Curator), Lieutenant-Colonel W. J. Gilling, MBE (Librarian) and Mrs D. Sutherland (Assistant Librarian), Royal Canadian Military Institute, Toronto.

For reading and commenting on the manuscript, and helping correct some gross errors on my part, I wish to thank Professor Richard A. Preston of Duke University, North Carolina; Brigadier H. T. Shean, OBE, Curator, RAEC Museum, Beaconsfield; Lieutenant-Colonel G. W. D. Glover, Army Apprentices College, Chepstow; Professor P. Morton, Trent University, Ontario; and Major J. J. Dobbs. Also, Loretta Beath for helping analyse the submissions of respondents; Doris Speakman for typing the manuscript; Charlotte Cockerill for editing; and Editor Leo Cooper.

Finally, and more by way of explanation than desire to excuse myself for the approach I have taken to this history, I should note the thread with which it is sewn. This is the collective consciousness of the military hierarchy through the ages for the care, succour and education of young soldiers. In this respect the achievement has been profound, for that hierarchy, from the highest-ranking officers to the regimental officers, has demonstrated a far greater awareness of the needs of young boys in their care than society at large.

ABBREVIATIONS

AAC	Army Apprentices College	PLO	Palestine Liberation Organization
AGO	Adjutant General Order		
A/T	Apprentice Tradesman	POW	Prisoner of War
ATS	Army Technical School	PRO	Public Records Office
Bdby	Bandboy	Pte	Private
Bdmstr	Bandmaster	QMS	Quartermaster Sergeant
Bglr	Bugler	QVS	Queen Victoria School
Brig.	Brigadier	RA	Royal Artillery
BSM	Battery Sergeant Major	RAF	Royal Air Force
CB	Confined to Barracks	RAOC	Royal Army Ordnance Corps
CIGS	Chief of the Imperial General Staff		
		RASC	Royal Army Service Corps
CSM	Company Sergeant Major	RATA	Royal Army Temperance Association
CTTC	Canadian Technical Training Corps		
		RE	Royal Engineers
DCGS	Deputy Commander General Staff (Canada)	REME	Royal Electrical & Mechanical Engineers
Dmr	Drummer	RFA	Royal Field Artillery
DYRMS	Duke of York's Royal Military School	Rflmn	Rifleman
		RGA	Royal Garrison Artillery
Fd B	Field Battery	RHA	Royal Horse Artillery
HE	High Explosive	RHMS	Royal Hibernian Military School
IRA	Irish Republican Army		
L/Bdr	Lance Bombadier	RMA	Royal Military Academy (or Royal Military Asylum)
L/Cpl	Lance Corporal		
Lt	Lieutenant	RMC	Royal Military College
Lt Col	Lieutenant-Colonel	RMP	Royal Military Police
Lt Gen	Lieutenant-General	RRA	Royal Regiment of Artillery
Lt Gov	Lieutenant-Governor	RRB	Royal Rifle Brigade
Maj Gen	Major-General	RSM	Regimental Sergeant Major
MGC	Machine Gun Corps	RUSI	Royal United Service Institute
MP	Military Police		
NAAFI	Navy, Army and Air Force Institute	Sgt	Sergeant
		SSM	Squadron Sergeant Major
NCO	Non-Commissioned Officer	TM	Trumpet Major
NSW	New South Wales	Tptr	Trumpeter
OBA	Old Boys Association	WO Doc.	War Office Document

INTRODUCTION

During the month of July 1944 there took place in Normandy a battle of small significance to the eventual outcome of the Second World War but of importance to the history of boy soldiers, for it was a conflict of unequal strengths —though unquestionably of equal wills.

The defenders in company strength crouched in comparative safety in their dugouts for as long as the bombardment lasted. They were armed with Spandau automatics (the German equivalent of the British Bren gun) which they wisely kept under cover, for to leave them in the open, exposed to all the HE flying around, would have been sheer folly. Similarly, the attackers, in brigade strength, remained on their side of the line, awaiting the signal to overwhelm the enemy with superior numbers. The brigade had the support of over 400 assorted field guns; the flame throwing crocodiles and flail tanks of an armoured division; and the armament of two warships standing offshore in the English Channel, the battleship *Rodney* which mounted 16-inch guns, and the monitor* *Roberts* equipped with 15-inch guns. 'In terms of manpower,' wrote Alexander McKee, 'this was quite ridiculous. Carpiquet was held by 150 teenagers . . .'[1]

The capture of the village of Carpiquet and its adjacent airfield was the objective of 'Operation Windsor' which, in turn, was part of the larger battle for Caen during the early stages of the Normandy invasion in the Second World War. Caen, the lynchpin holding back the Allied advance into France and Europe, had to be broken and Carpiquet was the split pin which held the German defence in place. Remove this from German control, the Allied commanders reasoned, and the floodgates would swing open. Eventually that is what happened, but not as a result of Operation Windsor, which was a costly failure. What characterised the battle for Carpiquet was not so much the repulse of the 8th Canadian Infantry Brigade (comprising the Queen's Own Rifles of Canada, the Royal Winnipeg Rifles and the North Shore Chaudière) as the extreme youth of the defending 25th Panzer Grenadiers, who ranged in age from 11 to 17 years.

The 25th Panzer Grenadier Regiment was part of the 12th SS Hitlerjugend (Hitler Youth) Division which had been formed less than a year earlier, in July and August 1943, and whose approximate strength was 10,000 in all ranks. The Division was commanded by experienced officers and senior NCOs and a

*A Warship of the US Fleet in the Monitor Class.

serious shortage of junior NCO leaders was overcome by training and promoting selected youths from the ranks of the boy grenadiers. So, in less than a year after its formation, the 12th SS Division marched into battle. Along the 70-mile-long route, from its forward base to its assigned sector of operations, Caen, the Division was strafed by Allied fighter bombers and suffered casualties. Nevertheless, it took up its battle station in and around Caen, still very much a fighting, if untried, formation. In its first action the Division destroyed 28 Canadian tanks for the loss of six of its own. Chester Wilmot, a war correspondent who covered the campaign, wrote: 'The troops of the 12th SS, who were holding this sector, fought with a tenacity and ferocity seldom equalled and never excelled during the whole campaign'.[2]

Operation Windsor opened with a massive bombardment to soften up the defences. The village, defended by 50 boys, was soon reduced to a heap of rubble while the airfield and surrounding countryside, held by the remaining 100 grenadiers, quickly resembled the worst of the Somme landscape almost 30 years earlier during the first Battle of the Somme in 1916. It seemed impossible that any living creature could survive so massive an onslaught of high explosives. Yet, in less time than it took the troops of the 8th Canadian Infantry Brigade to leave cover and cross the start line, the panzer grenadiers emerged from their ratholes, set up their Spandaus, and then delivered the same scourging fire with which their forefathers broke the first Somme offensive.

Operation Windsor was brought to a standstill and not until another Allied plan was launched and Caen outflanked did those young grenadiers who survived the battle abandon their position. The historian of the 43rd Division, who commanded one of its brigades at the time, wrote: 'The young SS troops were detestable young beasts, but, like good infantry, they stood up and fought it out when overrun.'[3]

Since before the war it had been well known that there was a national movement in Germany to organise German youth, but the existence of the 12th SS Division was something new and not to be equated with the Hitler Youth Movement in general. However, photographic evidence of the reality of the Hitlerjugend soon convinced the British public that what they had been told was indeed true. Many of the prisoners were children not yet in their teens and public reaction ranged from incredulity to disgust. To the majority of people it seemed inconceivable that the enemy could so callously arm and throw its young people into the fray.

It is of course entirely speculative to suggest that there existed in the public mind a psychological barrier to seriously considering the use of immature youths in the conflict. It might well be argued that in total war children are as much victims and sufferers as all other sections of society. Bombs and bullets themselves do not differentiate between the innocent and the guilty, between the young, the old, the crippled and the infirm. However, at the same time, while public consciousness admits to the inclusion of all in the conflict, it draws a sharp distinction between those who may actually participate by reason of training, skill and ability, and those who may not. As a general rule, this distinction rules out use of those below a certain unspecified age. So it will be part of our task to define the meaning of the term 'boy soldier' and to distinguish between public awareness and the actual military experience.

Memories are short and, by convenience or perhaps by some collective self-induced amnesia, it is easily forgotten that the use of boy soldiers is common to all nations. So, far from setting a precedent towards the close of the Second World War, the Germans were following an age-old tradition. The extent to which they followed the tradition at Carpiquet is simply one of degree. The same holds true for the entire 12th SS Division in the defence of Caen; for the legions of teenage girls who operated the searchlights and manned the anti-aircraft defences; for the ten- and eleven-year-olds who dug trenches under fire on the German-Russian front; and for the many thousands of youngsters who served their country in its hour of need—for whatever motives—and suffered accordingly.

What is deemed noble and courageous and self-sacrificing on one side is, of course, often viewed with contempt and derision on the other. The grudging admiration of the historian quoted—'The young SS troops were detestable young beasts . . .'—is typical of what one side may say about the other. We may be equally sure that the veterans of Napoleon's Old Guard made much the same sort of comment about the ten- to seventeen-year-olds who fought on the allied side, including those under Marshall Blücher, and at least two boy soldier regiments, one of Brunswickers and one English battalion. On the other hand, Napoleon's Old Guard was drummed into the valley and up the far slope by its own boy soldiers thumping out the very distinctive French tap 'Old Trousers'.

A great deal of this history, the whole aspect of which has been largely ignored by military historians to date, centres on an investigation of changing values, conditions of service, the treatment boy soldiers have received through the ages and, strange as it may seem in a sometimes harsh and brutal service, the intense concern for their welfare by the military hierarchy. This concern is not at first apparent, especially when we consider sparsely-recorded early military history; but it becomes more obvious from about 1750 onwards.

One further point will be made before we embark on our long journey of investigation. The emphasis of this enquiry must perforce be centred on the British Commonwealth armies in general and the British Army in particular. Some interesting facts relating to other armies will be unearthed during the course of our investigation—the early army of the USA for instance— especially where these facts may be usefully equated with the British boy soldier's experience; the experience of the Hitlerjugend Division is a prime example. But we cannot ignore the existence of the boy troops of the Palestine Liberation Organisation, those of the Viet Cong, the State of Israel, and contemporary 'armies' in Africa, Central America and the Middle East countries.

Also, to put this investigation in perspective, it is necessary to define clearly what we mean by the term 'boy soldier'. In recent years new terms have been coined to describe boy soldiers: 'Junior soldiers', 'Young soldiers' and 'Junior leaders' are phrases now commonly used in British military circles. These are euphemisms evidently coined to avoid the use of the word 'boy', which is perhaps considered too juvenile by the young soldier of today. One can sympathise with young soldiers and the authorities to some degree, for every generation must set its own standards of self respect and dignity. What they or contemporary military authorities decide best suits their status none are better qualified to determine than themselves. It matters little whether underage soldiers of earlier generations—but soldiers all the same—have accepted the term 'boy soldier' or not. Yet, to my mind, 'boy soldier' seems more descriptive of that state of being than any of the current euphemisms. Among those who entered adult service, boy soldiers have for many years been known as 'Rats', 'Brats', 'Jeeps' or 'Badgies' so that, once having left the most junior of all military ranks, they become known simply as 'Ex-boys', 'Ex-Rats', 'Ex-Brats', and so on. Perhaps the question of what term to use would be adequately served by paraphrasing Gertrude Stein in stating that 'a boy is a boy is a boy'.

On a personal note, as contemporaries of those young soldiers of the Hitlerjugend who fought at Carpiquet or who slipped through the Falaise Gap later in the Normandy Campaign, thousands of us who served as boy soldiers before and during the war years thought little of the name by which we went. As much, then, for those who were in a sense kindred spirits of the Hitlerjugend, as well as in deference to what is most generally understood by the non-military reader, 'boy soldier' is the working term to be used in this history.

Considering the all-too-prevalent negative attitude of the civilian population towards the military in times of peace, it is only natural to dismiss as 'not real soldiers' those who, though they may wear soldier's uniform, are obviously not men either by age or physical development (or both). Yet appearances can be deceptive on both counts, as in the remarkable case of James Gray, a marine who served in the mid-eighteenth century. Gray enlisted under the normal age of 18 and served in the ranks for seven years. In 1748 Private Gray landed in India where he took part in the siege of Pondicherry, sustained multiple wounds in both legs and took a ball in the groin. Not trusting, nor even allowing, the surgeons to attend to the wound, he extracted the ball himself and recovered—no mean feat in those days. Returned to England an invalid, Gray petitioned the Commander-in-Chief, the Duke of Cumberland, for a pension.[4] James Gray, it turned out, was a woman, Hannah Snell, who had originally enlisted seven years earlier to follow her lover who eventually fell in battle. Hannah received an annuity of £30 and was one of the few women to become a Chelsea pensioner, for she was neither the first nor the last young woman to masquerade as a man.

To return to boy soldiers, some 15-year-old youths are more robust and physically better developed than some full-grown men twice their age. Physique alone, then, cannot be the criterion by which to judge the fitness of a young male to serve as a front-line soldier. So if one cannot judge on the ground of physique, what about age? If we consider the lower end of the age scale, say a ten-year-old, we would clearly be dealing with a minor. On the other hand, from a strictly legal standpoint, anyone under the age of 18 is a minor in most, if not all, English-speaking societies. And to confuse the issue, as a soldier he is subject to military law, but with respect to civil law as it relates to property rights, legal contracts, *et al.*, he remains a minor.

There is here a contradiction between the application of civil and military law inasmuch as each set of laws, for example, applies to criminal offences. Whereas on home service he would be tried under civil law as a minor, an 18-year-old or younger soldier who commits a criminal offence on active service would be tried in accordance with the same military laws which apply to soldiers of 18 years of age and over. In point of fact, even though the law is applied differently today, boy soldiers, when serving overseas as well as at home, were at one time tried and sentenced according to the same military code which governed the conduct of their adult-serving comrades. They frequently received the same punishment meted out to men, without regard to either their age or boy soldier status.

Therefore it is neither age nor physique but, rather, what has come to be regarded as accepted convention that is the governing factor in defining the meaning of a boy soldier. In more explicit terms, a boy soldier may be defined as a minor less than 18 years of age who is accepted for military service. He is subject to military law (administered these days with due regard to his age) and, therefore, military discipline. In truth, we will find that long after corporal punishment was abolished as a deterrent to crime and indiscipline for the army in general, it was still very much in effect for boy soldiers. For many years in some sections of the army boys continued to be lashed, thrashed, caned and belted. That barbaric punishment the 'drumming out' ceremony, for instance, which may be thought to have ended with the nineteenth century, was not finally done away with until the eve of the Second World War. We will find, too, that some very young children were inducted into the military service. At one time ten-year-old boy soldiers were quite common; nine-year-olds not uncommon; even children as young as seven served in the ranks. Youngsters in this category are not to be confused with what Thomas Carter in *The Curiosities of War* (1860) terms 'commissioned infants', those babes-in-arms and older for whom commissions were bought as an investment, to be sold again like stocks and shares when the price was right.

Contrary to the popular opinion of contemporary society that the notion of employing children in military service is absurd, the practice is still quite common. Witness the use of teenagers and pre-teenagers by the Palestine Liberation Organisation, the IRA and by guerrillas in Central America. Yet it is here necessary to draw a sharp distinction between boy soldiers in the sense here employed and those part-time paramilitary organisations, such as high school cadets, who don a uniform once a week and parade at the local drill hall. To qualify for inclusion in this study, boy soldiers have to be, or must have been, regular serving military personnel, clothed, fed, housed, disciplined, educated and trained for military service in a *bona fide* military environment.

At this point it is certainly of value to ask of what earthly use children might be to military commanders, generals, field officers and regimental officers intent on conducting the grim business of war. Numerous are the complaints to be found in official military correspondence that 'these boys are incapable of handling their muskets' much less loading and firing them. In the cavalry, quite apart from the fact that they were no match for an experienced enemy, they had not the strength to wield a dragoon's sword. The same reasoning applied to the artillery: children simply lacked the strength to 'man a gun in action, to sponge the barrel, load the powder and shot, or to manoeuvre the weapon into its firing position'.

Nevertheless, taking all these drawbacks into account, boy soldiers have been a feature of armies the world over for many hundreds of years, so we must seek a rational explanation for this phenomenon. Rare has been the army put into the field for which adequate funds were available for provisioning and maintenance—Marlborough's army during the reign of Queen Anne is a rare exception—so there was no logic in squandering precious funds on a boy soldier element unless there was some return on the investment. On the other hand, to turn from the military experience for a moment, we accept as rational that children raised from infancy to, say, pursue an artistic career—music, painting, literature—stand a better chance of success than those who lack the benefit of such early training. The same may apply to those channelled into a military career. Examples are numerous: Frederick the Great began his military training at the age of six; Marshall Saxe, about whom more will be said in due course, began his military career when he was seven; and among the more famous British field commanders who will find a place in this history are Sir John Moore who was 14 when he began his military career; James Wolfe, Sir Thomas Picton (who fell at Waterloo) and Lt Col Stewart (of the Light Brigade) who were 13 when they joined the army, and Pakenham (Wellington's brother-in-law) who was 12. Indeed, the benefits of an early start in military life, a military apprenticeship perhaps, have held true for thousands of lesser-known commissioned officers and, still more, those lumped together as 'other ranks'. The military apprenticeship is one reason for a career soldier to make an early start, but there is another, more compelling and practical reason for the use of boy soldiers.

In the not so distant past, when nations were small and battles resulted in wholesale slaughter, fighting men were at a premium. Commanders had to cope with loss of fighting strength by desertion, battle casualties and those captured. Anyone not carrying a bow and quiver of arrows, billhook, pike, musket, sword or other offensive weapon did not contribute to the fighting strength of the unit. Leaders needed aides-de-camp and other handy noncombatants to transmit their orders, to carry messages and to bear away the wounded—and this is where the younger apprentice soldiers served a useful purpose. However, they did more than run errands or transmit orders by drum and bugle. They frequently became involved in the fighting when the situation became desperate. The use of the Hitlerjugend in Normandy is an already quoted instance of this.

Finally, there is one further aspect which must be taken into account, and this is certainly a subsidiary, if not a major, reason for employing boy soldiers. An analogy is to be found in the Roman Catholic Church where it has been said of the Jesuits that to be given a child up to the age of seven could be taken as a guarantee that he would be a devout Catholic for the rest of his life. Similarly, give the army a boy recruit till he reaches man service and he will be of that freemasonry of the military establishment until the day he dies. This has obvious advantages to the military establishment because, whether he dies in uniform or returns to civilian life, he will form part of that broad base of support on which military moral integrity rests. This support, in fact, works both ways, for the army has a reputation for taking care of its own, young or old.

Here, then, are some logical reasons for the use of boy soldiers, some explanation as to who and what they are or were. To seek definition is an attempt to explain fact, not to excuse it. For whatever reason, the use of boy soldiers stretches back into the depths of antiquity, so that we cannot point to any particular battle, war or military operation and say: 'Here! this is when they were first used. This is where it all began.' If we are to understand this little written about and much ignored tradition of the military experience it is necessary to expose the bedrock that is its foundation, for boy soldiering is as old as history itself.

CHAPTER I
DEVILS AND DEMONS

THE STUDY OF any kind of history is rather like viewing a jar of viscous oil holding particles in suspension. The upper section is clear but as one's gaze travels down the glass the view becomes more and more obscure until, somewhere near the bottom where the particles are settling, there lies a thick sediment which defies analysis. Mere probing to see what makes up the sediment results in clouds of confusion. It is no wonder that most histories begin somewhere up the jar, so to speak, and military history is no different in this respect. In fact, for most people, British history in general begins with the Plantagenets, Henry I, or, more particularly, the Norman Conquest beginning with the battle of Hastings in 1066.

Fortescue, the most diligent of military historians, is no exception. In his *History of the British Army*, he wrote: 'The primitive national army of the English, as of other Teutonic nations, consisted of a mass of free landowners between the ages of sixteen and sixty . . .'[1] This may have been so, but the ancient Britons were not Teutons, they were Britons. The Anglo-Saxon Teutons formed but one of the many streams which have been poured into the jar which makes up the British people. If we probe deeper to reach a more basic constituent, there we will find the Celtic civilisation. Bearing this in mind, with the glass jar held before a strong lamp some surprising facts come to light.

The Celts, who include the Picts, Scots, Celtic Ligurians, Gauls, Gaels, Bretons and a host of lesser-known tribes, were the largest indentifiable and homogeneous grouping of peoples to issue out of Central Europe in the dim dawn of history. They spoke a common language, worshipped the same gods, and developed an ornate and distinctive emblematic art for their pottery and metalwork. But for one inherent weakness in their psyche the Celts, instead of the Romans, might well have conquered the ancient world and imposed their collective will on it. That weakness was, in fact, the very lack of a collective will. Theirs was an anarchist society which resisted obedience to central authority. Despite their impressive numbers the Celts, in contrast with the Graeco-Roman world, were undisciplined, and this proved to be their undoing. They were the people who conquered Rome and sacked Delphi. But always, on the point of winning great victories, they quarrelled amongst themselves as to who would be their supreme leader.

Pushed further and further west by the Teutons, between 500 and 800 BC the Celts invaded the British Isles. There they conquered the indigenous Hyperboreans—the megalith builders of Stonehenge and similar colossi—and established Britain as the centre of their religious life under the sway of the Druid priests. This centre became for the Celtic civilisation what Delphi was for the more compact world of the Hellenes. (The Greeks believed that the god Apollo originated from among the Hyperboreans.) Branches of the Celtic peoples became firmly established in present-day Ireland, Wales and Scotland, as well as Britain. Their history was never committed to writing during the flowering of their civilisation because they placed no reliance on the written word. Theirs was the oral tradition as noted by Julius Caesar in his *Conquest of Gaul*. Of their religious leaders he noted: 'The druids believe that their religion forbids them to commit their teachings to writing, because they did not want their doctrine to become public property and in order to prevent their pupils from relying on the written word and neglecting to train their memories.'[2]

Despite this shortcoming in their national character, the Celts were a nation that refused to die, and the astonishing resiliency of that oral tradition has provided us with an insight into their social organisation, their history and some of their national characteristics. For example, the Celts relied on a kind of matrilinear succession whereby a man favoured his sister's children in preference to his own because, in that promiscuous world in which women had true equality with men, he could be certain that his nephews and nieces carried his genes, while he could not be certain this was true of his own children. In such a society, therefore, children were more generally assured of 'protection' from their uncles, fosterage was a common practice, and children could always be sure that someone in the tribe would care for them. In other words, concern for children was more widespread in Celtic society than might have been the case in the more common patrilinear society.[3] We will later have reason to refer to this phenomenon in explaining why the Irish, particularly, led the way in caring for the orphans of fallen British soldiers. By the same token, it is the Irish branch of the Celtic civilisation to which we must turn for knowledge of organised boy troops. Indeed, almost as much is known about the Celtic boy troops as about the training of Spartan youths, for the Celts, too, had training camps and sent selected youths across the Irish Sea for additional training. This evidence is to be found in the ancient Irish epic *Táin Bó Cuailnge*,[4] the events of which occurred between 300 and 500 BC.

The Tain, as it is commonly known (meaning 'cattle raid'), has much in common with the *Aeneid* and the *Iliad*, inasmuch as its subject matter lies more in the realm of mythology than in fact. However, although it was not committed to writing for well over a thousand years (circa AD 1200) after the events it recorded were supposed to have taken place, nevertheless, as scholarly research grows more confident in shedding light on the fabric of the

Celtic culture, it becomes increasingly evident that *The Tain*, and similar works, have considerable foundation in fact.

In *The Tain* it is revealed that ancient Ireland comprised four provinces: Ulster, Leinster, Munster and Connaught. Each province (or kingdom) was ruled by a king of kings (as we once spoke of the Persian shah of shahs) under whom there ruled numerous petty kings. Under the warrior King Conchobor, Ulster was bitterly opposed by the combined armies of the other three provinces. The hero of *The Tain*, however, is young Cúchulainn (pronounced Cuhollan), a mystical character with god-like powers of endurance.

As a small child, Cúchulainn begs his mother (not his father) to let him join the boy troops of Ulster. He sets off on his journey armed with 'his javelin and a shield made out of sticks', but he neglects to seek the 'protection' of the troops when he encounters them and so is attacked by them in force.

> They flung three times fifty javelins at him, and he stopped them all on his shield of sticks. Then they drove all their hurling-balls at him, and he stopped every ball on his breast. They threw their hurling-sticks at him, three times fifty of them: he dodged them so well that none of them touched him, except for a handful that he plucked down as they shot past.[5]

With the help of Conchobor, Cúchulainn is accepted, and the boys of the boy troops he laid low revived *with the help of their foster parents* (author's italics).

Some time later, after Cúchulainn has received military training in Alba (the ancient name of present-day Scotland, England and Wales, which survives in the French jibe 'perfidious sons of Albion') he returns to defend Ulster against its enemies. The men of Ulster at the moment of crisis have been incapacitated by an attack of the 'pangs' (the result of a curse put on them by a woman in labour whom they abused) and are consequently unable to defend the provinces. Cúchulainn, then only 17, holds the river crossing alone against the mighty host, just as brave Horatius in Roman history held the bridge. Cúchulainn fights the enemies of Ulster until even he must rest from his labours. While he sleeps for three days and three nights the boy troops (not affected by the curse of the pangs) march south to his assistance. When he awakes, his guardian warrior (guardian angel) tells him what happened.

> The boy troops came south from Emain Macha, three times fifty sons of Ulster kings, led by Follamain, Conchobor's son, and they fought three battles with the armies in the three days and three nights you slept, and they slew three times their own number. All the boy troops perished except Follamain mac Conchobor. Follamain swore to take home Aillil's head, but that was no easy thing, and he too was killed.
>
> 'Stay with us tonight', Cúchulainn said, 'and we'll avenge the boy troops together.'[6]

But this the guardian warrior would not do. He took his departure, leaving Cúchulainn, hero of *The Tain*, to engage in one final, grand 'donnybrook' before he too went the way of all flesh. Mythology or not, there has been no shortage of boy warriors since Cúchulainn and if there were to be a patron saint of boy soldiers it would undoubtedly be St Cúchulainn.

Before we take our leave of the boy troops of Ulster there is one final observation to make. The legend speaks of Cúchulainn's piercing war-cry. 'He uttered his warrior's scream on high . . . so that every living man in Ulster heard it, except those that lay asleep.'[7] The war-paint of many tribes has been used to strike fear into the hearts of enemies and all soldiers have been known to shout their way into battle, but the war-cry of the Celts was evidently particularly daunting, for it impressed many of their foes. Polybius (*The Punic Wars*) noted: 'The Gaels had innumerable horns and trumpets; and at the same time the whole army set up such a shouting that not only the instruments and the warriors but the hills around seemed to be raising their voices in echo.'[8] This war-cry was still very much in evidence in the nineteenth century, for the Royal Irish Fusiliers were nicknamed 'The Faughs' on the strength of their triumphant battle whoop shortly after their formation during the Napoleonic Wars.

Much of our knowledge of the Celts comes from the writings of ancient Roman and Greek scholars—Plutarch, Livy, Herodotus, Pliny, Caesar, Appian, Justinus, Pomponius Mela—who, not unnaturally, were biased. But the Mediterranean peoples were certainly not behind the times in the tradition of using boy soldiers in their military formations. We know enough from Thucydides (*Peloponnesian Wars*), Xenophon (*Return of the Ten Thousand*) and Plutarch (*Plutarch's Lives*) to accept as reliable the evidence that the Greeks and Romans used apprentice soldiers. They served as servants to the Greek hoplite infantrymen, provided music to the warriors of Roman legions and, no doubt, acted as stretcher-bearers to bear away the wounded from the field of battle.

Writing of the battle of Mantinea (418 BC) between the Argives and Lacedaemonians (Spartans), Thucydides told of the young musicians who accompanied the adult warriors into battle.

> They joined battle, the Argives and their allies advancing with haste and fury, and the Lacedaemonians slowly and to the music of many flute players, a standing institution in their army which has nothing to do with religion but is meant to make them advance slowly, stepping in time, without breaking their order, as large armies are apt to do in the moment of engaging.[9]

Sparta, the nation whose reputation for making war is synonymous with 'military state', was said to have trained its warriors from the cradle. New-born infants of Spartan society were put outside for the night and those who survived were then considered fit to endure 'the Spartan life'. There is, too, the story—which I heard in my own youth, but which I have been unable to locate in any literature—of the Spartan boy of a military training school who stole a chicken and hid it beneath the folds of his garments to avoid detection. He was stopped and questioned, but uttered not a sound while the frantic bird tore out his entrails.

Similarly, the Macedonians trained their young soldiers from an early age. In his 'Life of Alexander', Plutarch wrote:

> While Philip [Alexander's father] went on his expedition against the Byzantines, he left Alexander, then sixteen years old, his lieutenant in Macedonia, committing the charge of his seal to him; who, not to sit idle, reduced the rebellious Maedi, and having taken their chief town by storm, drove out the barbarous inhabitants, and planting a colony of several nations in their room [place], called the place after his own name, Alexandropolis.[10]

We have, then, established that boy soldiering, far from being a relatively new phenomenon, has a broad base, being recognised, practised and encouraged by the armies of antiquity. The Greeks, Romans, Celts all trained and used boy soldiers. Even during the so-called 'dark ages' of Europe and the long decline of the Roman Empire to the rise of Charlemagne the practice flourished. Cormac, the Irish Celtic king of kings (about AD 250), established colleges of military science, history, law and literature at Tara, Ireland; and the Arthurian legends (which are Welsh Celtic in origin) tell of King Arthur drawing the sword Excalibur from the rock when still a boy. This is not to suggest, much less to prove, that King Arthur was a boy soldier but rather to establish the general acceptance of youthful warriors—be they aristocratic of plebeian in origin. The Arthurian legends, being of Celtic origin, do, of course, predate the rise of medieval armies from about the eleventh century.

CHAPTER II
MEDIEVAL APPRENTICE
SOLDIERS

IN THE ARMOURIES of the Tower of London, among the array of jousting lances, plate armour, maces, pikes and other grim instruments of war, there is a glass case which contains an exceptionally small suit of half-armour. That is, it is a composite half-armour for a boy of about eight years of age. The helmet is German, the rest Italian (*c.* 1560). The armour consists of a long-waisted cuirass (the breastplate has movable gussets, a hinged lance rest, and is articulated once at the base); two fauld plates to which long tassets of eight lames are attached by rivets; and fingered gauntlets with pointed cuffs.[1]

Mr Ian Eaves, Keeper of Armour of the Tower of London, expressed an opinion that a boy's medieval armour, because it would have been worn only briefly and was not likely to have been handed down and worn out, had a high chance of survival. Later generations of owners would have preserved it not only as a charming curiosity but as an historic relic of the original owner. For this reason, he suggests, and in proportion to the total number of men's suits made more boys' armour survived because of its curiosity value. Further, the Keeper of Armour contends, if the total number of suits in existence was known it would probably give a distorted picture of the actual number that were made.

Although we know very little of medieval warfare, we know enough to get some idea of the part played in it by boy soldier apprentices. Fortescue has already been noted as mentioning the composition of King Harold's housecarls (aged 16 to 60) in the Anglo-Saxon army at the time of the Norman invasion in 1066. By our definition, then, underage soldiers formed part of the Anglo-Saxon army's front line troops.

It is worth noting that the Norman Conquest was not simply a contest between the Normans and Anglo-Saxons, as almost all historians have led us to believe. A good third of William's invading army was composed of Bretons from Brittany, the descendants of those West Country and Welsh Celts who had been pushed out by the invading Angles and Saxons, and who emigrated back to continental Europe to carve out a new home for themselves in Brittany (Little Britain). They had long memories—as was to be expected of a people who still relied on the oral tradition—and even though they came for plunder and adventure they undoubtedly seized the opportunity to wipe off old scores. In fact, the Norman Conquest was more successful than it might have been because of the help received from the West Country and Welsh cousins of the Bretons, among whom there was then still a common language. Did the Bretons bring their boy troops with them? There is no direct evidence that they did but it is quite likely. Whatever the case, this fusing of the Celts, Normans and Anglo-Saxons which occurred over the following centuries, to which later must be added the Scots and Irish Celts, produced that combination which I prefer to regard as the true beginning of the invincible succession of British armies and British peoples. They all had something to contribute: the Normans provided leadership and organisation; the Anglo-Saxons staying power; and the Celts a fiery imagination and astonishing vitality.

Early in the new century Henry I was on the Continent with an army of English and Norman knights to fight Robert of Normandy. Henry, the first of the Plantagenets, developed the English line of battle with dismounted knights drawn up in line, but in depth, and flanked by two wedges of archers. This combination was further developed by Richard Cœur de Lion who was able to draw on the national militia for his crusades in the Holy Land. Richard was the first to employ a paid army, which was a unique innovation in its day. He also copied the Saracens in using trumpets and drums for making music for military purposes and not particularly to while away the time between battles. Richard's minstrels were part of the battle line (as opposed to camp followers) and were used to 'indicate the rallying point'; for

> though at ordinary times the standards sufficed to show men the places of their leaders, yet in the dust of battle these were often hidden from sight; and it was therefore the rule to gather the minstrels . . . around the standards, and bid them blow and beat strenuously and unceasingly during the action.[2]

One is reminded of the Irish ballad of Thomas Moore (1779–1852):

> The minstrel boy to the war is gone,
> In the ranks of death you'll find him;
> His father's sword he has girded on,
> And his wild harp slung behind him.

Edward III was but a boy of 14 when he ascended the English throne, but he immediately set forth with an army to do battle with the Scots with whom the English had been warring from the time the Anglo-Saxons arrived on the scene. The English had already been defeated at Bannockburn and the Scots, sometime later, at Falkirk. They were at that time fairly evenly matched. Edward won the next round at the battle of Halidon Hill where 'the English minstrels blew aloud trumpets and sounded their pipes and other instruments of martial music, and marched furiously to meet the Scots.'[3]

For the purpose of this account we may safely ignore the causes of the Hundred Years War which began during the reign of Edward III. Suffice it to say that although he was nominally a vassal of Philip VI of France (a much smaller country than it is today), Edward laid claim to the throne of France, embarking on an enterprise of pure conquest when he shipped his first small army to France.

The composition of Edward's army, which underwent transformation and change during the 20-odd years he was in command, is interesting from the viewpoint of the younger soldiers in its ranks. In whatever capacity they served they were undoubtedly apprentice soldiers. There were two components in the English line: the men-at-arms and the archers. Knights, who travelled mounted, almost always fought as part of the men-at-arms contingent; there were mounted archers also, but they, too, fought on foot. Apart from three of four horses to serve him, each knight employed two pages or more to clean his armour and to tend the horses. A great many of these pages were young boys. What Alfred H. Burne (*The Crécy War*) describes as 'the rank and file'[4] of the men-at-arms were the squires, usually the younger sons of the nobility who aspired to a knighthood. Among the archers there were unquestionably many young sons along to learn the business, for archery was a national pastime taught from early childhood.

It would be naive to suppose that in the days of medieval warfare there existed any clear and sharp distinction between a man and a boy. Those boys capable of drawing a longbow or wielding a sword would automatically take their place in the battleline. However, there was one other category of apprentice soldier, minstrels aside, and these were included in the wagon train as apprentice saddlers, harness-makers, drovers, and the like.

Twentieth-century warfare notwithstanding, only once during the long period of British arms was the superb organisation developed by Edward III repeated, and this was achieved by Marlborough in the early 1700s. There are indeed many favourable comparisons to be made between Edward and Marlborough in the areas of organisation, tactics, the choice of lieutenants, the deceptive manoeuvring of their armies, and transportation arrangements. Edward is reported to have had a wagon train constructed of between 1,000 and 6,000 horse-drawn wagons to transport provisions. Each wagon required four horses, so even accepting the lower figure of 1,000 wagons (employed later in the campaign) there was ample opportunity for apprentice drivers, farriers and harness-makers.

It is no wonder that Edward or his field commanders invariably won the battles they fought. For all its primitive nature, the army he put in the field was superbly provisioned and trained. Marlaix, Auberoche, Crécy, Calais, Mauron and Poitiers are the famous battles of Edward's reign, actions in which hundreds of young boy soldiers took some part. At Crécy (1346) Edward's son, the Black Prince, then 16, commanded the right wing of the English line.

When the Earl of Arundel, who had been commanded to keep an eye on the young prince, sent to Edward for reinforcements for the hard-pressed wing, he received the message 'let the boy win his spurs'. No reinforcements were sent.

At this distance in time it is difficult to realise that in viewing the period of medieval warfare from, say, 1066 to the reign of Henry VIII (1509–47)—well over 400 years—we are dealing with a timespan well in excess of the period the British Army as it is now known has existed. This is, in round figures, 440 years as compared with 330 years.

As pointed out by Professor Richard A. Preston of Duke University, it is important to make a clear 'distinction between forces raised in the Middle Ages and down to the Civil War, and the period after the creation of the standing army by Charles II from the remnants of the Royalist and Cromwellian armies for the Civil War and for the ensuing campaigns on the continent.' He goes on to note:

> After the decline of feudal armies, forces were raised by commissions of array for temporary service in particular campaigns. There was no [standing] 'army' as such. Home defence was the responsibility of the Militia which was reorganised in . . . the reign of Mary I. With some modifications, these 'systems' lasted down to the Civil War.[5]

It is as well that we should take a rather large leap from the fourteenth century to the sixteenth, for over that long period there occurred a steady but certain decline in the force of English (we cannot yet say British) arms. The area of the Continent over which its sway and influence had been established during the reign of Edward III was gradually eroded until only Calais remained. Two factors were at work: firstly, the growing superiority of the continental armies and, secondly, the more important factor, a moral decline in the armies which successive Plantagenet monarchs were able to put into the field. This may seem an oversimplistic explanation of this decline, yet the facts strongly lead to this conclusion. The successes of Edward and his son, the Black Prince, gave rise to a certain arrogance, arrogance led to disorder, disorder to indiscipline, and a breakdown of discipline resulted in defeat by superior forces.

It seems clear that there is a strong relationship between military success and the public acceptance of military operations. Compare, for instance, the astonishing rise of the Swiss mercenary battalions which during this same period brought the long pike into prominence, both as a defensive and an offensive weapon. For generations the Swiss ruled the battlefields of Europe (until defeated by the Swabians and Spaniards in their turn) as the English yeomen had done before them. Public acceptance in the mountainous land of Helvetia was a reflection of this invincibility so that 'children turned out with drums, flags and pikes with all the order and regularity of full-grown soldiers'.[6] And this is the point to be made with respect to the youth of England during the same period. So we must surmise, history being largely a matter of speculation, that as English military prowess waned so must involvement of the nation's youth have diminished to a like degree.

Even so, we can say with reasonable certainty that over this long period of decline (Agincourt and other notable successes notwithstanding) young apprentice soldiers still tramped dutifully alongside, among and behind adult soldiers on campaign. Indeed, it is interesting to note that one of the main sources of boy recruits came from among the multitude of camp followers —the sutlers, merchants, soldiers' families and hangers-on—who have accompanied armies on the march over the ages. Those boys, as Fortescue notes, were employed to carry the men's weapons or harness on the march. 'Such boys, or rather fags, were called in French *goujats* . . .'[7] We will frequently come across the phrase 'a [boy] soldier born in the regiment', meaning the son of a soldier enlisted at the earliest opportunity, for he would then be one child less for the soldier's family to feed, clothe and shelter.

Despite the fact that Henry VIII made a promising start in martial enterprise when he ascended the throne of England, he did not really have the success that would put him in the Edward III class of warrior kings. His major contribution to the army (as opposed to the navy to which he was more favourably inclined) was the creation of independent artillery garrisons in the country's fortresses. He may therefore be regarded as the father of the Regiment of Royal Artillery (Henry VII, be it noted, also had artillery). Henry also showed interest in military music, thereby widening the avenue of employment for young musicians. He 'sent to Vienna for kettledrums that could be played on horseback, together with men to play them skilfully. Ten good drums and as many fifers were ordered at the same time to teach the English ministrels.'[8]

Sending 'to Vienna for kettledrums . . . and fifers' most probably referred to adult musicians, not boys, and frequent references in muster rolls and military histories to musicians could also mean men, not boys. But research confirms that boy soldiers more often than men served as drummers, buglers and fifers. So, referring to the music makers of the army, the inference in this history will be that we have boy soldiers in mind, not fully grown men.

Mary Tudor's sole contribution to our story must be to note that Calais was lost to the French during her reign. Elizabeth I's influence, however, is another matter, even if it has to be counted as a negative one. As one of England's most illustrious monarchs, she has to be counted among the worst of friends with whom hard-done-by soldiers have had to contend through the ages.[9] It is true she had to cope with an almost bankrupt economy when she came to the throne, but her record as a sovereign responsible for the care and welfare of the soldiers of the realm was appalling. She was tight-fisted, miserly and negligent of her troops, not just to those who served but to those also who, released wounded and crippled, were forced to depend on beggary for an existence.

However, her influence was not entirely on the debit side of the ledger. Elizabeth inspired her subjects in thought, word and deed, which indirectly affected the course of national affairs and therefore the military for generations to come. Apart from one important military operation during her reign, which we will come to shortly, there developed during the Elizabethan era an intellectual and philosophical reassessment of the military art of enormous significance. Given the power of hindsight this is no more than we would expect, for new ideas and concepts occurred at this time in all branches of the arts, in music, poetry, architecture, painting, literature and the sciences. It is a phenomenon of such surges in human thought that they occur on a broad front and are not confined to a single branch of artistic activity. Nor does this leap in intellectual activity favour one nation alone when it manifests itself. In the same way that population explosions affect large sections of the globe at one and the same time, all Europe was affected by, and contributed to, what culminated in the intellectual brilliance of the sixteenth century. We have come to know this period as the Renaissance, and in Italy it produced magnificent paintings, poetry and architecture. But Italy was also the cockpit to which numerous European armies flocked to sharpen their military wits and to blunt their swords. That much-maligned Florentine Machiavelli (1469 –1527) wrote his *Discourses* and *The Prince* during the first quarter of the sixteenth century. Nor was he the only brilliant writer on the art of war and political philosophy; other Europeans and Elizabethan Englishmen produced a prolific outpouring of literature on military science.

As early as 1544 Peter Nethan translated Jacopo di Poncie's *The Preceptes of Warre* in which he wrote '. . . the young of England do so flourish in warlike knowledge that they pass all other both Greeks and Romans to this day'. The point of this passage is not so much the reference to the youth of England as to the classical world of Greece and Rome. Other writers followed suit and leaning heavily on the lessons to be drawn from the tactics of the Roman legion, they became altogether too obsessed with ancient warfare. The trouble was that the Macedonian phalanx and the Roman legion were already 1,200 years out of date. Even if the principles of war were unchanged, weapons had changed and tactics with them. Armed with this military theory gleaned from ancient writings, the Elizabethans re-entered the European ring with disastrous results, and their underage soldiers went along for the experience. The Elizabethans also learned much from the Spanish whom they fought.

During the period of Elizabeth's reign when England was militarily weak, and still developing a political-economic cohesion which enabled it to begin its conquest of empire in the next century, the Ottoman Empire under Suleiman the First, Sultan of Turkey, was achieving major conquests. Training male infants in the manner of the ancient Spartans and Celts, the Ottomans created an elite corps of fanatical warriors called the Janissaries. In *The Great Siege* Ernle Bradford provided a vivid description of these warriors:

The Janissaries, Yeni-Cheri, or 'New Soldiers' were one of the most extraordinary inventions of the Ottoman Empire. It is fair to call them an 'Invention', for they were unlike any type of soldier known to history, before or since. The most unusual thing about this corps d'elite was that none of them were Turkish by birth. All were the children of Christian parents who lived within the confines of the Ottoman Empire. Once every five years a general conscription was made throughout the Empire, and all the sons of Christians who had reached the age of seven were subject to inspection. Those who seemed to show the most promise in physique and intelligence were taken to Constantinople.

Christian by birth, Spartan by upbringing, and fanatical Moslems by conversion, the Janissaries were one of the most amazing military corps in history. It was as if the Turks, remembering over the centuries the nature of the men who had defeated their ancestors at Thermopylae, were determined to raise a type of soldier who should combine the most arrogant militarism of the West with the religious fanaticism of the East.[10]

Meanwhile, one of the military operations to which I earlier referred was the expedition to the Low Countries under the command of Robert, Earl of Leicester. Again it is unnecessary to enter into lengthy explanation of the reasons why Elizabeth felt compelled to order this expedition, except to say that they stemmed from the rising tension between the church of Rome and the Protestant movement in Western Europe and Britain. The French and English were already separated by an enmity 500 years old, in which ancient argument, it will be noted, the Irish and Scots Celts favoured the French cause. Although this Celtic support for French aspirations has generally been equated with religious fervour, I am persuaded that the French-Irish-Scots relationship issues more from pre-Christian ties, albeit strongly influenced by religion.

Leicester was desperately short of men for his expedition and had to rely heavily on the press gangs for raising recruits. It is at this point that we introduce 'Drummer' Shakespeare, not that the Bard ever actually held that rank. It is bestowed on him more as an honorary title in appreciation of the services he rendered to soldiers throughout his literary life, for never has a poet more faithfully served the soldier's cause. Shakespeare's work is infused with the military metaphor, simile and imagery. Why he should have dwelt so heavily on the subject of soldiers is a matter for speculation. What is more, his understanding of the military mind is limited to those ranks below that of captain. Military commanders are revealed to us—Othello, Hotspur, Talbot —but without allusion to a knowledge of strategy and tactics. This is important, for it tells us a great deal about the writer himself.

Between the time he disappeared from Stratford where he deserted his wife and children, in 1585, until he resurfaced in London about 1592 (his 21st to his 27th year) nothing is known of him—or is it? It is inconceivable that a man of his genius, with no first-hand knowledge of the subject, should be able to write with such authority on military matters.

Duff Cooper has provided a most plausible explanation,[11] which is that when Shakespeare was compelled to leave Stratford because he was in trouble with the law in connection with a poaching offence, instead of walking to London (a distance of 90 miles) and risking falling foul of the press gangs, he journeyed the 13 miles to Kenilworth to seek the protection of Leicester. It is entirely conceivable that Shakespeare became 'Leicester's jesting player' referred to by Leicester's nephew, Sir Philip Sidney, in a letter to a friend in March 1586. He wrote: 'I wrote to you a letter by Will, my Lord of Leicester's jesting player, enclosed in a letter to my wife, and I never had answer thereof . . .'[12] Whether or not Shakespeare was the Will referred to, in any case it is a clue to what followed.

If the conjecture is accurate, Shakespeare was the messenger to whom the commander entrusted private letters to his friends. Cooper wrote: 'To be his postman required tact and discretion. He would not wish to give the job to a clumsy soldier, nor to deprive himself of the services of an experienced officer. Who could be better than a jesting player who seemed to have more brains in his head than the whole of his staff put together.'[13] Did Shakespeare then slip off to London, foreshadowing the messengers Rosencrantz and Guildenstern? Perhaps; and nor should we overlook the fact that Leicester, a patron of the arts, was owner of one of the six companies of licensed players in the capital, the very one which staged its productions in the Globe Theatre. It was that same company to which Shakespeare belonged, the one which passed to Lord Derby upon the death of Leicester in 1587. Duff Cooper, in his *Sergeant Shakespeare*, wrote: 'it is fair to assume that this was the company which Shakespeare orginally joined and adhered to through life.'[14]

That Shakespeare relied heavily on 'military experience', especially in his early plays when he was forging a reputation in a fiercely competitive world of letters, is clearly evident. *Henry VI* is a long play of inglorious defeats yet, from beginning to end, it is one of military enterprise. It is significant that Act I Scene 4 of the play deals with the master gunner of Orleans instructing his boy assistant. The French are holding the town but the English have penetrated to the suburbs and, pointing to the turrets, the master gunner tells the boy of the English presence. Says the boy

> Father, I know; and oft have shot at them,
> Howe'er unfortunate I miss'd my aim.

Left in charge with instructions to tell his father immediately he sees the English appear, the boy has no intention of obeying his father's commands. When the English appear the apprentice gunner fires the gun and dispatches Lord Salisbury and Sir Thomas Gargrave to the next world.

Either Shakespeare had the opportunity to observe young soldiers as well as men serving under Leicester's command (which is highly likely) or had knowledge of their use 200 years earlier when Henry VI was campaigning on the Continent. Fortescue's only reference to the poet at this period was the suggestion that he might have witnessed troops being paraded and exercised at Mile End under Captain Thomas Morgan. He may have been there, but more likely as a participant than as a spectator, for it is hard to imagine that, given his penetrating insight into the mind of the soldier, he was without first-hand experience of military life.

As with many peripheral matters which touch on the subject of this history, Shakespeare's military connections have fascinating potential for investigation. However, it is sufficient, and indeed satisfying, to note that the youngest and lowliest in the army received some small recognition.

CHAPTER III
A NEW BEGINNING

THE SEVENTEENTH-CENTURY BOY soldier is in many ways an ephemeral figure, a will-o'-the-wisp far more remote than the rambunctious, shille-lagh-wielding boy troops of *The Tain*, whom we at least know of by name, by reputation, by their dress, by the weapons they carried and by their exploits. In contrast, with the exception of Sergeant John Wilson of the 15th Foot, some soldiers in McKay's Scottish Regiment, and a few young commissioned officers, the boy soldiers who served in the seventeenth-century British Army are almost totally unknown to us. In regimental histories (few and far between for the period in any case), names and exploits of the boys, as well as the adult 'other ranks', have gone unrecorded; for the rarely-opened and dusty tomes in military libraries record only the actions and movements of the regimental unit as a whole.

To find the seventeenth-century young soldier, then, especially during the first half of the century, we must make a diligent search of the battlefields of Europe—because we may scan the Civil War battlefields of England in vain for him. Not until we come to the early campaigns on the Continent, in which the English soldier was once more engaged, does his younger companion begin to emerge with any sort of substance.

To understand the boy soldier's condition, his duties and way of life, no matter how slightly, it is again necessary to sketch in the background and to look at some of his commanders. Indeed, that understanding would be impossible without some knowledge of England's quarrels, military exploits, successes and—lest we forget—dismal defeats.

England entered the century fighting under Elizabeth I, who had but three more years to live. During the last 18 years of her reign, her soldiers had campaigned in the Low Countries and learned a great deal about warfare from their antagonists, the Spaniards. On the other hand, England had given Spain a sharp lesson in naval warfare. Robert Dudley, Earl of Leicester, acquitted himself well enough, aiding the fight of the United States of the Netherlands against their Spanish overlords; yet Leicester was only a general of ordinary competence. He was followed first by Lord Willoughby and then by a field commander of far greater stature who, with vigour and imagination, provided that kind of leadership which makes the difference between pedestrian achievement and heroic effort. This was Sir Francis Vere who, with his brothers, led his small army of English, Welsh and some Scotsmen (the Irish had yet to add their strength) in an unceasing struggle against the foe. With Dutch allies under the young Prince of Orange whose father, William the Silent, Philip of Spain had caused to be assassinated, Vere made brilliant use of slender resources.

The fight was long, the issues naked: freedom for the Dutch or subjugation to Spain. For 14 long years the allies under Vere fought the Duke of Parma and his successors, in 1600 defeated the Spaniards in open battle at Nieuport, and for a further three years kept the besiegers of Ostend at bay. Finally, at the instigation of James I, who succeeded to the throne of England upon the death of Elizabeth, a treaty with the Archdukes of the Spanish Netherlands was concluded and a shaky peace brought about. This, in short, was the background.

Vere's army was organised of independent companies of infantry of up to 150 men each. His horsemen were split into troops, or cornets, of horse. Captains of companies were personally appointed by the Queen who, being Chancellor of the Exchequer as well as everything else (for monarchs then were still absolute), personally financed the army at home or in the field. It is evident that a larger contingent of boy soldiers accompanied the companies than came to be included in regimental companies from the time of Cromwell's New Model Army and onwards. This was because there were 10 to 15 'comarado boys' per company in addition to the usual company drummer and fifer. Comarado boys replaced the pages and squires of medieval armies and were of lowlier origin on the social scale. The name by which they were known derived from the system of messing then in vogue, companies being divided into comarados of between 10 and 15 men each. The word 'comrade' stems from the Spanish 'comarado'. To each comarado two or more boys were attached. Their equipment included 'a small hatchet, a leathern bottle for water, a small kettle to seethe meat in, and a bag of salt.'[1] The Queen allowed 120 rations for each 100 men and by the standards of later armies the rations were exceedingly generous. I have said earlier that Elizabeth was a poor friend of the soldier, but in the matter of victuals she was indeed bounteous. A ration comprised 'one bottle of beer [half a gallon by modern measure], one and a half pounds of bread, half a pound of butter, one pound of cheese, six herrings, two pounds of salt beef, and one pound of bacon'.[2] There was no nutritionist present to say what constituted a balanced diet, but this ration list proves that Elizabethan soldiers ate heartily.

When settling into camp after the day's march (and during winter, the non-campaigning season) it was the comarado boy's task to forage for firewood, to prepare the meals, and to find straw to bed down the men of the comarado. If he was to supplement the diet and provide for the comfort of the men he served, an enterprising and efficient boy had to become a proficient scrounger and fowler. It is doubtful if these boys were paid but otherwise they were well looked after. Like the men, they received a fustian doublet, a cassock or cloak for winter wear, a pair of Venetian hose, two shirts, two bands (presumably in place of belts), three pairs of woollen stockings and four pairs of boots. Undoubtedly, they were infinitely better off than their contemporaries in the towns and villages of Elizabethan England.

That they were given wide latitude to forage and short rein when it came to military discipline is evidenced by the experience of John Coopman, a comarado boy present at the siege of Ostend in 1594. Ostend was then in the heart of enemy-held territory. Coopman crossed the sand dunes to catch fowl in the swamp and was captured by a Spanish cavalry patrol. Carted off to Nieuport, he was questioned on the artillery in place in the beleagured city but released on the understanding that he would return to report the positions of the posted sentinels. Upon rejoining his own lines, he reported faithfully to Sir Edward Norris, the Governor of Ostend, all that had occurred. A truthful report should have been sufficient to clear him, but since he had been given strict orders not to go near the dunes over which the enemy frequently patrolled, and also as he had been provided with a 'leaping pole' to move over the marshes where horses could not travel, he was held responsible for his folly and sentenced to be whipped. The matter was serious enough to be referred to the Lords in Council in London, for which we may be thankful, for otherwise Coopman's exploits would never have come down to us. Whether or not he received a more severe punishment than a whipping as a result of any debate by the Lords in Council is not known, but had a Vere, Marlborough or Wellington been in Governor Norris's place the incident would have been used as an ideal opportunity to mount some masterful subterfuge by sending Coopman back with false information.

Two items of interest concerning this first British campaign in the Low Countries are worth noting. The first is that the British and Dutch began their long association as brother-in-arms. There were, however, two short periods in the seventeenth century when their trading interests clashed and they went to war. They shared the common outlook of Protestanism, but were also drawn together into competition by trade and commerce. Secondly, the united English and Welsh had their first experience of fighting side by side with the Scots under Vere. It was a magnificent experiment but not yet the time for making a permanent combination of British arms; Culloden and other fierce battles between the English and Scots were a hundred years or more away.

After the agreement with the Archdukes of Spanish Flanders was ratified during the reign of James I there followed a 12-year truce but, because the Spaniards still held large tracts of territory having a Dutch population that would not submit for long, in 1616 hostilities again broke out. Present-day Holland was then a loose federation of independent states. Under their elected leaders, the burghers, they became the United States of the Netherlands, contributing men, arms and money to the rebellion against Spain, and submitting themselves to the direction of the States-Generals. Their first military leader, William the Silent, assassinated by order of King Philip of Spain, was succeeded by his son, Maurice, who fought his first action at the age of 17. Prince Maurice speedily took over command of the Dutch patriot cause and from 1621 with English, Welsh and Scottish help in men and material carried on the fight. A total of 6,000 soldiers from England crossed the Channel to lend a hand and this number was increased to 17,000 over the next four years. Many Englishmen who later fought in the great Civil War of England received their military baptism under Prince Maurice as mere youths. Philip Skippon and John Cromwell (a relative of Oliver Cromwell) fought at Breda (1625), while others—Doncaster, Throgmorton, Lambert, Astley, Craven and Culpeper—fought in the trenches at Bois Le Duc in 1629.

It is extremely difficult to form any clear picture of the conditions under which the common soldier lived and fought during this period and it is equally difficult to be factual about the younger element of the army. But we do know that in those days soldiers of every degree served their time where they could and whenever opportunity knocked, and thus it is reasonable to suggest that as change in such a conservative institution as the military comes about slowly, then drummers, fifers, comarado boys and drover apprentices must have been among those who served.

Robert Munro, an officer of Sir Donald KcKay's regiment of Scottish volunteers, raised for service in the Low Countries, writing of his youth in the 1620s, said: 'I was once made to stand at the Louvre Gate at Paris, being then in the King's regiment of guards passing my apprenticeship, for sleeping in the morning when I ought to have been at my exercise. For punishment I was made to stand from eleven before noon to eight o'clock of the night, sentry, with corselet, headpiece, braselets, being iron to the teeth, in a hot summer's day, till I was weary of my life.'[3] (Elizabethan and immediate post-Elizabethan soldiers still wore some body armour.)

We are indebted to Munro for knowledge of McKay's regiment because, in writing its history, he had a lot to say about the boy soldiers who served in its ranks. From his description of the regiment's later service, under King Christian of Denmark, it is evident that a large element of the regiment was made up of 15-, 16- and 17-year-old youths who made up in enthusiasm what they lacked in experience. Holding a pass at Oldenburg against Marshal Tilly's French army, the Scots found themselves alone, the Danes and Germans having prematurely retired to fight another day. Wrote Munro:

Ensign David Ross was hit in the chest, but stayed on to fight; Hector Munro of Coull was shot in the foot and he, too, stayed to fire his ammunition while Hugh Murray refused to bear away his brother's corpse until he had emptied his own and his brother's ammunition at the foe. Yet these were young soldiers of so little experience that they left their reserve of ammunition exposed and suffered heavily from the explosion of a barrel of gunpowder.[4]

Vastly outnumbered by Tilly's troops, the Scots beat a fighting retreat. When next we get a glimpse of them, brought up to strength by the indefatigable McKay with reinforcements from Scotland, the regiment had taken service under Gustavus Adolphus of Sweden. McKay's regiment formed part of the famous Scots brigade, joining the regiments of Hepburn, Stangate and Lumsden, all under the command of Sir John Hepburn. In hiring out their services to Adolphus, the Scots entirely separated from their English-Welsh brethren.

Meanwhile in England, James I had died and Charles I became king (1625). Being less pacific-minded than his father, he sent an expedition to sack Cadiz. The last attack on this Spanish port by the English had taken place under Raleigh and Vere in 1595 and was far more successful than Charles's expedition proved to be. The 10,000-strong force sent by Charles included the usual complement of boy soldiers, for there was a continuing need for drummers, trumpeters and fifers in the expeditionary forces of pre-Civil War England. That the boy soldiers were present—and that not all were volunteers—is suggested by the petition addressed to the Lords of the Admiralty by Sergeant Josias Broom in 1637.

Sergeant Broom had appointed one Cuthbert Collins of London (probably a broker contracted to deliver recruits) to search out likely young lads to serve as trumpeters in the King's service. Armed with a commission to press, Collins duly pressed John Digges to take service, but young Digges '. . . violently abused petitioner, calling him a base rogue, and challenged him to fight'.[5] By modern standards it might seem a petty thing for incidents such as this to be referred to that august body of Lords of the Admiralty (the case of comarado boy Coopman was, after all, referred to the Lords of the Council), but we have to remember that at that time those in authority were not as remote from the man in the street as they are today. The population was a great deal smaller and, for all the differences that existed between rich and poor, society operated more like an extended family, especially in London and the sea ports. The Industrial Revolution was yet a long way away so society was more static and settled. One suspects that Digges was prevailed upon to blow a trumpet for the King in the end, there being little choice in those days.

Of greater import to the realm and society at large was the widening rift between the King and Parliament, which culminated in the Civil War and resulted in the creation of the New Model Army. While the reasons for the war between the Cavaliers and Roundheads need not concern us, it should be noted that the seeds of trouble took root during Elizabeth's reign when, in the early 1580s, Puritan political ministers sought to introduce the rudiments of presbyterian order into the Church of England and the nonconformist tree sprouted. But this is a lengthy and obscure story best left to theologians to debate.

At the beginning of the war the Royalists had fourteen regiments of foot and eighteen troops of cavalry, called out by Commissions of Array—as in the later Middle Ages. Parliament had eighteen regiments of foot and eight troops of horse, of which five were troops of dragoons—mounted foot soldiers, that is, who fought in the line as did the knights in Edward II's day. They used their horses for greater mobility only, and they dismounted for action, though not always because cavalry still charged.[6]

Numerically, the advantage may seem to have lain with Parliament, but an over-abundance of men does not automatically make for victory, as small armies both before and after the Civil War have often proved. Victory finally went to the Parliamentary army under Oliver Cromwell, the Great Protector, and somewhere between the start and finish of that war the Parliamentarians discovered the secret of success. That secret lay in discipline and financial control; he who pays the piper calls the tune. The new national army was born with a silver spoon in its mouth, for whereas the Royalists had to rely on private subscription (wealthy though some supporters were), voluntary subscription was not enough. Parliament, on the other hand, had the power to tax, and taxes are virtually without limit, as we know.

With the issue of an Ordinance on 15 February 1645, Parliament authorised and financed the creation of 12 regiments of foot, each comprising 10 companies of 120 men. Each company, in addition to its officers, had two sergeants, three corporals and two drummers. As far as this history is concerned, the inclusion of drummers in the regimental establishment is important, for it set a precedent. Precedent became a tradition and that tradition, of employing company drummers, was maintained well into the twentieth century, a span of over 300 years. What is more, we will find that while the establishment of officers and non-commissioned officers per regimental company varied (and, in the long term tended to increase) the establishment of authorised drummers never changed until they were replaced entirely by modern telecommunications devices.

The drummer had the lowliest of all military ranks—and, in battle, among the most dangerous. It is therefore as well as well to say something about his lowly state, his drum, and the ancient art of drumming. First, the drum, which came in various shapes and sizes but which has changed remarkably little over the centuries. Weighing between eight and ten pounds when dry—considerably more when wet and becoming heavier in direct relation to the distance it was carried—the most common drum was about eighteen inches in diameter and eighteen inches in length. Its light wooden cylinder was covered at both ends by cured pigskins which, stretched and bound on a hoop, were held in place by slightly larger hoops, one on each end. The clamping hoops were drilled with equally-spaced holes and bound together by a single length of thin rope that so formed a continuous V-pattern around the outer surface of the drum. The small end of each inverted V thus formed was bound by a leather pad by which the clamping hoops might be drawn tightly together to stretch the drum skins. The leather pads were known as snares; hence the term 'snare-drum'. Drummers soon got the knack of spitting on the ropes to increase the grip of the snares, and of using the thick end of the drum stick to force the snares down the V-ropes. The further the snares were forced down, the sharper the timbre of sound produced.

The time needed to teach a boy the basic beats varied of course, but six weeks of constant practice was sufficient for even the least gifted child to learn his calls. A boy with a sense of rhythm would take less than six weeks to master the instrument. At the same time, a boy 'born in the regiment' would learn the drum beats long before he was taken on to the regimental muster roll between the ages of 7 and 10. When the New Model Army was first formed there were but five beats to master: the march, troop, preparative, battle and retreat.

Drummers wore the same uniform as the private soldiers, except that there was some variation in the facings of their uniform, a distinction which set them apart from the rest of the regiment, perhaps to pander to the whims and vanities of the colonel. Drummers also had the same accoutrements as the men, except that in place of a musket, pike or other weapon, they carried the drum. This was slung from the buckle of a leather carrying strap hung over one shoulder. The drum, normally strapped to the left leg above the knee to prevent it bouncing against the leg on the march, in foul weather could be turned on its side to protect the skins from the rain.

On the march drummers were placed at the head of their companies, alongside the leading sergeant and behind the company commander mounted on his horse. When the regiment formed into line for manoeuvres, practice drill or on those rare occasions when going into battle, one drummer was posted out in front with the company officer, who went into action on foot. Therefore, in battle, officer and drummer were first into the fray when engaging the enemy.

Regimental drill, or evolutions as drill practice was known, formed a major part of the soldier's life. When manoeuvring into position for battle, the speed with which companies and battalions formed into line, the distance between companies and the accuracy of their movement might mean the difference between victory and defeat. Sloppiness in wheeling into line could result in the men crowding one another or getting into a hopeless tangle. Regimental pride had to be considered, too, for whether in a brigade or wing or army there were always critical eyes watching how this or that regiment performed. The drummers, taking direction from the regimental and company commanders, had to have their wits about them to beat out the correct orders—not an easy task with cannonballs flying indiscriminately about the field of battle.

If the drummers survived long enough to reach manhood—and often before—they exchanged their drums for musket and their places were taken by other likely lads who, in turn, served their time. Odd though it may seem, drummers were for a long time paid more than the private soldier of the line, not because they filled a more important role but because they needed more food to grow and soon grew out of their uniforms. However, the pay was little enough and with stoppages and 'off reckonings' for their keep, losses of equipment and other means by which they were cheated out of the money, the actual cash they received was minuscule. In 1686, for example, the pay scale for other ranks was

Sergeants	1/6 per day
Corporals	1/- per day
Drummers	1/- per day
Privates	8d per day

If a drummer received 8d a week he was lucky.

In the interior economy of the regiment, boy soldiers were treated exactly the same as the men and for a long time (well into the nineteenth century) no effort was made to keep them separated. They shared the same food, the same accommodation and the same harsh discipline. When it came to corporal punishment the drummers served a special role, which we will describe later.

Over the years there was a great variation in the number of drummers maintained on regimental establishments, despite the fact that only two drummers per company were officially sanctioned. To take the 14th Foot (first formed in 1685), a typical regiment of the line, the accompanying table gives some idea of the variation in drummers on strength over the years. These figures, taken at random times, are not necessarily those of the same battalion but they serve well enough to illustrate the variation. It will be noted that a dramatic increase occurred towards the end of the eighteenth and beginning of the nineteenth centuries (at the time of the Napoleonic Wars) when children were inducted into the army in their thousands. This, too, is representative of the general pattern throughout the army.

	Total strength, all ranks	Drummers
1689	617	9
1727	1119	16
1746	359	11
1759	702	20
1807	1249	59
1815	630	11

As the century progressed a steady increase in the size of the army is certain proof that the military hierarchy consolidated its newly-won position, even though there were numerous attempts on the part of Parliament to disband it. This was an important experimental period for British arms in expansion by conquest, particularly in the Americas. By 1650 the colonies of English America were well established and, by reason of the base they provided, new island territories in the Caribbean were won. The Great Protector, Oliver Cromwell, had mounted an expedition against Spanish possessions in the New World which, save for the capture of Jamaica, ended in disaster. As part of her marriage dowry, Catherine of Braganza presented Charles I with Bombay and

Tangier. Nevertheless, the army remained relatively small. John Churchill (born 1650), the future Duke of Marlborough, became an ensign at the age of 17 and served with the 1st Guards in Tangier. He later served under Turrene, the great French commander of the day, unquestionably a master in the art of war comparable to the Duke of Parma and Francis Vere.

Despite the possessions England had acquired overseas there were few places where aspiring soldiers could win their spurs. Like Munro and others before them they went where they could. Such practice after all is common for artists, composers and writers. So why not for soldiers?

However, during Marlborough's formative years there were troubles enough in the British Isles and religious differences were at the root of them. In an essay, George Orwell said that society is in a constant state of catastrophe but, despite the sense of hopelessness which appears to confront each generation, the rate of change from one generation to the next is quite gradual. Orwell called this phenomenon 'catastrophic gradualism'. The year 1685 was no different from any other in this respect. James II was on the throne by then and as secure as any monarch in good health could be. Indeed, there was no reason, given good sense and wise council, why he should not have enjoyed the loyalty of his subjects for the rest of his life. The cause of his eventual downfall was his openly avowed intent to curtail his subjects' liberties and to bring them back, even though kicking and screaming, into the arms of the Church of Rome.

As far back as 1668, when he was the Duke of York, James's vigorous encouragement of the Roman Catholic cause gave rise to a rollicking ballad called *Lillibullero* (which satirised James and the papists) which swept the country. It had a catchy melody and became a firm favourite with the army, especially as it was admirably suited to the fife and drum. Although few people today recognise the name *Lillibullero*, most would recognise the tune which has been played with gusto by the 'spit and dribbles' (the army name for fife and drum bands) ever since it delighted the Protestants of 1668.

After his accession in 1685 James's attempts to change the religious basis of the country by means of the Declaration of Indulgence, by which Roman Catholics were permitted to practise their faith as they wished, led to the Monmouth Rebellion. The Duke of Monmouth, bastard son of Charles II, landed at Lyme Regis on 11 June 1685 to claim the throne and to restore the ascendancy of Protestanism in the country. Monmouth, however, was ahead of his time, for James had not gone far enough to provoke his subjects into general revolt; the army and bulk of the population remained loyal to their elected king. The Lord-Lieutenants of the Western Counties ordered out their militia and six regiments were recalled from Holland to deal with the crisis. All regular troops in the country converged on Salisbury and were placed under the command of Brigadier-General John Churchill.

Lord Feversham was given command of the artillery, specially raised to put down the rebellion. The artillery train assembled at Chippenham, and was joined there by the Wiltshire Militia for its 'protection'. Then the whole assembly moved to Axminster. The composition of artillery trains of the period deserves attention for these invariably included a high proportion of boys. The train raised for Feversham was 255-strong and included gunners, mattrosses (gunners' assistants) and 118 drivers, of whom some 30 were boys. A single drummer was engaged at a shilling a day to serve the entire formation.

The position of the boy drivers was an ambiguous one, for the entire body of drivers and carters (almost always drawn from the rural areas in the vicinity of London) was, and remained throughout any campaign, of civilian status under contract to the army. As far as is known, these civilians were left to their own devices for the purpose of feeding themselves and their horses. Soldiers of line regiments were detailed off to escort and protect the train, but this was as much to prevent the drivers from running away as to guard against attack by any enemy. The sole duty of the drivers was to move the artillery and its supplies to and from the field of battle, and given the deplorable state of the roads that was a difficult enough task. Once the guns were placed in the position selected by the officer of ordnance, the civilians and horses retired to some convenient marshalling area where they were kept under armed guard until further instructions were issued.

Three years later, in 1688, James II raised another artillery train to resist the invasion of William of Orange; but by this time the political situation had undergone a dramatic change. James had become insufferable in his efforts to re-establish Roman Catholicism by turning his attention to the army and replacing Protestant officers with Irish officers. The result was the popular revolt which Monmouth had hoped for three years earlier. James was not an incompetent commander; as the Duke of York he had won two sea battles against the Dutch and acquitted himself reasonably well as Commander-in-Chief of the army. However, faced with the enemy, he had a nose bleed and wanted to retreat. His deputy commander, Churchill, then deserted him and welcomed William of Orange. James was forced to flee to France and as a consequence lost his throne. Had he stayed in England he might well have lost his head.

William, the husband of James's daughter Mary, brought trusted Dutch officers with him and installed them in prominent positions in the army over the heads, and to the chagrin, of the English-born officers. This was no less than James had tried to do with his Irish adherents, but whereas James forfeited his throne the army, headed by Churchill, swallowed the bitter pill administered by William. The difference was that William not only supported the Protestant cause, but was prepared to prosecute it, firstly by mounting an expedition against James's Irish supporters and, secondly, by using the English army he had inherited from James II against Louis XIV of France. To aid the Dutch against France was more to the nation's liking.

Before William could move his English army to the Continent he was compelled to deal with James II in Ireland, where the deposed king, with French help, had gathered an army in an attempt to regain his kingdom. William ordered his master gunner to assemble artillery enough to accompany the army to Ireland and so the nation's artillery—or what could be spared

—was gathered together for crossing the Irish Sea: 16 guns of various calibres, 20 wagonloads of supplies, 186 horses, 36 carters and 36 boys made up the train. On the move it stretched out for more than a mile, creaking and croaking its way over the countryside. It was an impressive sight with the young boys mounted astride the backs of the draught horses, urging the beasts on. These were country boys who with the drivers lived and worked with the forebears of those shire horses, the Suffolk Punch and Clydesdale, beasts which normally worked on the farms of rural England.

The frequent use by the artillery of boys is an important element in the history of boy soldiers. At first civilians, hired and fired as suited the master of ordnance, they became so numerous along with the cadet gunners that it was inevitable something special should be done by the army to care for them. Because the RRA (Royal Regiment of Artillery) was the first military unit to establish a training school for boys, this is an opportune place to explain the composition and organisation of the artillery at the close of the century.

From the earliest times the artillery was under the command of a 'master of ordnance' appointed by the commander-in-chief. Under the master of ordnance there were two subordinate commanders: the surveyor-general, controlling the care and custody of all military stores, and a lieutenant-general who served in the field and was responsible for the 'general efficiency of the artillery, both as regards men and guns'.[7] For operations artillery was commanded by the master gunner, a position of the highest importance requiring a man of experience and artillery knowledge.

Although the RRA was not formed until 1719 its life began in the shape of artillery trains many years earlier, as has been described. Indeed, the first commander of the RRA was very actively involved with artillery from the time he became a gunner in 1676. This father of the RRA was Albert Borgard (1659–1751), a Dane by birth, who began his military career at the age of 16. As a cadet he served at the siege of Wismar (Mecklenburg) with the Queen's Regiment of Foot before becoming an artillerist in the fledgling British Army. It was as much Borgard's influence as anyone's which gave the impetus for the establishment of the cadet training school at Woolwich (see Chapter 4).

The events which occurred towards the close of the seventeenth century set the stage for the Duke of Marlborough's campaigns and British alliance with the Dutch, Danes and German states in the War of the Spanish Succession. One of these events was the mutiny of the Royal Scots on being ordered to embark for Flanders at Ipswich in 1689. As a consequence the government passed the Mutiny Act which effectively separated civil and military law, for that Act affected all military personnel including boy soldiers. Because the Act drew no distinction between those on adult service and the younger soldiers, it meant that all were subject to the full rigour of military law and discipline. In a word, boy soldiers who became disenchanted enough with military life to desert were subject to the same corporal punishment meted out to the men, and there is ample evidence that boy soldiers found guilty of breaches in discipline were punished severely. However, there is also no doubt that the majority of officers and NCOs dealt humanely with their lowliest of subordinates and showed, in the main, extreme consideration. One of the first personal records we have, from an ex-boy soldier, is evidence of this claim and comes from Sergeant John Wilson of the 15th Foot.

Just how old Wilson was when he enlisted on 25 March 1694 is not known. He was undoubtedly under 14 because 14-year-old recruits were common at that time, and even Sir James Leslie, Colonel of the 15th, was taken aback at Wilson's extreme youth. As Wilson wrote, upon his being introduced by a friend, Ensign Halliday, the colonel said:

> 'What my friend Halliday, do you bring me children for soldiers? I did not expect this from You, for You know Wee want men'. Sir James asked whose Childe I was and if he [Halliday] had knowledge of my parents. The ensign [sic] mentioned to Sir James my father's name, whom Sir James knew, and he said he knew my Grandfather also, whereupon Sir James turned to me with a frown, and Said, 'You young Rogue, how come you to Run away from your Parents?'[8]

Wilson persisted in his design to be a soldier, affirming that he had the full permission of his parents. Upon this, convinced, the colonel gave him three months' pay in advance and he was escorted home to finish his schooling. The following April, being paid his arrears of pay, Wilson was shipped on board a transport to Flanders, where, with other recruits, he was inspected by Sir James who asked Ensign Halliday if he was the 'Furloe Boy'. When told that Wilson was indeed the furloe boy, said, 'Very well, take care and have an Eye over him.'

Such was the welcome John Wilson had when he joined the army, a welcome to be repeated frequently over the years for the boys who followed the same path Wilson trod—yet we must neither forget nor ignore that many met a welcome that was less gentle.

Two weeks after Wilson arrived in Flanders the 1695 campaigning season began. Long, wearing marches, bad food, harsh discipline, wet nights, hot and dusty days were all the common lot of infantrymen, trooper and gunner alike. There had to be better days ahead and there were for those who survived. Young Wilson survived his first campaign and many to come, for he lived to tell us of his life.

CHAPTER IV
A PUSH FROM CORPORAL JOHN

A SONG GOOD enough to shorten a long march is a rare combination of words and music. *Lilli Marlene* was such a song; *Tipperary* was another. At the turn of 1700 a new marching song became popular enough to rival *Lillibullero* and found such favour among regiments of the line that it lasted well into the twentieth century. This was *Over the Hills and Far Away*, and its appealing melody is still played by concert bands on Sunday afternoons in the park. The words, which convey a message germane to this history, are worth quoting.

> Over the hills and over the main
> To Flanders, Portugal and Spain
> The Queen commands and we'll obey,
> Over the hills and far away.

> Our 'prentice Tom may now refuse
> To wipe his scoundrelly master's shoes,
> For now he's free to sing and play
> Over the hills and far away.

The lusty flavour of *Over the Hills* is one peculiar to the early eighteenth century and it stirs memories of Fielding's *Tom Jones*, Tom and Squire Western, or the equally ribald characters of Smollett's works. These characters and the song share something in common, which has none of the pious moralising of the Puritans who went before or the lofty grandeur of the Regency period that was to come after. For this reason, no one doubts that Tom's master was any worse than many of his real-life contemporaries. The Queen to whom the lines refer was the younger daughter of James II, Queen Anne, who became Queen of England in 1702 upon the death of William III. Because of her friendship with Sarah and John Churchill—during the early part of her reign at least—the star of the Churchills was soon in the ascendant.

The self-willed but easily led young queen needed a stong hand to guide her and John Churchill, Duke of Marlborough, willingly provided this.

The Protestant struggle against the expansionist policies of Louis XIV of France had virtually continued unceasingly since it began under the leadership of William of Orange in 1685. It was given fresh impetus over the single vexing question of succession to the recently-vacated throne of Spain. As a result the full-scale war which began in 1702 became known as the War of the Spanish Succession. The long and fierce conflict saw the old allies—the Dutch, Danes, some German states and the British—pitted aginst the armies of France, Bavaria and Spain.

It is human nature to dismiss all that has gone before as essentially primitive; this is especially true of the commonly-held opinion of war when viewed in retrospect. Historians often write of primitive weapons and simple tactics as though any schoolboy of the age in which they write could have done better. However, war at any period in history is always a serious undertaking, for it is one thing to have abundant manpower with which to create an army, but quite another to organise it into a fighting force, to equip it with weapons, and to provide it with the necessary supplies for a long campaign. By some means raw materials had to be converted into usable form by civilian industry and in the age immediately preceding the Industrial Revolution this was a substantial endeavour. With the exception of sulphur, which was imported from Italy, all the raw materials were available in the British Isles in 1700, but considerable organisation was needed to make use of them.

It may seem that a discussion of the ingredients of war in the early 1700s has little bearing on the history of boy soldiers. However, that the two subjects are not incongruous will become clear with some explanation of the factors which determine a nation's ability to make war. Firstly there has to be a cause worth fighting for, but as children cannot possibly influence the decisions by which war is declared we can safely leave discussion of this subject to the Machiavellis and Clausewitzes. We then come to the question of how to organise manpower, manufacture arms and produce the army's necessities, and in these endeavours we will find that children were directly affected and intimately involved.

For example, in 1702 Parliament voted into law the Act of Enlistment (or the Recruiting Act as it soon became known). Under this law parishes and corporations were required to furnish recruits for the army. The Act stipulated what bounties were to be paid to parishes and corporations for those enlisted and a £5 fine was imposed on those councils found guilty of neglecting the Act. Regular meetings of justices were held to systematise the law and changes were legislated from time to time to meet the changing circumstances of demand. (In 1707 the enlistment bounty was raised from £1 to £2 during the campaigning season, but remained £1 out of season.)

Parish councils and corporations were for the greater part dominated by the squirearchy and landed gentry. These men, as the employers of the labour force, had a vested interest in who should go off to war and who should remain, so they were unlikely to skim the cream off the top for the army. It was natural, therefore, that they chose those who were either too young or too old to be of use to them. As a consequence, 'vast numbers of boys enlisted as well as men in their 50s and 60s'.[1] Sergeants Little and Hall, both infants when they joined, testify to this in their memoirs. Such abuses of the Enlistment Act gave rise to increasingly stringent enforcement.

There was another prime source of recruits which yielded a large number of young boys, though not in as high a proportion to full-grown men as those produced by the Enlistment Act of 1702. This was the Mutiny Act of 1703, which empowered the Queen to pardon criminals on condition that they enlisted in the army. Debtors, however, were permitted to find a substitute recruit to serve in their place, with the result that fathers willingly yielded their sons to the army in return for their own release from prison. This Act, added to the large number of young people serving sentence, produced a large crop of boys. Nevertheless, in the main, those recruited under the Mutiny Act were sufficiently well developed physically to shoulder their muskets.

Historians frequently refer to criminals as constituting the main element of the army from the time of Marlborough onwards, so unjustly condemning the great bulk of men who served in Great Britain's foreign wars—and those of other European armies for that matter. The word 'criminal' has to be interpreted with great caution, bearing in mind the petty offences for which justices awarded harsh sentences. Pilfering, poaching, unlawful trespass, insolence to one's betters, and other minor infractions of the law resulted in severe punishment: prison, pillory or shipment to the colonies. The majority of those so convicted would today be astounded by the leniency with which the law treats first-time offenders. Considering this conception of crime in the early eighteenth century, it should come as no surprise that competition among the regiments for this type of recruit was so great that a roster was maintained to ensure that colonels each got their fair share. It is of course equally true that the criminal element included footpads, cutpurses, highway robbers and other thieves, but more often than not these criminals met the swift justice of the gallows.

The commissioned ranks, too, included a large number of boys, although a line was drawn in accepting the extremely young. Marlborough, in a letter to Lord Cadogan in 1705, refused a commission to a 5-year-old infant as 'contrary to the rules the Queen has proscribed for herself in that matter'.[2] It is again necessary to draw a sharp distinction between commissioned infants absolutely incapable of serving—as in the obvious case of the 5-year-old—and youngsters who actually took up their duties and saw active service. This distinction was recognised at the time, for in 1705 Queen Anne directed '. . . for the future no person that is not of age sufficient to serve shall be admitted into any of HM troops *except children of officers who have been slain or suffered extremely in the service . . .*' (author's italics).[3] Not more than two officers *under 16* were to be appointed to any regiment; and when regiments went abroad the boy officers were to be transferred to home-based regiments. That this specific command was frequently ignored will be demonstrated when we come to describe some incidents during Marlborough's campaigns. Marlborough wrote to Mr Walpole in 1708 admitting an obligation to Lord Portmore regarding Portmore's son (then aged 12): 'and though I am by no means for encouraging children in the service, yet his Lordship (rest assured) I intend to write two words to the prince upon the present vacancy.'[4]

So much for the commissioned ranks and the fifers and drummers, but there were also many hundreds of boy soldiers in the fighting ranks. However, before dealing with the field service experience of these young boys I want to examine two other aspects of the war effort which affected the lives of the young: the manufacture of arms and the provision of materials.

The Brown Bess musket, the weapon with which the British Army was to conquer her empire, was invented in the 1680s, and this muzzle-loading weapon remained virtually unchanged for the next 200 years. (Used in the early stages of the Crimean War, the Brown Bess musket continued to see service in India until it was replaced by the rifle in the 1800s.) As famous a weapon as the English longbow, the Brown Bess was manufactured over the years by the hundred thousand.

It is generally not realised that the production of arms, gunpowder, shot, boots, uniforms and accoutrements for both the army and the navy was a national effort in which children were directly and closely involved. Indeed, the evidence suggests that the needs of the army or, rather, the national effort made to satisfy those needs was one of the concomitant causes which led to the Industrial Revolution in the 1740s. Manufacture of the Brown Bess certainly became a major industry and was the first effort at mass production ever attempted in Western society. It was mass production by cottage industry, for the factory system had not yet come into existence.

The manufacture of arms was controlled and organised by the Master of Ordnance from the Tower of London, for centuries the national armoury. It was therefore natural for the Tower armourers to enlist cottage craftsmen from within striking distance of London when organising the mass production of the musket. Carpenters, woodworkers, blacksmiths, metal workers, village craftsmen in the villages and hamlets of the Home Counties were contracted to produce specific parts of the weapon. With the aid of jigs and gauges supplied by the Tower armourers, adequate accuracy and quality control were maintained. One worker made flashpans, another the flintlock, while still others fashioned the barrels, stocks, springs, triggers and multiplicity of parts which made up the complete musket. At regular intervals government carters and their assistants made their rounds checking and collecting the parts produced.

Tower armourers assembled the muskets and, by way of a test to ensure that the weapon did not blow up in the soldier's face when used in battle, loaded them to one and a half times the allowable gunpowder capacity. (Components for pressure vessels are, today, still tested at one and a half times their design pressure.) Each weapon was then hallmarked with the Royal Crown and the word 'TOWER' and pronounced ready for issue to the army. Boy armourers served their apprenticeships in this trade.[5]

The manufacture of gunpowder was equally well organised, except that a steady supply of sulphur from abroad was needed. Of the other two elements required for making gunpowder, charcoal was obtained from government-licensed charcoal makers operating on the edges of woodlands, and saltpetre was collected from as far afield as hamlets and villages in Suffolk, Sussex, Essex, Kent and Berkshire. Since the earliest days the earth of cottage floors was a major source of saltpetre, a constituent element of urine. Government carts regularly made the rounds of villages to remove cottage earth and to replace it with fresh earth from the fields. Apart from helping the war effort, the practice was hygienically beneficial. Later, to improve the collection system, villagers were encouraged to urinate in wooden buckets of earth called pissers (the inelegant forerunner of the chamberpot?). The material collected was then taken to refineries along the Thames for the saltpetre to be removed.

When blended, the gunpowder was coarse, black and flaky, the flakes having the consistency of finely-chopped newspaper. To ignite the powder, a chemically equal but more finely ground blend called corn powder was placed on the musket's flashpan. When struck by a flint, the ignition went through the touch hole to ignite the charge.

Lead shot was manufactured by means of shot towers where molten lead poured through an iron mesh grid into cold water. Five shot towers were located along the banks of the river Thames, two for the Royal Navy and three for the army. Two of these towers were still standing in 1975.[6]

On active service, soldiers made their lead balls once government-issue shot had run out. For this purpose the lead presses carried by every regimental company were used. Filled with molten lead, the presses were dipped in cold water to solidify the lead. Ball-making was one of the soldiers' main occupations between battles or when in winter quarters and the supply of lead for shot was a constant cause of concern to regimental officers. A victorious army could always rely on captured stores to replenish powder and shot, even if different calibre lead shot had to be melted and re-pressed. If routed in battle, an army could be faced with severe supply problems.[7]

All of these activities involved the use of children so that even before young boys joined the army they were conditioned to accept a disciplined life. Some sense of this conditioning can be appreciated considering the experience of civilian populations during the First and Second World Wars.

This experience of the nation's youth was not confined to the production of arms, powder and shot, for adequate and continuous supply of clothing and accoutrements has also to be taken into account. The manufacture of cloth for uniforms, and the uniforms themselves—again produced by cottage industry —was carried on mainly in the northern counties of Yorkshire and Lancashire. The production of boots, belts and other necessary accoutrements for both men and beasts was mainly the contribution of the Midland centres: Leicester, Nottingham, Northampton and Bedford. The provision of so many war stores by those cottage industries helped push the country far along the road to the Industrial Revolution. More to the point, children no less than adults contributed hugely to the military successes of Marlborough. Indeed, the country remained for generations on a war footing, with the result that young boys who joined the army, whether by reason of the Enlistment Act of 1702, the Mutiny Act of 1703 or as willing volunteers to recruiting parties, were conditioned in large measure by the social, political and economic struggles of the nation.

The situation in the British Isles was reproduced in every country of Europe embroiled in the conflict of the War of the Spanish Succession: France, Italy, the German states, Austria, the Netherlands, Denmark and Belgium. In the same way the children of these nations served in their national armies and the anecdotes of their experiences in the military histories of those nations are numerous.

Ultimately, success depended on organisation and ability to finance the struggle. In the case of the British they had an incomparable organiser in Marlborough, while the finance to underwrite his campaigns came from the country's burgeoning foreign trade and commerce. The English settlements in America provided a firm base for offensive operations in the Caribbean and West Indies for which, however, there was always a dire shortage of men. Recruits for service in the West Indies had always been difficult to find ever since Oliver Cromwell embarked on his profitless venture in that part of the globe. Yellow fever was the real enemy and thousands of men and young boys perished from the disease without firing a single shot in anger. Early in the 1700s, 'old men and boys were sent across the Atlantic only to be at once discharged, at great loss, by the officers who were ashamed to admit creatures of such miserable appearances into their companies.'[8]

In distant India a similar tale is to be told—and it will be dealt with in detail later—but it is to Marlborough's contingent of redcoats in Europe that we must turn for for the experience of boy service during the opening decade of the eighteenth century. This is where Marlborough acquired the nickname 'Corporal John'—why it is not known for sure, but it is no wonder that the men gave him this simple accolade, for understatement is often a more powerful reflection of respect than all the politicians' polished rhetoric. And there is no doubt that he was a popular commander-in-chief; no commander before or since, with the possible exception of Montgomery, cared for his men as did Marlborough in providing for their sustenance and protecting them from unnecessary risks. During his astonishing march from Bedburg in the Low Countries to the Danube his arrangements for the comfort of his troops was impeccable: short marches of 10 to 15 miles; bread and meat to await the men at their daily halt; frequent rest days; all supplies paid for; even new boots were provided when they reached Frankfurt.

Needless to say numerous boy soldiers were on that march. They went unheralded, unrecorded and barely mentioned in the paeans of praise that followed the victories at Schellenberg, Blenheim, Oudenarde, Malpaquet and the breaching of the lines of Ne Plus Ultra. But they were there all the same, marching, living, dying, growing to manhood to take their places in the line.

Some were exceedingly young but not, on the whole, as young as their descendents would be a hundred years later. Yet, even under Marlborough, there were exceptions.

At the siege of Lille in 1708, 'during the enforced inaction of the army for the next few weeks, the monotony was broken only by the arrival of a distinguished visitor, Augustus the Strong, Elector of Saxony and King of Poland, together with one of his three hundred and sixty-four bastards, a little boy named Maurice, who ran away from School to join the army.'[9] This child was six years of age. He grew up to become the famous Marshal Saxe who, at Fontenoy just 20 miles from Lille, gave the British a difficult time in 1745.

While it was permissible for a boy of any age capable of carrying a drum to serve in the ranks, commissions for children were eventually forbidden by royal decree in 1711. Even so, some slipped through the net to take to the field, for there are records of 12-year-old officers on active service. One is reported as 'behaving with more courage and conduct than could have been expected from one of his years who later ruined his career by killing a man in a duel when he was but 16.'[10]

There was a decided difference in value between those boys who served in the ranks and those commissioned. Though their activities may offend our modern sensibilities, drummers, fifers and apprentices served useful functions which satisfied those under whom they served. Those boys holding commissions were in an entirely different category for they were, superficially at least, filling positions calling for a modicum of leadership. The idea of such boys providing leadership in any degree must have seemed as strange then as it does today and it is no wonder that the practice came to be prohibited.

This is an opportune time to discuss one of the most odious duties in the entire army which came to fall to the lot of boy soldiers. This was the administering of the cat-o'-nine tails or lash. It cannot, however, be discussed without qualifying the whole subject of military punishment in general.

Professor Sylvia R. Frey of Tulane University, an authority on the eighteenth-century British Army, has analysed over 2,000 criminal cases brought before general courts from 1666 until 1782.[11] The offences included murder, plunder, mutiny, desertion, treason and sexual offences. She grouped her findings into three periods: 1666–1718, 1719–53 and 1754–82 (see accompanying table)[12]. From these groupings Frey deduced there was a progressive enlightenment and diminishing severity of punishment from one period to the next. The most dramatic changes over the three periods were in the increase of corporal punishment and the number of acquittals. As a percentage, the death penalty decreased while a form of mercy by which condemned men were permitted to cast lots was abandoned by 1719.

1666–1718: TOTAL CASES 524

Punishment	Number	Percentage
Death	166	31.68
Cast lots	24	4.58
Corporal punishment	81	15.47
Pardon	206	39.31
Acquittal	41	8.97

1719–1753: TOTAL CASES 636

Death	140	22.01
Corporal punishment	257	40.41
Pardon	60	9.43
Acquittal	33	5.18
Service at a foreign post	137	21.54
Other (reprimand, prison, fine, black hole)	2	.31

6 (.93%) were released because the Articles of War were not read to them, 9 (1.30%) because of illegal confinement.

1754–1782: TOTAL CASES 893

Death	206	23.07
Corporal punishment	411	46.02
Pardon	41	4.59
Acquittal	230	25.76
Service at a foreign post	1	.11
Other (reprimand, prison fine)	4	.45

There were many forms of corporal punishment in use early in the century. These included the barbarous wooden horse (a wooden bar straddled by the victim weighed down by loads tied to his legs), picketing (being strung up with feet resting on pointed stakes), and the gantlope (a form of running the gauntlet and being whipped by the halberds of the regiment—by which a soldier could receive up to 3,000 lashes). The most common form of punishment, however, was the cat-o'-nine-tails.

Much has been written about the lash and little needs be added, except what serves to explain the part boy soldiers played in its application. Opinion is divided as to when boy drummers were first employed for this grisly duty. Professor Frey, writing of the gantlope punishment, states: 'After 1740 that savage and degrading form of punishment was apparently abandoned; thereafter punishment was carried out by a drummer or drummers, under the supervision of a regimental surgeon'.[13] The historian Major R. M. Barnes, writing in 1950,[14] inferred that drummers had this duty much earlier, although he neglected to quote his source.

Whatever the origin of involvement of the drummers in the punishment was, it is a fact that flogging was a public spectacle. The regiment was drawn up in open square with the prisoner and escort assembled for all to witness in a central position near the open side. The prisoner was then stripped entirely and lashed to a tripod of sergeants' halberds (the halberd was a modified form of the pike pole), hence the expression 'going to the halberds'.

The regimental drummers took turns in delivering 25 cuts each to the measured beat of a drum. Military law forbade the use of the same lash on two prisoners on the same day, for which reason regiments kept a stock of lashes. Behind the drummer stood a sergeant or sergeant major armed with a cane to make sure the drummer delivered manly cuts. In turn, behind the sergeant stood the regiment's adjutant ready to thrash the sergeant if he thought the drummer's strokes too light. One hundred strokes for petty offences were common and 1,000 strokes or more were given for the more serious crimes of desertion, cowardice or stealing from a comrade—followed by hanging or shooting should the regiment be on active service. As victims of the lash were all too frequently likely to die from an excess of cuts a musket ball was often sweet release.

The duty of the drummer was repulsive in the extreme and many boys vomited while performing the duty or simply from witnessing the punishment. Nor should it be supposed that because boy soldiers were so young they were spared the lash themselves. However, generally they were dealt with more lightly but, while there are happier tales to tell of their experience, we are bound to note that boys did receive the lash. In one recorded case a boy, who began his service as a drummer in Gibraltar in 1727, collected 27,000 lashes during his 14-year service and still lived to tell the tale.[15]

To retrace our steps to the beginning of the century, there is enough evidence from Professor Frey's table to suggest that discipline in Marlborough's army was severe, but otherwise his soldiers were well treated. Nevertheless, because the cat-o'-nine-tails was administered for almost 200 years, and with increasing frequency, the important question to be answered is why boy soldiers and not men wielded the lash. The answer, though entirely speculative, has to be that any soldier surviving the ordeal of flogging was less likely to take revenge on a mere boy than he might have done on a fellow soldier. No evidence whatsoever supports this conclusion yet, because there is generally a sound and rational explanation for any military tradition, the need to avoid vengeance seems the most plausible reason for using boy soldiers to administer this form of punishment.

The Treaty of Utrecht in 1712 spelt the end of the War of the Spanish Succession, by which time Marlborough's fortunes had sunk to such a low ebb that he had been relieved of his command of the allied operations for more than a year. Political intrigue at home, incurring the disfavour of Queen Anne during the latter part of her reign, and being outmanoeuvred by his political enemies, brought about his ruin. Nevertheless, with the exception of those who had taken over the helm of national affairs, Marlborough's achievements were universally acknowledged.

During the nine continuous years of war, Marlborough had fashioned an unbeatable military machine. Its morale, discipline and sense of self-worth had never been higher. Despite the rigours of service and the brutal system of punishments, the outlook was not entirely black. There was still useful work to be done and fresh fields to march over because, in fits and starts, the nation embarked on a programme of foreign conquest, to open new markets for the goods it was now able to produce. War, as so often happens, produced more sophisticated political and economic organisation in the country and set the scene during the first half of the century for the Industrial Revolution which followed.

CHAPTER V
SCABBY SHEEP

IN THE VICTORIOUS postwar world of Great Britain (the Act of Union occurred in 1707) following the Treaty of Utrecht, it was natural that the politicians and statesmen who brought about the peace should want to dismantle the army which Marlborough had hammered into shape. They did so with alacrity. Ten years or more of war had made the nation heartily sick of fighting, though the army was more than willing to continue and loud were the protests against making a premature end of it when complete victory was in sight. The reaction which set in followed what came to be realised over the next 200 years as a predictable pattern; that is, having enjoyed the nation's bounty in the form of money, arms, men and provisions, the army suffered the nation's neglect once peace was declared. Nor was the army given the courtesy of being disbanded according to the established tradition of the youngest regiments first. The military historian Fortescue was of the opinion that the Jacobite ministers perpetrated this insult preparatory to the Jacobite Rebellion of 1715,[1] but as those ministers, presumably, were intent on aiding the rebellion there would seem little point in their caring which units were disbanded first.

Between December 1712 and 1714, 33,000 soldiers were discharged, leaving less than 30,000 to garrison the homeland and the country's foreign possessions combined.[2] (H. C. B. Rogers[3] quotes a combined England and Scotland total of 8,000 men.) However, based on the practice of retaining the younger, enlisted for life, soldiers, few of those discharged were of the boy soldier element. Of those who remained in uniform every persuasion was used by the authorities to obtain volunteers to serve in the East Indian and West Indian stations, a prospect that meant they would be condemned to perpetual exile if they did volunteer.

Having noted the nation's neglect of the army as a 'predictable pattern', I am well aware that this has been the complaint of the military hierarchy through the ages. No professional body suffers cutbacks in silence, be it a government bureaucracy, the teaching community or organised labour. Unfortunately, the attitude to the army of successive governments, of whatever political hue, always ensures that the country is unprepared for the next war in which the nation becomes embroiled. The cycle of raising, training, equipping and disbanding a national army appears to have run a complete cycle every 50 years. Beginning about 1650, the cycles (give or take a few years) can be plotted with reasonable accuracy by the major conflicts which have occurred in the history of Great Britain: 1650, the Civil War; 1700, the War of the Spanish Succession; 1750, the Seven Years War; 1800, the Napoleonic Wars; 1850, the Crimean War (and the Indian Mutiny); 1900, the Boer War (closely followed by the First World War); and 1940, the Second World War. If we extend this pattern prophetically, with Cassandra-like foresight we might warn our children to expect another major conflict around the year 2000.

This prediction is not so far removed from the theme of this history as it might seem. We will later describe the current pragmatic policy of the British Army in regard to young soldiers—which policy lends credence to the observation that, in synchronism with the cycle just noted, increasing reliance over the years has been placed on boy soldiers, both to provide a core of trained soldiers and experienced commissioned and non-commissioned officers. From one half-century to the next there is evidence of the increasing concern by the military authorities for the welfare, care and treatment of its boy soldiers. Although this pattern is barely discernible in the post-Spanish Succession War period, it is there and it is as well to remind the reader of this trend for future reference.

Rapid disbandment of the army ceased with the outbreak of the Jacobite Rebellion of 1715 so that, with the return of many thousands of those soldiers discharged and the recall of officers on half pay, some semblance of prestige was restored to the national army. Damage to its morale, though not irreparable, had nevertheless been done and a mournful period spanning the next three decades followed. Despite the efforts of some good military administrators, such as General Wade (who put down the '15 Rebellion and kept the occupation troops of Scotland usefully employed building roads), continued political interference in the army's affairs resulted in low morale. Officers neglected their men and the debilitating punishments described in the last chapter were visited on the soldiery with unprecedented ferocity. The army's relations with the civilian population deteriorated in equal measure.

Riots, insurrection and lawlessness in the urban centres became commonplace and in the absence of an organised national police force, the army was called upon to restore order. Accusations of military brutality flew thick and fast as musketballs in battle and no one was appeased; the army disliked its distasteful task of keeping order and the civil population resented the military curb on its traditional freedoms.

Although historians frequently dwell on the dislike of the civilian population for the military, relations between the two have in fact fluctuated widely from good to bad to good again at different times. However, there is little doubt that from about 1720 to 1740, as reflected in the literature of the period, these relations were at a low ebb in Great Britain. Soldiers were then billeted in inns and taverns and, as innkeepers were paid little enough for the accommodation and food they provided, frequent trouble ensued. Fleeced by the innkeepers, cheated by those who paid them (and those who did not), our sympathy must be with the common soldier of the period. At the same time, while soldiers in general were having a rough time at every turn the fortunes of boy soldiers, taken as a whole, were improving in tangible ways.

To begin with, more boys were being taken on the strength of military units and this opened opportunities for children otherwise condemned to the workhouse. For example, in 1720 the 107-strong Honourable Artillery Company included two drummers, five cadets (boy) gunners, and five cadet matrosses (assistant gunners). By 1727 the regiment had increased to four companies with a total of 48 boy soldiers, mostly cadet gunners and matrosses or what one might call gentlemen apprentices.[4] The line regiments were also busy expanding their ranks by taking in more boys. A youthful drummer was most frequently included in the recruiting party when a regiment sent one out to drum up recruits. Throughout 1737 the 24th Foot had two parties constantly on the road, each one comprising a captain, two sergeants, two corporals and a drummer.[5] Young infantry drummers in their three-cornered hats, red coats and facings, white breeches, and toting brightly-painted drums, all contrasting vividly against the drab dwellings of rural England, could be counted on to appeal to impressionable country lads.

Furthermore, an exciting new idea had germinated in the minds of some regimental officers. Although officers in general had the improvement of their men at heart, whoever first conceived the idea of educating soldiers remains a mystery. For the army to concern itself with such a revolutionary concept of education a good hundred years before there was any such thing as even the most rudimentary publicly-funded education is astonishing. Yet to those who gave any thought to the subject, the need for soldiers to be able to read and write was perfectly obvious.

There have been two schools of thought in military circles concerning efficiency and discipline. The first and most popular view in the past held that soldiers must obey blindly and not think for themselves, but because drill sergeants pummelled this idea into the heads of soldiers for centuries (a practice not confined to the British Army) it does not automatically follow that it is a universal truth or that disciplined ignorance ever produced the best soldiers. If this doctrine had prevailed without question no one would have raised a finger a good century before the earliest publicly-funded school came into existence. As far back as 1662 the officers of the East India Company had asked for, and had been provided with, an army schoolmaster for its Madras garrison. In 1675 the garrison at Tangier, where Marlborough began his service, was provided with two schoolmasters for the troops but not, as might be thought, for their children.[6]

The second and more rational view is that the educated soldier was of more value than the soldier who could neither read nor write. Those officers who fostered the idea of educating the soldier had two ideas. Firstly, it was important to educate the NCOs and, secondly, to teach the rudiments of education to the boy soldiers under their command. Literate NCOs were necessary for the increasingly complex company system which emerged from Marlborough's campaigns. Muster rolls on which names, unit strength, casualties and ranks were recorded were becoming increasingly common. Also, because there were reports to read and write, it followed that senior NCOs, at least, needed to have some knowledge of the three Rs. And since the most likely future NCOs would be drawn from the youngest soldiers in the army, it was natural that the officers should direct their first efforts to giving a rudimentary education to underage soldiers.

It is difficult to grasp the enormity of the task regimental officers faced in educating an army largely composed of illiterates; indeed, many of the officers were illiterate themselves. Gradually, however, in fits and starts, colonels of regiments began by financing their own schools. We should not laugh at these puny efforts in experimental education. There was no model to go on: preparatory schools were beyond the reach of the great bulk of the population and universities were for the privileged few. Those officers who were literate had either been taught to read and write by their own parents or by hired tutors, not at a school.

It was an almost insuperable effort for conscientious officers to add to their normal regimental duties the problem of educating their men. In addition, they were finding themselves with an increasing number of very young soldiers on their hands, mere boys. This situation cannot be better illustrated than by describing the experience of the Royal Artillery.

While regiments of the line might continue to rely on the lash to lick their men into shape the Royal Artillery, simply by the nature of the function it served, was forced to give its officers and men the rudiments of artillery science. In addition, the RA had always had a larger proportion of boy soldiers in its ranks than other arms of the service, not so much by choice as economic necessity, especially to attend to the horses needed for hauling the guns and supply wagons. Towards the end of the War of the Austrian Succession (1742–8), for instance, over 1,400 horses were needed for the Flanders campaign to haul 32 guns, 2 howitzers, 6 mortars, 244 wagons and 30 pontoons.[7] Civilian carters were still employed at this period, yet there were many boys in regular service in the Artillery, both rankers and cadets. They were no doubt a hard lot to control and they plagued the life out of the men with whom they marched, as shown by the record of their behaviour when stationed at the regiment's Woolwich base. The cadets were no better disciplined than the rankers as recorded in the regimental reports for the period. Here it is again necessary to distinguish between boy soldiers in the ranks—drummers, apprentice farriers and harness makers—and cadets. Cadets were officers-in-training who, until the Royal Military Academy was established, initially served as matrosses who otherwise enjoyed the same privileges as ensigns in the line regiments.

In the records for the year 1739, the commanding officer was obliged to report on the bad behaviour of the cadets. Having noted that one was lame for six months and another had 'lost his memory', he wrote of the others: 'I know not where they are'. Six were detached, two were at Portsmouth and one, he thought, was on board a bomb vessel while another was in the Tower. (This sounds ominous, but he was probably with the Tower Artillery Battery.) The commanding officer thought that something more than he could undertake would have to be done to cope with all these boys. It was a cry from the wilderness, but evidently heard by those on high.

In 1741 the Royal Military Academy (RMA), Woolwich, was established to teach these young soldiers a sense of discipline and to give them the rudiments of an education. It should not be forgotten that these boys were 12 to 14 years old. From the regimental records, they were as wild and truculent a lot as ever wore the King's uniform. They were, wrote the regimental historian, 'the sons of Ishmael'.[8] One of the duty officer's main occupations was to protect the masters from being pelted with any handy missile by these outrageously undisciplined youths. The RMA was not an auspicious start for the education of boy soldiers, but it was a beginning.

To bring the boys to order and instil a sense of discipline the authorities created junior NCOs, sergeants and corporals, and the promotion of boy soldiers to junior NCO ranks became a regular practice whenever large numbers of boy soldiers were gathered together in one place, a practice still in force today. However, in the early days of the RMA, experience proved that the promotion of boy NCOs was not the solution to the problem of discipline, for those boy soldier NCOs turned out to be more unruly than those over whom they were put in charge. A constant problem was that they considered themselves the elite among 'the Lilliputians in their constant warfare with the Gullivers of authority'.[9]

The boys fought like wild animals whether on parade or at school. In one report, they were described as 'Scabby sheep, whom neither lenity will improve, nor confinement to a dark room [the black hole] and being fed on bread and water will improve.'[10] On parade, the cadets, drawn up on the right of the line, quarrelled so much among themselves that the adult soldiers were frequently sent among them to restore order. They were of course eventually brought to heel, but not until some years after the RMA came into existence. For the vile crime of 'skinny dipping' in the Thames a cure was soon found, however, when culprits were carried naked to the guardroom for all to see.

One has to admire the pluck of these 11, 12 and 13-year-olds; neither whip nor black hole nor all the retribution their officers or NCOs could devise could quench their rebellious spirits. The more lowly boy rankers were every bit as bad, except that they were, as yet, thinly distributed among the various batteries. When gathered together in what nuclear physicists would term a 'critical mass' (a dozen or so seems to be the critical number for boy soldiers) their behaviour became explosive.

Shortly after the RMA experiment got under way there was a fresh outbreak of hostilities in Europe, sometimes called the War of Jenkins' Ear (1740).

Britain and Spain clashed while France remained tacitly neutral, although France did send two squadrons to assist the Spaniards. Hardly had this conflct ended when the War of the Austrian Succession broke out. Increasing numbers of underage soldiers began to be inducted into the army about this time; brought, not simply as drummers, but as foot soldiers. This led to frequent complaints from commanding officers to the Commander-in-Chief, the Duke of Cumberland, and others in high command. A pithy comment to Lord Newcastle was typical. Lord Cathcart, assembling troops on the Isle of Wight for yet another assault on New Spain, wrote of the young recruits of the 27th Foot: 'They may be useful in a year hence but at present they have not the strength to handle their arms.'[11] For service in the West Indies, four battalions of infantry were raised in the American colonies and placed under the command of Spotswood of Carolina. In common with the established model of battalion organisation in the British Army, the American units included a complement of boys. Because of the lack of accurate records and muster rolls, it is not possible to give more than an estimate of the underage element of these battalions, but the number of boys was between 20 and 25 per battalion. The American settlements had for a long time provided manpower for military adventures in the Americas, but this was the first occasion on which a substantial force had been raised.

By 1742 the British Army was again in Flanders fighting the French and was having a difficult time; they had the Duke of Cumberland to lead them and he was no Marlborough.* The French, on the other hand, had as their comman-der the incomparable Marshal Saxe, the same 'little Maurice' whom we first met at the siege of Lille under Marlborough, proving once again that it pays to make an early start. Yet not even Saxe had it all his own way. At Dettingen the British won a victory in the face of overwhelming odds. It was in this action that James Wolfe got his first blooding. Wolfe, then aged 16, commissioned and the adjutant of his regiment, fought beside his 15-year-old brother. On the other side, the young Count Boufflers, aged 10, had a leg smashed by a cannonball and, according to Voltaire, watched impassively while the surgeons amputated his leg. He died a short time after the operation.

A rash of fighting again flared up in the mid-eighteenth century, and the energy with which Great Britain marshalled, organised and used its resources is astonishing. It is no wonder that, probably more than other European countries, it enlisted so many of its very young to join in the struggle. At times it is obvious that an acute shortage of men was made good by employing boys in the battleline, as happened during the early stages of the '45 Rebellion.

The Rebellion in 1745 was the last attempt by the House of Stuart to regain the English crown. Charles Stuart, the son of the Old Pretender, who led the first rebellion in 1715, landed in Scotland and persuaded enough Highlanders to support his cause and provide him with an army. However, the Presbyterian

*However, for the early part of the campaign, including at the combat at Dettingen in 1734, King George II commanded the army in person, the last occasion on which an English sovereign commanded in the field.

lowlanders as well as the majority of Highlanders held the Stuart cause in contempt and refused to join Charles in the rebellion. Undaunted by this lack of popular support, Charles moved his small army across the Highlands, invested and won Edinburgh, then met the hastily gathered troops of General Sir John Cope at Prestonpans, some little way south of Edinburgh. By a ruse worthy of Marlborough, Charles's army of Highlanders penetrated the British lines and took Cope by surprise. The raw untried British soldiers, many so young they were mere boys enlisted to meet the northern threat because the main army was already in Flanders, were overwhelmed by the Highlanders and utterly defeated. In the space of ten minutes the battle was lost and won. What followed was butchery more normal to the abattoir than to the battlefield. A few fled and escaped to tell the tale, but of those who remained not one was left alive, for the Highlanders hacked to pieces men and beasts alike and not a living creature was spared.

Following the victory, Charles spent the night at the home of a supporter where 'young boys of fourteen and fifteen were brought to him to tell how they had killed a dozen men. Each tale was better than the last.'[12] With such young warriors had Charles Stuart won a victory. The rest of his rebellion was a series of reverses which, following an abortive advance into England as far south as Derby, ended with an equally bloody massacre—this time of the Highlanders on the field of Culloden, where many a brave young Highland boy perished in the vengeance administered by veteran battalions brought back from Flanders to quell the rebellion.

CHAPTER VI
GENTLEMAN FROM VIRGINIA

IN OCTOBER 1753 Major George Washington, then a 20-year-old youth in the Virginia Militia, set out from Williamsburg on a long and perilous journey to Venango, 60 miles south of Lake Erie. Washington's mission was a considerable undertaking, for not only had he to cover a distance of over 400 miles, but his small party of lightly-armed militiamen was forced to traverse an unknown hinterland of mountains, rivers and trackless, virgin forest. In his saddlebag he carried Lieutenant-Governor Robert Dinwiddie's letter of expulsion to the commander of a strong French force which, that same summer, had built a wooden fort and was solidly entrenched.[1]

Judging by his despatches to Congress during the American War of Independence, and from the evidence of his correspondence, Washington was frequently depressed and often ready to resign his command, but still was one of the most successful field commanders of his century. If his military career has to have a beginning it must be with that first journey to the French stronghold, Fort Venango. Within five months he was back in Williamsburg. Dinwiddie's ultimatum, of course, was flatly rejected, but the French were hospitable enough and were pleased to give the young major an extensive tour of the fortifications before bidding him adieu. The events leading to that first visit are worth summarising because they are important in considering the British operations which followed in North America.

The Peace of Aix-la-Chappelle in 1748 brought to an end the War of the Austrian Succession, but it provided no more than a breathing space in the continuing struggle for supremacy among the nations of Europe. In 1753 the French military command of New France decided on a bold move: by setting out to construct a string of forts along the western flank of English America they hoped to cauterise the colonies and prevent further movement west. When the news of the French enterprise reached Dinwiddie he became justifiably alarmed; hence his decision to despatch Washington with his letter of expulsion. If nothing else, this gave the Lieutenant-Governor time to appeal to the home government for help and to acquaint the governors of English

America with the seriousness of the situation. The northern settlements of New England were well occupied in coping with continuing French incursions by way of Lake Champlain. As it turned out, Dinwiddie had to counter this new threat with his own resources and what he could winkle out of the Governor of Carolina in the way of men.

Upon the return of Washington, Dinwiddie issued a proclamation for the raising of the Virginia Provincial Regiment. (English settlers were known in England and America at the time as provincials; the word colonial is largely post-revolutionary.) The proclamation promised volunteers a share in 200,000 acres of His Majesty's land on the east side of the Ohio River, 'as an encouragement to the people to enlist with spirit'.[2] Colonel Joshua Fry was appointed Colonel of the Regiment and Lieutenant-Colonel Washington (promoted on receiving the appointment) was made second in command. The Lieutenant-Colonel, however, had effective command of the Regiment, as remains the practice in the British Army regimental stystem.

Of Virginia's 170,000 population the province could raise no more than 120 men. With this tiny force, comprising two captains, five lieutenants, two sergeants, six corporals, one surgeon-major, one volunteer (rank unknown), one boy soldier drummer and 102 men, Washington, in March 1754, set off to meet the foe. An additional 50 men under Major Robert Stobo marched behind boy soldier James Carson to join Washington in May. The pay of these troops was 15 pounds of tobacco a day which, presumably, would be sold by public auction upon their return from active service, assuming they were fortunate enough to survive.

To James Carson, with some qualification, must go the distinction of being the first identifiable boy soldier of the Amercan Army. In 1754 the Virginia Provincial Regiment was, of course, a unit of the British Army, but in the same way that we cannot consider General George Washington of any other national-ity than American we must also in simple justice so regard Drummer James Carson. Since the time of Oliver Cromwell the American colonists had provided a share of men and boys for British adventures in the West Indies and there is no doubt that many a boy served in the militia of the northern New England settlements, which were frequently at odds with the forces of New France. Drummer Carson's age may be put at 12 or 13; this is not known for sure although he was later joined by his elder brother whose age, according to Stobo,[3] was 16. It is also evident that the ensigns of the Virginia Provincial Regiment (identified as lieutenants) were not much older than the younger Carson.

One of Washington's first actions was to construct a stronghold at Great Meadows (near modern Uniontown, Pa.), naming it Fort Necessity. He also built a small fort at Wills Creek and left Ensign Edward Ward, 16 years of age, in command while he led the main force away to seek contact with the French. During Washington's absence Captain François du Mercier arrived at the head of a French scouting party and, in the company of an Indian and two French drummers (drummers almost always accompanied their officers to beat a *parlez*), called upon the fort to surrender. The captain offered generous terms: surrender within the hour or be blown to pieces. Ensign Ward, no doubt enjoying his first independent command, wisely yielded the premises to the French and surrendered.

A few weeks later Washington was joined by 100 South Carolina regulars under the command of Captain James McKay who, with the prejudice of the full-time soldier against the part-time soldier, was as contemptuous of the Virginians as a regular soldier could be. Nevertheless, largely owing to Washington's tact, there was accommodation on both sides and relations became cordial. Washington retained overall command and his ideas on the future course of action prevailed. Clausewitz said that everything in war is simple, but the most simple thing is often achieved with great difficulty. With such slender resources, Washington's simple aim was to contain the French until sufficient reinforcements arrived to throw them out. His task, therefore, was to make his tiny force seem ten times larger than it was, and this could only be done by rapid movement from one threatened spot to the next. He moved his men with skill and energy: whether retreating from Fort Necessity (the fort was called upon to surrender by a superior force, but he marched out with the honours of war) or slipping off to 'Gist's by way of Chalk Hill',[4] he made the most of what he had. The lessons he learned during this first encounter with the French he applied with crippling effect many years later during the lean and trying times of the Revolutionary War. However, wherever he moved on the frontier in 1754 we do know that his faithful drummer James Carson went with him.

By June 1754, Washington's force numbered 293 all ranks, among whom there were 15 officers and an undetermined number of boy soldiers masquerading as men. Carson's older brother, already mentioned, was there, some regular boy soldiers of the South Carolina contingent, and John Mercer, age 16, an officer who was present at the council of war Washington held at his camp at Great Meadows. The French having moved further south in force, the situation was desperate and Washington had to move with agility to keep his force out of harm's way. That he did so all that year is sufficient testimony to his skill, following another of Clausewitz's tactical rules, that the successful commander should not seek battle unless there is a reasonable chance of achieving an objective.

The next year (1755) Major-General Edward Braddock arrived with two infantry battalions. Unfortunately, as too often has been the case, the arrival of regular troops resulted in disaster. Washington, the local commander familiar with the territory and conditions of warfare peculiar to his own field of operations, was replaced by a commander with greater authority but less skill. It was not that Braddock was incompetent, but his experience was of an entirely different school from that of the North American. Washington joined the attack on Fort Duquesne, which the French had constructed at the confluence of the Ohio and Allegheny rivers (the present site of Pittsburgh), and was present at the following disaster when Braddock's 2,000-strong force was caught in an ambush in virgin forest and virtually destroyed by 900 French and Indians. A fearful slaughter followed the ambush. Braddock fell in the action, mortally wounded. Among the slain and scalped lay John Mercer, with many of his equally young companions. Washington survived and was largely responsible for leading the survivors to safety. Whether James Carson was among the survivors or not we do not know, for all track of him is lost following the ambush.

Although this chapter is mainly concerned with North America it is necessary to return to the British Isles to maintain the chronological story of events and to learn how boy soldiers were faring elsewhere.

Conditions for boy soldiers in the line regiments were virtually unchanged; the fixed number of drummers and fifers per regimental company remained as before. In 1756, the strength of the Royal Artillery stood at 576, including 12 drummers and 7 fifers, not counting the cadets who were still making life miserable for the staff and masters at the RMA, Woolwich. In contrast, the cavalry was having second thoughts about enlisting youths in its ranks and the best way of illustrating the attitude of the cavalry as a whole is to deal with a single regiment. For this purpose I have chosen at random the Inniskilling Dragoons.

In 1750 the Inniskillings were known as (Major-General) Cholmondeley's Regiment of Dragoons. As military units went, the Inniskillings were among the elite of mounted regiments. In a total strength of 246, the regiment had 12 drummers who were expensively outfitted and accoutred: caps, cloaks, breeches, boots, breastplate and cruppers, gloves and a full set of equipment for the horse. The cost of outfitting a mounted boy dragoon drummer amounted to £56 9s 8d, a considerable sum. Dressed in yellow coats with a scarlet lining ornamented with silver lace and a blue striped cuff, waistbands and scarlet breeches, the drummers were a striking sight—and a drain on the colonel's pocket. For no other reason, it seems, than the expense of outfitting growing boys who soon outgrew their clothes and had to be reclothed, in 1756 the colonel decreed that the regiment would take no new recruits under 18.[5] Who can blame him!

Although the injunction banning boy recruits seems to have been fairly general among cavalry regiments at this period, there were exceptions and these occurred among the commissioned ranks. These boys, presumably, had private means to outfit themselves, thus saving the regiment expense. Cornet ffloyd, aged 12, of the 1st Dragoons was in action with his regiment at the Battle of Emsdorff (1760). Before the action, along with the rest of the regiment he happily obeyed his major's instruction to twist an oak leaf in his helmet. Major Erskine said, 'Remember the English oak', and with that encouragement the 1st Dragoons charged the French lines, not once but three times. ffloyd had his horse shot from under him and, at the mercy of a French dragoon about to sabre him, was saved by one of his officers who despatched the attacker. Later, as a memento of his first battle, ffloyd was given a French sabre, a trophy of war. ffloyd made the army his life, fought Tippoo Sahib in

India under Arthur Wellesley, the Duke of Wellington, and was made a baronet in 1816. He died at the age of 86.[6]

The Seven Years War broke out in 1756 and quickly developed into a slugging match. The Holy Roman Empire (Austria) joined with Russia, Sweden, Saxony and France to contain Prussian expansionism under Frederick the Great. Great Britain, true to its policy of maintaining a balance of power, threw in its lot with Prussia. In any case, Britain was already deeply involved in its war with France for domination of North America. The new conflict in Europe was sufficient reason for British-French hostilities to spread—with renewed intensity—to the Mediterranean, India and the West Indies.

In order to avoid an excess of general history, we may safely ignore the conquest of Canada under Amherst and the efforts of Ligonier in Europe and turn for a moment to the Caribbean. Not only was that theatre directly related to events in North America but we can get another glimpse of boy service in that part of the world. We obviously cannot deal with every regiment which saw action in the West Indies during the 1750s and 1760s but, as in the case of the Inniskillings, which we used to illustrate a trend in the cavalry, we can look at some particular line regiments to understand the appalling loss of life.

By 1760 the conquest of Canada was complete; Governor Vaudreuil surrendered and ended French dominion of New France. In the south, regiments which had arrived to reinforce English America were suddenly available for operations against French possessions in the West Indies. Among those regiments was the 15th Foot, 858-strong with 14 drummers and two fifers. First it was employed in amphibious operations against Bermuda and Cuba in 1761 but, while battle casualties undoubtedly occurred, by far the greater loss to the regiment was from disease, chiefly yellow fever. During that year more than 219 perished from disease and that number included more than half its complement of boy soldiers.[7] Given the bad food on which the soldiers subsisted, they lacked the proper nourishment to resist disease and it is remarkable that any survived. The situation was to get worse, for the army was slow to learn and failed to take even the most elementary precautions in matters of health care.

The 58th Foot, employed in similar actions, was one of the strongest regiments and well served by its energetic recruiting parties in England which, over a two-year period, made good the regiment's losses from disease, combat and capture at sea. With a nominal strength of 586 total rank and file (including 15 drummers) when it began its service in the West Indies and Caribbean, the regiment first suffered capture at sea by a French squadron and lost ten drummers among those taken prisoner. Brought up to strength by fresh recruits from Great Britain, the 58th joined the attack on Havana and helped bring about its capture. Indeed, this was one of the few occasions on which there was prize money for those who survived. Drummers and privates each received £4 1s 8½d. The table of casualties for 1762, which excludes those captured at sea, tells a tale on which additional comment is unnecessary.[8]

	Officers	Sgts	Drummers	R & F	Total
Killed	11	15	4	260	290
Wounded	19	49	6	576	650
Died of wounds	4	–	1	51	56
Died of disease	39	14	11	630	694
Missing	–	1	4	126	131
	73	79	26	1,643	1,821

These casualty rates were the common experience of every regiment engaged in the Caribbean and West Indies during that period. The losses were truly appalling, including those for regiments raised in English America at this time, but about which comment will be deferred. Moreover, even though many interesting observations on the table may be noted, over the two-year period the total casualties of the 58th exceeded three times the nominal strength of the regiment when it began operations. This rate of loss could not fail to be felt in the mother country, but it is to Ireland that we must turn for some conception of the problem suffered by the children and families of serving soldiers.

A census in Dublin for the year 1765 revealed that there were 1,400 children whose fathers were either dead or serving overseas.[9] Multiply a reduced figure of, say, 1,000 children by the number of garrison towns in the British Isles at this time and some idea of the total number of fatherless children may be gauged. Conservatively, the total figure cannot be less than 50,000 for serving men alone.

At the beginning of this history I referred to the tradition of fosterage among the Celts, the dominant racial group in Ireland. Ignoring the religious groupings, one is persuaded that it was this characteristic of people of Dublin that gave rise to the founding of the Hibernian Society in 1764, in the parish of St Paul's. This society dedicated itself to alleviating the suffering of the destitute families of soldiers on foreign service. Generous public subscription enabled the society to open a 'school' in 1765 for 20 children and so was born, but not yet named, the Royal Hibernian Military School which has a most important place in this history of boy soldiers. Money flowed in more freely than expected: from the public, from military units, from King George III himself who contributed £1,000 per annum for upkeep of the premises.

George III has been treated slightingly by some historians, but he was in many ways a fine and compassionate monarch. He also donated a site of 3 acres for a projected 'hospital'* in Phoenix Park. The Irish Parliament voted £3,000 for the construction of the buildings, which were designed to accommodate 400 children, and in 1769 it voted an additional £4,000 to furnish and enclose the premises. The institution was opened on 6 March 1770 when 140 children,

---

*The word 'hospital' is here used in its old sense, derived from 'hospice' meaning a place of hospitality, and not in the modern sense meaning a medical care institution.

including 50 girls, moved in from various temporary placements in the city. The event was recorded in the Governors' Minute Book.

> This day the children, in their new clothing, appeared before the Committee and were afterwards received into the Castle Garden by His Excellency the Lord Lieutenant, the Marquis of Townshend, and then marched to Phoenix Park to the new Hospital, attended by the Artillery Musick.[10]

The Royal Irish Artillery was then stationed a short distance from the hospital. In the early days of its existence the Hibernian Society Hospital was more of a public subscription orphanage than a military training establishment. Only later did it come to be part of the British Army Establishment, and is dealt with more fully in Chapter IX. Nevertheless, from the very beginning the Hibernian Society Hospital developed strong ties with the army, not unsurprisingly considering that it was staffed by military and ex-military personnel. Support among the military for the institution was widespread: regiments which had served and recruited in Ireland donated money, material and gifts and staff. 'The Irish Society in London gave an annual theatrical performance, the proceeds of which were given to the Governors to provide portions for such girls that married with their consent. The establishment of girls was not to exceed fifty.'[11]

Having accounted for the establishment of what was to become the Royal Hibernian Military School it is again necessary to recount some general history concerning the American Revolutionary War, in order to meet some of the boys of the RHMS and others who took part in that conflict. The causes which led to the American Declaration of Independence in 1776 were many and complex. No one who impartially studies the events of the period can fail to view the subsequently written accounts—British or American—with a jaundiced eye. Minor players have been eulogised and equally minor events distorted beyond recognition for their symbolic value to the myth which patriotic historians deemed it necessary to create. It is a study worth deeper treatment than is possible in this history without straying too far from the main theme.

Washington, by degrees and growing conviction, came to identify himself with the cause of the Disunionist party which led to the fight for independence. He was of a good family, a man of high principles and it was undoubtedly because of him and men like him that Major-General Amherst, the British commander who conquered Canada, declined to command the British Army when the strife in New England made war unavoidable. Major-General Howe later resigned his command for similar reasons.

Accepting the command of the Revolutionary Army, Washington was soon faced with the insuperable task of fashioning a force out of indifferent militiamen and some British Army deserters. At an early stage in the war Washington recommended an increase in the bounties offered for enlistment. States offered thousands of pounds for a few months of service and one,

Massachusetts, whose citizens had been among the most vociferous clamouring for liberty, sent children to Washington's army 'hired at about fifteen hundred dollars for nine months'.[12] Washington's correspondence to Congress and governors is riddled with complaints and lamentations regarding the quality of men with which he had to fight. He reported to the President of Congress, 10 July 1775: 'So great was the dearth of recruits . . . it had been necessary to enlist . . . boys unable to bear arms, old men unfit to endure the fatigues of the campaign, and deserters from the British ranks'.[13]

He had to resort to the same administration of punishment as practised in European armies of the period to maintain order. Chaplain Emerson, who joined the army early in the war, reported that 'every man was made to know his place, or be tied up and receive thirty or forty lashes'. Later this form of punishment was greatly increased to as many as 500 lashes for some form of offences and capital sentences became more severe than in other armies.

In the British Army, the first boys of the Royal Hibernian Military School to join were seven 12- and 13-year-olds who enlisted in the 24th Foot in 1770.[14] The regiment was one of several shipped to New England under General Thomas Gage and arrived in Boston in May 1774. Gage was no stranger to North America. He had served at Fontenoy and Culloden, and with Washington at Monongahela.

The 24th was part of General Burgoyne's force which moved south from Ticonderoga on the understanding that General Clinton in New York would strike north. Disappointed in this hope, Burgoyne's force, increasingly short of supplies, fought a number of actions and was eventually forced to surrender at Saratoga. By the terms of the 'Convention of Saratoga' the British troops were to be disarmed and shipped back to Great Britain on parole, but this proviso of the Convention was repudiated by the American Congress and the captured British and German troops (in British pay) were made prisoners of war.

By this time, of course, the seven young lads of the RHMS were in their late teens and no longer boy soldiers. Their places had been taken by other, younger, boys who shared the same fate as the older captives. However, of the seven RHMS recruits only three returned from captivity, which leaves open the question of what happened to those who didn't return. No evidence is available to describe their fate but it seems likely that they were persuaded to join Washington's Continental Army. There are good reasons for this supposition, for there is no doubt that Washington was desperately short of troops throughout the war. His army never exceeded 30,000 men. According to the American Joseph Galloway,[15] a participant in the war who ought to have been in a position to know what was happening, the great majority of the Continental levies were immigrant volunteers of Irish birth, not the Roman Catholic Celts of the south, who served in the British ranks, but the Presbyterian Anglo-Caledonians of the north. 'These Anglo-Caledonians constituted the flower of the Continental Army.' Galloway contended that they formed one half of the whole army, one half of the remainder being Scots and English.

As there were several loyal American regiments in active service it some-times happened, when opposing forces met in conflict, that the majority of those fighting for colonial independence were of British and Irish birth, while, substantially, all those fighting for King and Parliament were native Americans.[16]

While the loyalty of Americans to the British crown was without question based on their genuine regard and respect for the British system of govern-ment, foreign troops (with few exceptions) fought in the Continental Army as hired mercenaries. Eventually a total of 100,000 Loyalists gave up, or were forced by proscription to give up, everything they possessed and move elsewhere, to Great Britain as refugees or to Canada, where they became the United Empire Loyalists of the Maritime Provinces and Upper Canada.

That hundreds and thousands of young boys fought in the War of American Independence there can be little doubt. The records of the Loyalist families testify to the fact and there are numerous written accounts of those who served. For instance, Spencer Thomas Vassal of Cambridge, Massachusetts, was a child of 12 when he joined the British Army in 1776. He rose to command the 38th Foot and fell, mortally wounded, at Montevideo in 1807. Frederick Phillips, age 12, served and lived to fight in the Napoleonic Wars under Wellington.

We can get some conception of the extreme youth of those who took sides from the account of Captain Stiel of the 24th Foot at the time of the surrender at Saratoga. Upon his eventual release in 1784 Stiel was 26. He was therefore 19 years of age at the time of the surrender. The average age of the nine lieutenants in the regiment was 25 and their average service was nine years. Their average age on joining, therefore, was 14, which meant that at least one or two were younger.[17]

Washington's Continental Army, similarly, had a large number of boy soldiers in its ranks and it is for this reason we surmise that at least some of those made captives at Saratoga were persuaded to transfer their allegiance to the other side, mostly from the British to the Continental Army.

Of the existence of young soldiers of American birth in the Continental Army we can be more certain. The source of the accounts given here is the military pension records of the US National Archives, prepared for publication by John C. Dann, director of the Clements Library, University of Michigan.

Eli Jacobs of Killingly, Connecticut, was aged 14 when he enlisted for his first term of service in April 1776. Jacobs served as a substitute, probably for an adult. His six months' substitute service as a private was spent 'guarding the shore and in drilling' at Roxbury, after which he was given an honourable discharge.

General Israel Putnam's personal servant (batman) was Joseph Rundel of New Fairfield, Connecticut, and he tells not only of the General's escape from the British at Horseneck but of his own.

I enlisted at Horseneck in the town of Greenwich, state of Connecticut, on Long Island Sound, on or about the first day of February (the day I cannot recollect), 1778, for the term of three years in the Continental service. I was thus enlisted by Charles Bush, a Continental recruiting officer. He was called Captain Bush. I never joined any company or regiment and cannot tell in what company or regiment I did enlist, not being able to recollect. The reason is this. On the day or day after I enlisted, General Putnam, whose headquarters were at Reading, Connecticut, was visiting Horseneck, one of his outposts. He saw me at that place, at what was called the Picket Fort. He told me I looked too young (I was then in my sixteenth year) to go into the line and said he would take me as his waiter. I told him I should like it. He took me with him to Bush, the person who enlisted me, and told him he should take me as his waiter. I then went into his service in that capacity.

A few days after I enlisted, the British, being a part of General Tryon's forces, I believe, attacked our men. Our men had stationed near the meetinghouse a cannon or two, which fired upon the enemy till they approached in so great force and so near that General Putnam ordered his men to retreat and save themselves the best they could. He also retreated on his horse at full speed, pursued closely by the British horse. He made down a flight of stone steps, the top of which were about sixty rods (I should think) from the meetinghouse. He did not ride down more than fifteen or twenty of them (there being, I think, about one hundred of them in the whole). He then dismounted and led down the horse as fast as possible. I was at the bottom of the steps as soon as he was. He then mounted his horse, told me to make my escape to a swamp not far off, and he rode off.

By the time the British horse, who had gone around the hill by the usually travelled road, come in tight pursuit, I ran towards the swamp. One of the dragoons (I think there were six who come round the hill) took after me. As I was getting over a stone wall, he overtook me. He hallowed, 'Stop, you little devil, or I'll take your head off.' In attempting to get over the wall, my foot slipped. He struck my left arm with his cutlass and inflicted a wound, the scar of which is still visible. I surrendered. He took me to Kingsbridge near New York City. From there I was sent with other prisoners to the Sugar House in the city of New York and there confined. I remained there about three months.

As I was young and small of my age, they permitted me in the daytime to be out, and I was sent to bring water and do chores about the yard. Some others of the prisoners were also permitted to be out. It was the custom at night to lock us up. The names were called over, and care taken to see all were in. I had gained the confidence of a Hessian soldier named Michael Hiderbrand. He could speak broken English. He was one of our guard at the Sugar House. I proposed to him to go off with me. He at first declined, saying that they would catch and shoot him. He finally consented, and we agreed upon a plan. When he stood sentinel, it being dusk, when our names

were called over to go in and be locked up, he secreted me under his watch
cloak. When my name was called, he said that I had gone in.

After dark, we started from the Sugar House and went with all haste out of
the city about three miles on the Hudson River. We then made a float of
some posts we procured from the fence and some slabs and boards and got
over the river on the Jersey side. We slept in the bushes. Early next morning
we went to a house. They asked us to come in. We declined, as we were
lousy. They brought us out some victuals. We then made our way to West
Point, where we arrived the next day about dark.[18]

Rundel rejoined Putnam and continued to serve as the General's waiter.

Henry Yeager of Philadelphia, aged 13,

volunteered as a drummer in a company commanded by Captain Weed
towards the close of October or beginning of November, 1776. The regiment
to which his company was attached was commanded by Colonel Ayres or
Eyre, and Major Boyd, in his rank as major, was attached to the same
regiment. The regiment went up the River Delaware in boats from Philadelphia to Trenton, where they encamped. General Washington, with the
army, was on towards Princeton, and Colonel Ayres's or Eyre's regiment
had drawn three days' provision and raised their tents to march onward in
pursuance of orders, when they were directed to retire to Philadelphia,
General Washington having determined to retreat in consequence of the
British, in a larger force under Cornwallis marching upon him from New
Brunswick. Colonel Ayres or Eyre with his regiment therefore retired to
Philadelphia in boats and encamped in the district of Kensington, in the
country of Philadelphia, where they remained under orders for about ten
days, when they were dismissed in December, about the middle of the
month, 1776. In this your declarant served not less than six weeks. Upon
Washington's retreat, as herein mentioned, he crossed the Delaware from
New Jersey and destroyed the bridges and removed all boats to prevent the
British, who were very close upon him, from following.[19]

The lack of full-time serving troops on whom he could depend was, for
Washington, an exasperating experience. American volunteers served for very
limited periods of a few months at a time, and one of his greatest difficulties in
prosecuting the war was having to contend with volunteers of all ranks who
came and went almost at will. Yeager repeatedly took his discharge only to
volunteer for service again, always as a drummer until, eventually, he volunteered for service as a privateer only to suffer capture and imprisonment in
Plymouth, England.

American boy soldiers were as close to their senior officers as boy soldiers in
the European armies were to theirs. John Suddarth, aged 13 when he enlisted,
was a boy soldier throughout the war. His narrative is interesting for its report

on an incident involving Washington at the siege of Yorktown. Suddarth, be it noted, served as a private.

That he volunteered in the army of the United States about the last of June (he recollects it was just before harvest), 1778, as a substitute for his brother James Suddarth under the command and in the company of Capt. John Burley or Burleigh and in the regiment of Colonel Bland of the Virginia troops, but he cannot state whether of the state or Continental line. Under the command of these officers he was engaged as a private in guarding the prisoners in the county of Albemarle, about four miles westwardly of Charlottesville, Virginia, which prisoners had been taken by General Gates in the defeat of General Burgoyne. He continued in this service until the last of September (a period of three months), when he was relieved by the return of his brother for whom he had substituted as aforesaid and who had been compelled to leave the service in consequence of sickness. This declarant, at the time of joining the service, resided in the county of Albemarle, Virginia. He recollects that Capt. Holman Rice and Captain Garland were in this service at the same time with this declarant, and that Captain Garland was shot by a sentry whilst there.

This declarant again joined the army of the Revolution from said county of Albemarle and state of Virginia about the middle of July, 1781, in the company of Capt. Benjamin Harris and joined a portion of the main army at Williamsburg, which to the best of his recollection was under the command of Major Merriweather. He will not say that Merriweather was the highest officer in command there, but from his indistinct recollection, he now seems to him to have been so. From Williamsburg we marched to Travis Point, at the mouth of Queen's Creek into York River, where we remained a few days guarding a number of beeves, etc., belonging to the American army. From thence we were marched down to the main encampment before Yorktown. We were here immediately placed to work in rearing the breastworks around the town. We were put on duty during this time at eight o'clock in the morning and not relieved until the succeeding morning at eight o'clock, only taking time to eat our meals. We then rested the succeeding twenty-four hours and so on till the works were finished.* He was present at the taking of two British redoubts, the one stormed by the French and the other by the Americans. He was not a participant in the storm, except so far as that he was drawn out with a large body of other troops to render such aid as might become necessary. Each man of the troops with him had a fascine, and as soon as the redoubts surrendered they were thrown down and the work of circumvallation was recommenced.

Your declarant, during the progress of these works, witnessed a deed of personal daring and coolness in General Washington which he never saw equalled. During a tremendous cannonade from the British in order to

---

*The mid-passage change to first person appears in the original declaration.

demolish our breastworks, a few days prior to the surrender, General Washington visited that part of our fortifications behind which your declarant was posted and, whilst here, discovered that the enemy were drowning their horses, etc. Not, however, entirely assured of what they were doing, he took his glass and mounted the highest, most prominent, and most exposed point of our fortifications, and there stood exposed to the enemy's fire, where shot seemed flying almost as thick as hail and were instantly demolishing portions of the embankment around him, for ten or fifteen minutes, until he had completely satisfied himself of the purposes of the enemy. During this time his aides, etc., were remonstrating with him with all their earnestness against this exposure of his person and once or twice drew him down. He severely reprimanded them and resumed his position. When satisfied, he dispatched a flag to the enemy, and they desisted from their purpose.

Your declarant continued at Yorktown till the surrender of Cornwallis. He then marched as a guard to the prisoners as far as Nolan's Ferry on the Potomac, where we delivered them to the Maryland troops. Thence he returned and was discharged about Christmas of that year, making this period of his service five months and a half, thus making the entire period of his service eight months and a half.[20]

Lastly, as a sampling of the accounts of boy soldiers in the American Army during the Revolution, there is the testimony of Israel Trask, aged ten, of Colonel Mansfield's Regiment.

In the year of our Lord 1775, having completed the tenth year of my age the fifth day of February of that year, I volunteered in the service of the United States as a soldier in a company commanded by Capt. John Low, Lieutenant, I believe his name was, Eveleth, Lieutenant Trask, Ensign Cooper, and Sergeant Major Widger in the regiment commanded by Colonel Mansfield, Lieutenant Colonel Hutchinson, and Major Putnam. In my application to the secretary's office for a certificate of service, I stated that the enlistment took place at Beverly, and the certificate itself purports the same, but the fact is, as I believe, it took place in Gloucester, as Lieutenant Trask, my father, procured a number of recruits there as well as other places, and Beverly was assigned for their meeting, and from thence marched to headquarters.

The precise time of the enlistment or that of joining the encampment of the army, my memory does not save me, and I can only state that Captain Low and the officers under him as well as the soldiers were bivouacked and under light tents during the summer months and part of the autumn. When cold weather set in we were put under barracks and quartered on Winter Hill during this period. I had various duties assigned me such as the care of the baggage and the property of the mess. When the officers were called on duty, which was daily the case, either to mount guard, or fatigue duties in fortifying the camp, the entrenchment of which had a line of continuity from

Winter Hill to Waterdown when finished, my duty alternately was to take the edibles prepared at the mess to the officers on duty, which in some instances [were] miles distant.

My knowledge of the general officers of the army during this first term of service was quite limited. General Greene I knew well. Mounted on a white horse, he made frequent visits of inspection to our regiment, from which I infer I was attached to the brigade he commanded. Major General Lee I also knew, from the circumstance of his angry threats to cane an officer of considerable grade in the army for unsoldierly conduct and the high excitement the fact created among the officers of the army.[21]

The year 1780 was one of the gloomiest of the century for Great Britain. Menaced by the combined arms of France and Spain in Europe, by the victorious Hyder Ali in Asia, the only force, a paltry one, she could spare from her armies needed for the protection of the homeland was fully engaged in this conflict with her insurgent subjects. At home the Gordon Riots were in full swing and London lay at the mercy of the mob.

It was an equally melancholy year for Washington, who clearly saw no hope but to make peace. He wrote to Congress: 'Indeed, I have almost ceased to hope . . . The circumstances of our allies, as well as our own, call for peace. We may expect soon to be reduced to the humiliating condition of seeing the cause of America, in America, upheld by foreign arms,' for it is impossible to expel the British forces 'till we derive more effectual aid from abroad.'[22]

Washington was being his usual pessimistic self and not entirely right, for time, the political situation, 3,000 miles of ocean, and the circumstances of beleagured Britain favoured the cause of the American Revolution. The isolation of what remained of the British forces under General Cornwallis in Yorktown, enabled Washington, with the help of 7,800 French regulars under General Rochambeau, to force a British surrender which, effectively, brought to an end the Revolutionary War.

CHAPTER VII
LIKELY LADS

Captain stiel's account of the 12th Foot during the American Revolutionary War is testimony to the extreme youth of the junior officers of that regiment, beginning their active service as 12 and 13 year olds. There is ample evidence from similar sources to support the view that this experience was general throughout the army and not restricted to the 12th. Not only the junior commissioned ranks but the lowly soldiers shared in the infant military apprenticeship.

From 1780 onwards the principle of training large numbers of very young boys became firmly entrenched among senior commanders of the army. The fact was that there never had been a nationally accepted age of, say, 18 for enlistment into the ranks. Rather it was more a case of thrusting a firelock into the hands of a boy—of whatever age—as soon as he was strong enough to handle one. Even this problem was soon overcome by the introduction of a lightweight musket known as the fusil. The ready acceptance of young boys sprung without doubt from the attitude of the regimental commanders who were always desperately short of recruits to fill their regiments' authorised strength. However, not until the closing years of the century was there a concerted national effort to enlist the very young in large numbers. Before explaining how this effort was organised and hopes realised we must look at the youthful experience of those who were to command the country's youth. Then we can examine the 20-year period from 1795 to 1815 to show how the principle was put into practice.

Among commanders during the Napoleonic Wars who served early apprenticeships in North America—and on other fronts too for that matter—some stand head and shoulders above their contemporaries: Lieutenant-Colonels McKenzie and Stewart of the Light Brigade, the Napier brothers and Generals Picton, Craufurd, Moore and Pakenham.

McKenzie was already in his mid-forties when, soon after the turn of the century, he helped shape Colonel Coote-Manningham's experimental corps of light infantrymen, later to become the famous Light Brigade. By that time

McKenzie had served for 35 years, having begun his career at the age of 13 as an ensign in the 33rd Foot.

Sir Thomas Picton rose to command the Third Division of the Peninsular Field Army under Wellington. Picton also began his military career as a 13-year-old ensign, in the 12th Foot in 1771. His biographer, writing in 1835 and referring to the young age at which Picton became an ensign, remarked:

> The present age would condemn the admission of so young a soldier into our army as unnatural and dangerous; for it is surely unnatural to expose to all the perils and privations of war those who still require maternal care.[1]

He was also moved to say that it was dangerous to place in authority those who had neither judgement nor resolution to perform arduous military duty. Picton spent a long period in the wilderness of civilian life as a half-pay officer before obtaining a senior appointment in the West Indies. While there he was accused of whipping a young slave girl and, although vindicated of the charge, carried the stigma of cruelty with him until his death at Waterloo.

Of all the great commanders who began military life in his youth, none was more renowned than Sir John Moore of Battle of Corunna fame. He joined the 51st Foot as an ensign of 14 but began his military training earlier than this. When he was 12 he accompanied his father, a travelling tutor to the Duke of Hamilton (a youngster the same age as John Moore), on a tour of Europe. In 1774 the trio visited Brunswick where Field-Marshal Sporken, Commander-in-Chief of the Duke of Brunswick's Army, assigned a sergeant to teach the boys the rudiments of Prussian drill and how to handle the flintlock musket. Writing to his mother, John Moore related that 'We are both pretty alert, and could fire a charge five times a minute'.[2] Considering that he was writing about the muzzle-loading firelock, one ball every 12 seconds was, if true (and this we must doubt), amazing.

At the same time that McKenzie, Moore and Picton were in training, other, equally young, boys were enjoying no such luxury, for they were in the battleline. Why? Because by that time the American Revolution was in full swing. 'When Picton joined the army it was not uncommon for a captain of a company to be a schoolboy while many of equally tender years were already on active service.'[3]

With continuous fighting in progress on all fronts by 1776, it might be thought that, with so many overseas possessions and a fast expanding empire to garrison, those in charge of troop movements would have provided regiments with a change of scenery from time to time; but no such consideration was given to those stationed overseas. Regiments were relieved of their stations but rarely and only then for the most compelling reasons.

The 58th Foot, for example, was so shattered by service in the West Indies that it became urgently necessary to withdraw it from the fighting zone to replenish its strength. This was accomplished not by returning the battalion to Great Britain, but by transferring it to Gibraltar. It arrived in time to receive its new recruits from England and to take part in the great siege beginning in 1779. It continued its existence at that station for many years and was considered one of the luckier battalions.

Boy soldiers of the Royal Artillery serving on the Rock were fully employed during the siege, helping service the guns. Boy soldiers of the infantry regiments, on the other hand, were found different employment. There was much for the infantry to do and, as recorded by the historian of the Northamptonshire Regiment, the 58th was used to keep in good repair the breastworks under fire from the Spanish batteries. Two boys of the regiment were posted as lookouts to warn the working parties when Spanish fire was directed at them. The sharp-eyed boys became so proficient that they could pinpoint the target directly a cannonball left its gun's barrel. The men became complacent until an occasion when, having chastised the others for ignoring one of his warnings, one of the lookouts turned to see a well-aimed shot. 'That one's not for us, lad,' someone said, but the ball scattered limbs over the rubble on which the men were working and from then on the survivors paid more attention to the lookouts. When the siege ended, the boys of the regiment each received the magnificent sum of £1 9s 1d as their share of the prize money.

The military experience in late eighteenth-century England has to be viewed against a background of civil disorder. English Jacobinism (closely related to the French Revolution) was on the rise. The Jacobins were the extreme radicals of the day, but the Dissenters and corresponding societies of a new working-class intellectualism were also at work stirring up the masses. In the absence of a police force, the army was called upon to cope with the rioters and, with serious rioting stretching far into the nineteenth century, was unable to stem the tide of insurrection which became endemic to the life of the nation. A long and sorry story of strife filled the next 50 years, during which the working population suffered chronically: the Gordon Riots (1780); the Luddites (1811 –13); the mobbing of George III in London (1795); the Bristol Riots (1839); the Labourers' Revolt; the East Anglia, Rebecca and Plug riots; all these constituted a lengthy period of upheaval.[4] The unrest initially was influenced by the French Revolution which, in turn, had a model in the American Revolution.

It is important to recognise the condition of Great Britain at this period, beginning about 1780, and the attendant misery of the working population, in order to juxtapose the plight of children in general with the relative good fortune of the young boys who joined the army. In the matter of clothing and personal belongings alone, there was no comparison. For example, each boy soldier in the Royal Artillery carried in his knapsack four white shirts, one check shirt, six false collars, a canvas frock, a pair of canvas trousers, a leather cap, two pairs of shoes, a pair of black cloth gaiters, a pair of white stockings, a powder bag and puff, a clothing brush, shoe brushes, a pair of worsted stockings, three pairs of Welsh yarn socks, a pair of shoe buckles, knee and stock buckles, one badge and one small comb.[5] If he was a drummer he was also provided with a warm fur hat.

We need only compare the rich material state of the boy soldier at that time with the condition of poverty-stricken villagers to get some measure of the differences. Commenting on poverty and parish relief, Rowland Parker, author of *The Common Stream*, dealing with the village of Foxton, writes: 'It is not easy to imagine the degradation of these wretched people as they trudged along to the overseer's house each week to collect the pittance on which they had to survive until the same time the following week.'[6] Nor was the poverty restricted to widows, orphans and the aged. 'So serious did this aspect [poverty] become that an Act of 1781 gave able-bodied men entitlement to parish relief for the first time . . .'[7]

The causes which gave rise to widespread poverty throughout the country at this period stemmed from conflicting social phenomena: a population explosion between 1780 and 1820 and a declining death rate. As described by Professor E. P. Thompson,[8] the population explosion was a European phenomenon brought about by improved medicine, 'nutrition' (potatoes), hygiene (soap and cotton shirt), water supplies and housing'. In other words, while social conditions improved there was less work and food to go round.

It was not only in food, clothing and shelter that boy soldiers enjoyed a privileged state. There was also the important consideration of education, the value of which in an age of general illiteracy cannot be overestimated. Increasing emphasis was being placed on this aspect of their lives and evidence of this occurs with increasing frequency from widely-scattered locales.

We have already come across the Hibernian Institution. In 1789 it was granted a Royal Charter and renamed the Royal Hibernian School. This meant, in effect, that it became part of the military establishment, so that from 1789 onwards the cost of running the school formed part of the annual budget, today known as the Defence Budget. This is an important distinction to make, even though at that time there was no emphasis on regarding the establishment as a sort of military kindergarten—that was to come later. However, a stronger military flavour was added to its daily life: medals were introduced as tokens of recognition of achievement (campaign medals were then unheard of in the regular army); defaulter reports were introduced; a band was formed and used on parades; the 'turncoat' concept was introduced for pupils found guilty of wrongdoing. More important, education and trades training were stressed. Also, older boys were employed to assist in the instruction of the younger pupils.[9]

Regimental officers everywhere were being more strongly urged to open schools. In London, officers of the Guards regiments contributed freely to a fund to start a school. The idea was taking root, but it was in distant India that the most important development took place. This was a system of education devised in an army-run school in Belem, Madras, by a clergyman, Dr Andrew Bell. (Belem crops up again in the most peculiar circumstances in 1846, so it is as well to keep this place in mind.)

The system developed by Bell became known as Bell's monitorial system and it dominated army education for the next 50 years. It was based on a novel principle. Bell selected and taught the brightest pupils the three Rs step by simple step. Once satisfied that these pupils, called monitors, had grasped their lessons, Bell gave them each charge of a certain number of other pupils to be taught what they had learnt. Theoretically, this system of pyramid teaching could be extended indefinitely. It ensured that Bell and his assistants could make the best use of their talents with limited resources. In its day it was both unique and simple although, like many new ideas, the same scheme of teaching was independently pioneered by Joseph Lancaster, a teacher in Scotland. Bell's monitorial system was at the root of a major upheaval in military education in 1846, but at the start it was a system without equal.

Late in the century (1797) the Royal Artillery Regiment, on the recommendation of a Captain William Rabe, began a second military school at Woolwich (not to be confused with the Royal Military Academy), which was soon taken over by the Board of Ordnance. Boy soldiers were made to attend the school along with children of the garrison, but here we must distinguish between boy soldiers and the children of soldiers. The first pupil, the son of a gunner in the Invalid Battalion, blew off both arms when firing a gun for his father. Because of these injuries he was granted a pension for life as a boy drummer, although in fact he had never been enlisted as a boy soldier. The story of the education of the children of the army has been told elsewhere.[10]

Lastly, in the matter of young soldier education and training, the army's commanders were waking up to the need to give boy officers a grounding in their basic duties, so that in 1799 'The Grand Duke [Frederick, Duke of York] established a military school at Great Marlow for cadets between the ages of 13 and 16'.[11] After four years' training the cadets were commissioned in the infantry and cavalry. Commanded by John Gaspard Le Marchant, the famous cavalry commander of Wellington's day, this school became the Royal Military College, Sandhurst.

Other things, too, were happening to help shape the course of history of boy soldiers and here, barely mentioned but hardly forgotten, was the outbreak of the French Revolution in 1792. Already alluded to is the connection between the French and American revolutions, separated by a mere 16 years. Whether by osmosis or a cross-fertilisation of ideas among the politically-conscious people of the two nations, a good case could be made for connecting the upheavals. As already indicated, Great Britain came close to revolution in the 1780s. In any case, numerous factors were at work, with the result that the armies of Revolutionary France burst upon a complacent Europe with devastating results and the Napoleonic Wars engulfed the continent.

Frederick, Duke of York, second son of George III, was sent to the Low Countries in command of a small British army to help stem the French tide, but try as he might he was not the man for the job. His contribution to the army, as events proved, lay in his worth as an influential reformer and administrator, a role to which he was particularly well suited. Lampooned by the wits of the day and dismissed as a useless popinjay by his opponents, the Duke of York was, nevertheless, a true friend of the ordinary soldier. Among his many achievements none was more beneficial to the life and comfort of the soldier than his programme to construct barracks, which began in 1792.

The use of barracks was not a new idea. It went back to the Elizabethan times and originated with the Spanish Army of the Duke of Parma. Also, barracks had existed in Ireland almost from the time that Cromwell's soldiers crossed the Irish Sea. By 1805 there were 203 barracks either built or under construction in England, Wales and Scotland capable of accommodating 146,000 infantry and 17,000 cavalry.[12] Boy soldiers had formerly shared the same accommodation as the men, but in the new barracks they were housed in the 'hospital' under the care of the drum major.

There was a huge expansion in the size of the British Army between 1792 and 1796. In 1792 there were 32,000 men in the home establishment (which did not include Ireland) and 164,000 (excluding 42,000 militia) in 1796.[13] The continuing appalling loss of men in West Indies garrisons, caused by tropical diseases, was the initial reason for the greatly increased enlistment of boy soldiers. Some regiments, notably the 22nd, 34th and 56th Regiments of Foot, were so reduced in strength that it was decided to turn them into experimental boy regiments and to acclimatise these youngsters in South Africa for eventual service in India. Consequently, the Adjutant General issued the first of a series of circular orders on the subject on 28 October 1795.[14] This permitted the commanding officers of the 9th, 16th, 22nd, 34th and 56th Regiments to enlist as many boys as need be to reach their authorised establishments. Advertisements similar to that which appeared in the *Ipswich Journal* of 17 December 1796 appealed for young recruits.

> Wanted, a Number of Boys, from 12 to 14 years of age, who will answer for Drummers or Music. The Commanding Officer assures their friends that the greatest care and attention will be paid to them. Any person bringing a boy of the above description, to Lieutenant Colonel Mercer, commanding the regiment at Colchester Barracks, shall receive ONE GUINEA, if approved of.[15]

An estimated number of 6,000 boys, aged 10 to 14 years, were enlisted under this first AG order.[16] It was undoubtedly under this programme that John Shipp, aged 10, an orphan of the village of Saxmundham, enlisted in the 22nd Foot. In his autobiography, written after he left the army for the second time, he gave a detailed account of boy soldiering in the 1790s a period when soldiers still wore their hair greased, powdered and shaped in a 'queue'. Shipp wrote a vivid description of this painful operation. Having had most of his curly locks shorn by the regimental barber, he graphically relates

> After this I went into the town to purchase a few things that I needed such as a powder-bag, puff, soap, dandles, grease and so on. As soon as I got back I had to undergo the operation of having my hair tied for the first time, to the no small amusement of the other boys. A large piece of dandle-grease was

applied first to the sides of my head, and then to the long hair behind. After this, the same operation was gone through with nasty, stinking soap, the man who was dressing me applying his knuckles as often as the soap to the delight of the surrounding boys who watched the tears roll down my cheeks. That part was bad enough, but the next was worse. A large pad, or bag, filled with sand, was poked into the back of my neck, the hair twisted tightly round it, and the whole tied with a leather thong. When thus dressed for parade, the skin of my face was pulled so tight by the bag stuck at the back of my head, that it was impossible so much as to wink an eyelid. Add to this an enormous high stock, which was pushed under my chin, and I felt as stiff as if I had swallowed a ramrod or the Sergeant's halbert. Shortly after this we were called to dinner, but my poor jaws could hardly move, and at every attempt to do so the pad behind went up and down like a sledgehammer.[17]

Within a year of Shipp's enlistment the 22nd Foot was in South Africa where it was in action against the Kaffirs, protecting Boer settlers, though the idea of boy soldiers (Shipp was in his twelfth year) protecting hardy Boer families seems incongruous. In many ways Shipp had, as he himself claimed, 'a most extraordinary military career'. He had the unusual, but not unique, experience of twice rising through the ranks to commissioned rank. The first time he sold his commission; the second time he lost it—for reasons not clearly explained but evidently for 'conduct unbecoming of an officer and a gentleman'—when he was found guilty of a charge related to shady horse dealing. (The feat of rising twice to commissioned rank was not again repeated until the Second World War, by Canadian boy soldier Ernest Cloutier: see Chapter XIV.)

The experimental boy soldier regiments were evidently successful because the 1795 order was followed by more in 1796, extending the scheme to other regiments. One order directed that

All healthy lads under sixteen years of Age, who are likely to grow, may be taken as low as five feet one inch. It will be necessary to pay particular attention to the make of these lads, and not to take any who are not properly straight, open chested and what is commonly called, long in the fork; nor any who are small limbed in general.[18]

Another order directed that boys be 'sent to Gibraltar to grow'[19] while the Duke of York in yet a third AG order objected to the enlistment of boys in Fencible regiments.[20]*

The orders stipulated what bounties were to be paid for, and to, boy recruits, and commanding officers were advised not to accept apprentices, being instructed to 'procure a certificate from the parish officers' to attest that such boys were not bound apprentices. In the circular the purpose for which the

---

*A Fencible regiment was a regular battalion raised for service in the country but not to be sent overseas. The militia, of course, was a formation of part-time soldiers for use in times of national emergency.

boys were recruited was made perfectly clear in the injunction 'They are to be enlisted as privates without any hope being held out to them that they are to be employed and paid as drummers.' The boy recruits were then trained to handle the fusil which, as already pointed out, was a lighter version of the regulation musket specially designed for boy recruits.

It had taken the authorities a century or more to recognise what a rich vein there was to be tapped for young recruits who could, with care, be rendered down and recast in the military mould. The Duke of York's hand and influence was clearly at work in this scheme, for numerous references to 'HRH, the Commander-in-Chief, has directed me to . . .' in AG orders of the period reminded regimental officers of the need to treat these young soldiers with kindness, care and consideration.

> It will be needless to suggest to you the necessity of more than ordinary regularity in the article of Messing, Cleanliness and Conduct in Quarters, which can only be enforced . . . by the unremitting care of the Officers and NCOs of the Regiment. HRH recommends in general terms the utmost Mildness and Lenity as the best modes of establishing Discipline and attaching Lads to H.M.'s service and commands me to suggest for your consideration the expediency of establishing a Regimental School for the instruction of such as them as discover Abilities in the necessary Qualifications of reading and writing with a view of their becoming hereafter useful and valuable NCOs.[21]

From 1795, when the first order was issued, until 1811 at least 25 AG circular orders were issued which dealt exclusively with the enlistment, training and use of boy soldiers. Some were directed to individual battalion commanders, such as that in January 1805 to the commanding officer of the 96th Foot,[22] while the majority were addressed to large numbers of regiments.

By 1811 the extensive use of boys was firmly established, for that year a new order was issued by which all previous orders on the subject were cancelled. This order was dated 17 January 1811[23] and under its authority, colonels of regiments were permitted to enlist boys under 16 years of age at the rate of 10 boys per regimental company. The emphasis placed on the care and attention to be paid by officers and NCOs to the welfare of the boy recruits was unremitting. The January 1811 order, like those which preceded it, was specific.

> The utmost attention is required to be paid by their officers and NCOs to the messing, cleanliness and general conduct of the boys, as from their unremitting care and superintendence, the gradual formation of these boys into useful soldiers is (ultimately) to be expected, and on their exertion must depend the ultimate success and benefit which is expected to accrue for the service from the (adoption) of these measures.*

*The words in parenthesis are not clear in the original document.

Arms were not to be put into the hands of boys until they had been trained in their field exercises and, because it was recognised that they had not the strength to handle the regular musket, additional supplies of the fusil were to be provided.

Given the regiments authorised to enlist a high complement of boys, and the authorised strength of boy soldiers in all units, we may reasonably compute the total number of boys aged from 10 to 16 in the British Army at the height of the Peninsular Campaign (1811). There were 180 battalions* of infantry, each with an average of 20 boys or a total of, say, 3,600. Added to this there were roughly 100 additional boys allowed to each of the regiments listed in the January 1811 AG circular. Some of these regiments were single battalion formations; others had two battalions. Allowing 30 battalions for the 22 regiments listed in the order we get 3,000 boys. In 1811, therefore, the infantry had some 6,600 young soldiers in its ranks. Add to this figure the boy soldier strengths of the Royal Artillery, cavalry and miscellaneous formations, and the total number of boy soldiers in the British Army was more probably in the order of 11,000.

The youngest soldier on record to enlist was Drummer James Wade of the 9th Foot who joined on his seventh birthday, 10 July 1800. One suspects from his age that he was 'born in the regiment'. The families of serving soldiers were a regular source of boy recruits, for as soon as a soldier's son was taken on the strength of a regiment he became one less mouth for the hard-pressed family to feed. In many respects, these healthy sons of soldiers were more fortunate than their contemporaries in civilian life—not the least of these advantages being in having a career already mapped out for them.

The year 1800 also saw the army reform movement, which had been gathering momentum under the Duke of York, make enormous gains in the influence it exerted over military life. As a result, serving soldiers of all ranks benefited in many tangible ways: in training, discipline, living conditions and the reduction of corporal punishment meted out to them. The queue hairstyle had by then been done away with—and though boys still had their locks shorn by the regimental barber they at least no longer had to suffer the ordeal John Shipp and his companions endured. By modern standards army life was still extremely hard, but the first faint winds of change which had begun to blow with the construction of barracks in 1792 were now more strongly in evidence.

The reforms were not the work of any one man. Rather, they were the outcome of a changing military philosophy characterised by the actions and influence of a small group of officers. This group, headed by the Duke of York, is easily identified by its achievements which, tested in the field, both in the Peninsular Campaign and at Waterloo, contributed in large measure to Wellington's victories. This is not to diminish Wellington's greatness as a battle commander, but there is no doubt that the weapon he wielded was fashioned for him by others.

*This number includes the 104th Foot, the New Brunswick Regiment, generally omitted from military histories covering the period under discussion.

The most prominent members of the group, other than the Duke of York, were Moore, Le Marchant, Manningham and Stewart. There were others, of course, whose influence was felt to a greater or lesser extent, but none brought about fundamental changes anywhere near approaching those wrought by these five architects of army reform.

The Duke of York had good reason for seeking and promoting reform. As commander of the army during the Flanders Campaign of 1794-5, he suffered greatly from having to contend with 'boys and idiots' for officers, and from a lack of support from the government. This was especially true in the matter of what today is termed 'logistical support'. He therefore knew from firsthand experience that an army to be successful, must be provided with adequate supplies of food, clothing, arms and money. He was opposed to the practice of young men with no military training and experience buying commissions. He tried hard to put a stop to it, despite a later charge, indirectly brought against him in the celebrated case of the impeachment of his mistress, Mrs Clarke, that he himself peddled commissions and promotion. Not surprising, then, was the support and help he gave Le Marchant to start the Royal Military College.

He was equally concerned for the children of the rank and file, for orphans and the destitute families of soldiers killed in battle or who died on active service. In 1800 he obtained a Royal Charter to found an 'Asylum for the orphaned children of fallen soldiers'.[24] The Royal Military Asylum (asylum here means 'haven') opened its doors in 1803 on premises adjacent to the Royal Pensioners Hospital, Chelsea. The Royal Military Asylum thus became, after the Royal Hibernian Military School, Dublin, the second military school on the military establishment. (The Asylum is hereafter referred to by its present name, the Duke of York's Royal Military School or, simply, the Duke of York's.)

These two schools—and a third which will be introduced later— occupy an important place in the annals of British military history, and, so far as is known, are unique in the armies of the Western world; the nearest parallels to be found are in the military systems of Sparta and the Irish Celts. Their contribution to the army, in providing a constant supply of young soldiers superbly trained and educated to army life, cannot be overestimated. Furthermore, being *bona fide* military units, the place of these military schools in the history of the British Army is explored in detail in Chapter IX.

Of the reform group, Manningham and Stewart were primarily responsible for creating the Experimental Corps of Riflemen that was to become the 95th Foot, and later to form part of the Rifle Brigade. Both Manningham and Stewart began their careers as boy ensigns: Manningham at 14 and Stewart at 13. Similarly, having both served in the American War, they learned the harsh lessons of reality in fighting sharpshooters, of taking advantage of ground cover, and of skirmishing in open order.

The formation of special riflemen units was by no means an original idea; Prussian skirmishers and French *tirailleurs* were already features of those European armies. Colonel de Rottenburg published his *Regulations for the*

Exercise of Riflemen and Light Infantry in 1797 and the English translation of this work, published the following year, formed the basis for training Manningham's Experimental Corps. These two officers persuaded the Duke of York and others of the need for such a corps and so the 95th came into existence.

To obtain suitable recruits for the new regiment an AG order was sent to 14 regiments of foot, requiring each to draft two sergeants, two corporals and 30 men for rifle training. The order also stated that

> Eight drummers will be required to act as bugle horns, and I request you will acquaint me, for the information of His Royal Highness, [the Duke of York] whether you have any in the . . . Regiment qualified to act as such, or of a capacity to be easily instructed.[25]

Initially, 13 drummers were transferred to the 95th and by the end of the year the number had increased to 18. The reason for wanting buglers in preference to drummers becomes obvious when it is realised that the new rifle corps was to operate in open or extended order as opposed to the close-packed formation of the infantry of the line battalions. In such densely-packed units everyone was within hearing of the commanding officer's drummer who beat out the orders to advance, retire, extend, close up, and so on. Riflemen would need the instructions of their superior officers transmitted over greater distances, for which a bugle sound was more satisfactory.

The transferred drummers therefore exchanged their drums for 'bugle-horns' and buckled down to learning their calls, which by 1805 totalled 57 in all. Some were borrowed from the Prussian Army; others were specially written for the 95th and other light infantry regiments and either gained recognition or came into existence soon after 1800. The calls published in de Rottenburg's *Regulations* were borrowed in their entirety and to these were added the balance as published in Captain T. M. Cooper's *A Practical Guide to the Light Infantry Officer*, which came out in 1806. The calls provided for every contingency and emergency with which the new rifle corps was likely to meet, either in or out of battle. These included such gems as 'The Enemy is Infantry' and 'The Enemy is Cavalry'—as though it would not be obvious who might be bearing down on them. The buglars also had to master longer pieces, post calls which included 'Reveille', 'Officer's dinner', 'Last Post', and a repertoire of marches.

The new riflemen in 'Manningham's Sharpshooters', as the 95th soon became known, soon proved their worth as the eyes and ears of field commanders by forming a protective screen around the slower-moving regiments of the line. The new corps was created in a new spirit unknown to regiments born in the previous century, and the quality of leadership had everything to do with it. The regulations which governed the riflemen were novel, for they showed a refreshing enlightenment on the part of the commanders. Under this new order the boy soldiers were equal beneficiaries with the men.

Under the ponderous title *Regulations for the Rifle Corps formed at Blatch-ington Barracks under the Command of Colonel Manningham, August 15, 1800,* the new weapon of the British Army took shape. By the time the 95th was joined by the 43rd and 52nd Foot at Shorncliffe in 1803, to form what later became known as the Light Brigade, it had already seen active service. The new formation was placed under the command of Sir John Moore.

With Moore in command an even more ambitious system of training was instituted and the rank and file, no less than the officers, took to it with verve and panache. Under Moore's direction the men found themselves well fed; they were encouraged to read, to write, to educate themselves and—what must have been a blessed relief—the mind-dulling drill of the infantry was abolished in favour of the new (for British infantry) system of open-order training. More important than anything else, the lash was all but (not entirely) dispensed with. A pairing-off of the rank and file as devised by Manningham and Stewart was undertaken by Moore. This was especially important to the boy buglers because each was placed under the care of an older, experienced, soldier by which means, consciously or unconsciously, the commanders provided them with surrogate father figures. The passage dealing with this subject (in the regulations) read

> The captain . . . having formed his company thus equally, will arrange comrades. Every Corporal, Private and bugler will select a comrade of the ranks differing from his own, ie, front and rear rank, and is never to change him without permission of his captain. Comrades are always to have the same berth in quarters; and, in either barracks or the field, will form the same file on parade and go on the same duties with arms . . . The Corporal's comrade should either be the *Chosen Man* or some steady man of the squad or who can occasionally help him in his duty; and the buglers' comrades the odd man of any two squads where there are any.[26]

It may be suspected that the system of berth sharing led to a more than comradely companionship, especially as far as the boy soldiers were concerned. Perhaps; it is hard to say, but there is no evidence in available regimental records to lead one to such a conclusion.

Training under Moore was intense and revolutionary in many ways: all ranks mixed together on the sports field; the rank and file lived in decent quarters for a change; they were divided into messes, hence the improved quality of food; and the officers were considerate towards the men. The whole concept of the officer-soldier relationship was revolutionary; nor were the buglers neglected or ignored.

Not all boys were buglers, for some marched in the ranks of the riflemen, as will be understood from the army orders previously cited. Rifleman Harris, for example, formerly a shepherd boy, was by his own testimony quite young when he joined the army, first in the militia as a result of The Army Reserve Act of 1803, then in the 66th Foot, followed by a transfer to the 95th. His father, who was not a military man, tried hard to dissuade him from listening to the recruiting sergeant but, as Harris records, 'The Sergeant, however, said I was just the sort of little chap he wanted', and so proved himself the more persuasive.[27] His age on joining is not known. However, writing of himself as, say, a 14-year-old he was more likely to use the term 'little chap' than had he been 16 or 17 when he joined.

The newly-established Duke of York's immediately proved to be an important source of boy recruits. The Asylum (there were two branches at the time: the main institution at Chelsea and an 'overflow' branch at Southampton) accommodated children of both sexes but with a total number exceeding 2,000. I estimate that boys in the order of 250 were available annually for military service during the first few years of the institution's existence. Competition among infantry, artillery and cavalry units to secure the enlistment of these young recruits (known as 'Dukies') by the time they reached their eleventh and twelfth years was fierce. Taken together with the Royal Hibernians, the army was assured of an estimated yearly intake of 300 boys from this source. Many, but not all, boys automatically enlisted in their fathers' regiments, a tradition that was maintained until the beginning of the Second World War.

Private (later Sergeant) Wheeler of the 51st Foot records that in 1807 when the regiment was stationed at Chichester under the command of Colonel Mainwaring, several boys from the Duke of York's 'with other boys born in the Regiment, were put on pay'.[28] Dukies from the outset had been a proud and rambunctious lot and those of the 51st were not in the regiment long before they were in trouble. They organised a raid on the cherry orchard, but unable to lay hands on a single Dukie, the farmer reported them to the Colonel. Mainwaring had the regiment's boy soldiers mustered for identification but the farmer was stymied.

> Said the Colonel, 'I see, was not this the case. When you looked over the hedge, they young rogues popped over the opposite.'
> 'Just so, sir,' the farmer replied.
> 'I thought as much. They have learnt something from the crows that robs you of your corn. Like them they had thrown out their sentries, so they out-generaled you, but I am too old a soldier to be done by such a set of young spalpeens . . . I will make the whole of the rascals disgorge the contents of their stomachs at our feet.'[29]

He ordered the Sergeant of the hospital to bring him a supply of emetics, but the threat of a dose of laxative each was enough to make the scrumpers identify themselves. What happened to the guilty is not recorded, but knowing the character of Mainwaring it is doubtful if the punishment was severe. The Colonel was neither a vindictive nor a brutal officer and, once the farmer was satisfied the culprits had been exposed, he probably treated the escapade as a joke.

Not everyone agreed with the scheme to enlist boys and at least one recruiting officer expressed himself in strong terms on the subject in an official report. This was Major Grey of the Nottingham Recruiting District who, in writing to the Secretary of State in 1809, deplored the practice and suggested that most of them would enlist if left till they grew up. When taken so young, he said, they contracted the bad habits of their seniors and many died.[30]

Without being callous, bad habits and premature death before they went into action were not the major problems. It soon became evident that the cost of their upkeep and maintenance placed an insuperable burden on their regimental officers who, by and large, were acutely conscious of their responsibilities. Reports of enlistment bounties, rates of pay and subsistence allowances during this period are conflicting and confusing, but these facts emerge. First, the bounty paid to boy recruits, being £5 5s 0d, was about half that paid to adult recruits; second, a boy's pay and allowances, amounting to 6s 11d, was considerably less than that received by an adult private soldier. The army was obviously getting its boy soldiers on the cheap. The lack of adequate financial support presented enormous problems to the regimental officers because, whereas in the past all due allowance was made for growing boys, the authorities now seemed to think that boys needed less for their upkeep than grown men. The inadequacy of pay and subsistence allowances was a constant cause for complaint from commanding officers.

In a lengthy submission to the Commander-in-Chief, Adjutant-General Henry Calvert summarised the opinions of four of the most experienced commanding officers with whom he had consulted on this vexing subject and asked to submit reports. These were the COs of the Royals, the Regiment of Royal Fusiliers, and the 14th and 36th Regiments of Foot. He tabled a breakdown of disbursements (see table). The remaining sum of 1s 1d per week, amounting to £2 16s 4d per annum, was required to maintain a boy's uniform, to replace worn-out clothing, and to pay for barrack damages. Lieutenant-Colonel Nicholls of the 14th, abstracting figures from the regimental accounts, reported by way of example that the debt of one boy for the year was £3 14s 9½d; of another £3 17s 0d.[31] The reports of the other commanding officers told similar stories. All this meant that the boy soldiers, in effect, were subsidising the army since they were always in its debt.

	Royals	Fusiliers	14th	36th
Board & Meat	3s 6d	3s 6d	3s 6d	3s 6d
Vegetables	7d	7d	7d	7d
Washing	3d	4d	4d	5d
Subsistence	6d	3½d	5d	2d
Badges of War & Other Necessities	1s 0d	1s 1½d	1s 0d	1s 2d
Weekly Cost	5s 10d	5s 10d	5s 10d	5s 10d

In this account of the massive boy soldier recruiting programme during the

Napoleonic Wars, three sources of recruits have been noted: the civilian population (which included the children of the poor houses), the military schools, and children born in the regiment. However, it was not only in England, Wales and Scotland that the programme was put into operation. In Ireland, too, there was extensive enlistment of boys into the ranks as opposed to service as drummers and buglers. And although we are primarily concerned with the regular army, the record of the Irish Militia gives some measure of the boy soldier complement. In any case, the Irish Militia between 1793 and 1816 served in Ireland full time, to all intents and purposes as a fencible force.[32] Further, as thousands of militia soldiers were persuaded to transfer to the regular army throughout the great war with France, the militia records are a significant indicator.

Under the Militia Amending Act of 1811[33] it was provided that not more than one quarter of militia recruits raised annually in each county of Ireland should consist of boys aged 14 and up. A total strength of 21,660 rank and file had been authorised. The Amending Act, therefore, ensured that many thousands of boys would be in militia service, trained, and ripe for transfer into the regular army.

When it is remembered that young boys in uniform were continually being replaced by other boys when they themselves reached man-service age, there can be only one conclusion: a large proportion of the British Army consisted of mere youths. It would appear then, that the land battles fought by Great Britain from 1800 to 1815 were fought not by grizzled veterans of 20 years and up, but by 14 to 20 year olds. It was an exceptionally young army, and it is probable that Napoleon's army was similarly constituted.

To summarise, the many orders dealing with the enlistment of boys brought thousands of likely lads to serve the army for life, at a period when life was often short and death swift. Many of them we will meet in the next few years as experienced NCOs who, thanks to the education they received in the hands of concerned and dedicated officers, were able to write reminiscences of military life never before equalled by the 'rank and file', for they formed the core of Wellington's army. In the light of what we now know of their extreme youth, one has to wonder at Wellington's remark that the soldiers of his army were the 'scum of the earth'. Scum indeed! They were the very flower of the nation.

CHAPTER VIII
FIELD ARMY BRATS

IN THE SAME month that Drummer Wade enlisted in the 9th Foot, July 1800, an unknown field commander in distant India, far removed from the battlefields of the great war with France, began earning his reputation as a sepoy general. This was Arthur Wellesley (later the Duke of Wellington), who took to the field in the state of Mysore against the Dhoondiah Waugh, described by one of Wellington's biographers as a 'Mahratta Freebooter'.[1] While the future duke, thus gainfully employed, was building his incomparable reputation, others, as we have shown, were equally busy shaping the invincible army he was to command in the Iberian peninsula during the Peninsular Campaign.

Having described the massive recruiting programme for boy soldiers it is natural that we should want to know how they acquitted themselves on the field of battle; but first a sketch of Drummer Wade, for his brief history is known.

While he could have no way of knowing it at the time, nor anyone else for that matter, he was to become a minute part of Wellington's army. Even as a child Wade joined for life as was then the common practice, and did not enter man service* until his eighteenth birthday in 1811. By that time he had taken part in half a dozen major battles, numerous combats, and had tramped a thousand miles or more, for the 9th Foot was in the force sent to Portugal at the outset of the Peninsular Campaign. Despite the fact that Wade joined for life he was given a sick discharge after 25 years of service because of wounds received when a boy in one of the peninsular battles.

John Shipp of the 22nd, from whose company we parted in South Africa before the turn of the century, was promoted to corporal before he was 18 and soon regarded the lowly drummer as 'little better than his drum'.[2] His regiment was transferred to India, where it took part in numerous campaigns against the Mahrattas. More than once did Shipp join the 'forlorn hope',** to

---

*The term 'man service' has always been used by boy soldiers to distinguish between their own service and that of adult-serving soldiers.
**Forlorn hope was the name given to storming parties or any desperate enterprise in which the participants had little hope of surviving the ordeal.

assure himself of attracting the attention of his superiors and of rising through the ranks to his first commission.

Elsewhere there was enough active service to satiate the appetite of the hardiest soldiers: there were expeditions to Egypt, the Mediterranean, South America, the Scheldt, Sweden and the West Indies. We could look at any one of these compaigns to discover what ordeals boy soldiers experienced, but for the sake of continuity and in view of the abundance of material it is more expedient to concentrate on the Peninsular Campaign and the Battle of Waterloo.

Briefly, the decision to mount an expedition to the Iberian Peninsula was the result of a Spanish appeal to the British government in June 1808. A token force of 9,000 men (comprising cavalry, artillery and infantry units), which some military historians would refer to as 9,000 sabres and bayonets, was allocated to the expedition. A short time after it sailed an additional 5,000 reinforcements were added. The original number included 229 boy soldier drummers and trumpeters, together with an unspecified but large element of underage soldiers who, from 1805 onwards, had enlisted under the AG orders already discussed.

So it was that in the autumn of 1808, with colours unfurled, drums beating and fifes trilling, the various contingents of the expeditionary force converged on England's south coast embarkation ports. The troops, their scarlet, blue and yellow uniforms contrasting vividly against the sombre autumnal hues, snaked along the King's highways, oblivious to the fate awaiting them once they crowded on to the dirty, stinking wooden ships that were to carry them from Britain's shores. They marched as on many occasions before and after, little realising how many British soldiers left and never returned. Nor perhaps would this have troubled them, for the enthusiasm for active service was general.

Private Wheeler reported that Colonel Mainwaring had written to the Duke of York on behalf of the 51st, he told the regiment, to say 'We were all tired of eating the bread of idleness and longing to go out on service'.[3] The Commander-in-Chief's reply had been to grant the request so that the 51st, content to a man, found itself among those converging battalions selected for the expedition.

The first clash on the peninsula occurred at Roliça when Wellington defeated 4,000 French under General Laborde. Wellington then advanced on Lisbon to meet the hastily-gathered forces of Marshal Junot's 30,000-strong army of occupation. At the Battle of Vimeiro 17,000 British clashed with 14,000 French, and that too ended in a victory for Wellington. He was then joined by Moore who brought reinforcements from an abortive expedition sent to help the King of Sweden.

Following the success at Vimeiro an armistice was negotiated at Cintra. Under the terms of the Convention, Junot's troops were permitted to leave Portugal by courtesy of the British transport ships which had brought Wellington's and Moore's troops to the country. Odd that one enemy should be so

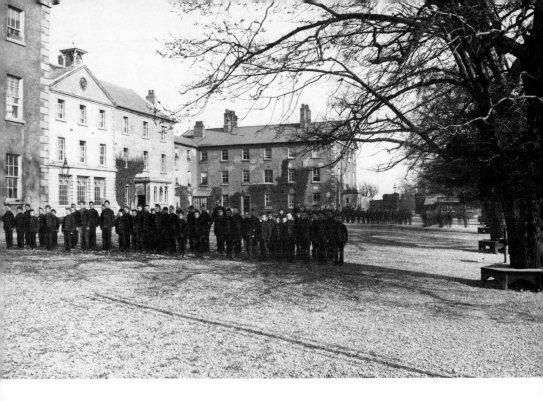

The Royal Hibernian Military School,
Phoenix Park, Dublin. Muster Parade
(c. 1898).

Royal Hibernian 'old sweat' with pensioner of
the Royal Irish Pensioner's Hospital, Dublin
(c. 1898).

Two brothers in the Duke of York's Royal Military School, Dover – 1940.

Brothers in Arms, England 1943. Ages 18, 17, 14 and 13 years.

Duke of York's Dover, 1981. Trooping the colour.

Army Technical School, Arborfield, 1946. Passing out Parade. The Inspecting Officer is Field-Marshal Viscount Montgomery.

Army apprentices at lunch (c. 1947). The gentleman in the trilby is Emanuel Shinwell, MP, who was a conscientious objector and Minister of War, 1945.

Pay parade at Army Technical College, Arborfield, 1980.

Boys Troop. Mounted Squadron, Corps of Royal Engineers, 1936.

Boy Bob Kennelly, second from right, with companions of RAOC in walking-out dress (c. 1965).

Boy Robert C. Thompson, Canadian Army, enlisted aged 13 during World War I. He was a Sgt-Major when the armistice was signed.

Trumpeters J. J. Dobbs and Greenhow, RA on arrival in Quetta, India, April 1930

Trumpeters of the Royal Artillery Depot, Woolwich, 1929.

Pte Walter Beck, aged 15, of the Nova Scotia Regiment, 1918.

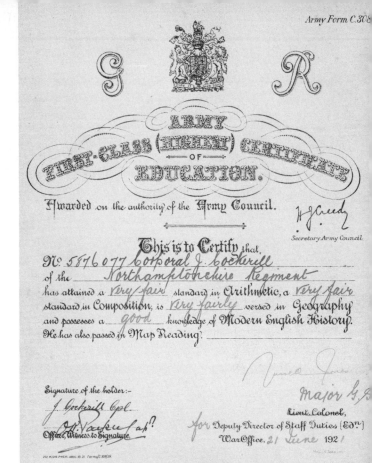

Example of the Army First-Class Certificate of Education awarded to soldiers in the 1920s.

Roy Kennelly, far left, with companions of RAOC 'junior soldiers' in fatigue dress (circa 1965).

Recruit Apprentice
Tradesmen during room
inspection by Sgt. K. S.
Edwards, RE.

Boy recruits of the 5th Batt.
Rifle Brigade during the
1914–18 war.

accommodating, but it was an age in which enemies were still civil to one another and there were many occasions on which the French demonstrated equal regard for a vanquished foe. Although Wellington was not a party to the Convention he signed the document at the behest of his superior, Sir Hew Dalrymple, who had arrived on the scene while Vimeiro was in progress. Wellington then handed over command of the army to Moore and returned to England to face the music, once details of the Convention became known to the public.

With the road to Spain now open, Moore led his small army across the Portuguese-Spanish frontier to challenge the lion in his den, for Napoleon, who had complained that the army in Spain seemed to be commanded by 'post-office inspectors', was now in the country himself at the head of 194,000 men. Vastly outnumbered, the small British army trekked towards the Douro River with its women, children, camp followers and baggage wagons bringing up the rear. Moore felt justified in making this move because he had promise of support from the Spanish who had asked for British help in the first place. Nevertheless, this was unlooked-for boldness on Moore's part and prompted Napoleon to change his plans for the subjugation of southern Spain, to deal with the impudent intruder. There then occurred a sharp reverse in Moore's fortunes. The Spanish help he expected failed to materialise, which compelled him to beat a hasty retreat. So began the dreadful march of Moore's army across the northern mountains of Portugal in the dead of winter.

There have been many retreats conducted under appalling conditions and, while the experience of Moore's troops cannot be compared with the great retreat of Napoleon from Moscow, it must stand among the worst soldiers have had to endure. Carried out over treacherous mountain tracks in foul weather, without food, shelter or the means of sustaining themselves, the soldiers, their women and children suffered to the limit of their endurance.

Going by the available muster rolls of the units of Moore's army, there were 350 boy soldiers, including those Dukies of the 51st who had mounted the cherry orchard raid at Chichester the previous year. The 350, however, excluded that large number who had enlisted 'with no hope being held out to them that they would be paid or serve as drummers'. How many of these youngsters fell out from exhaustion along the way is not known. That many did perish between the Douro River and Corunna is certain.

The drummers were as badly off as any on the retreat, for a drum is a burdensome thing to carry at the best of times. Slung over the shoulder by its lanyards it was more awkward to carry than the musket. Bugler John MacFarlane, aged 16, who two years earlier was outside Montevideo with 'other youths who did their duty',[4] took part in the retreat. MacFarlane, of the 71st Foot, was well under man-service age but, by any standards, he was a veteran soldier. Enlisting in 1802 at the age of ten he was by 1808 old enough to be issued with a musket in addition to his bugle. MacFarlane wrote of the retreat:

We came to Astorga. We expected to get into it, but it was full of Spanish troops, and the fever had broke out there, we halted outside, and got some bread served out. We went further on till we came to some houses and halted for the night. The weather was very changeable, sometimes rain, then frost and snow. It was difficult to get houses to shelter us for the night. We went off the road to a small village. There were six or eight of us put into one house. The people were baking bread, and got it into the oven, but they were keeping watch over it, and we were watching them. But it was managed to divert them off their guard and a load of bread was stolen out. It would be six or eight pounds weight. It was carried out, and by the light of the moon, divided into shares. They soon found out that one of the loaves was stolen. We had to march early in the morning. I put a pair of dry stockings and shoes on to keep my feet comfortable. But we had not gone far when came to a river. There was no bridge. We had to go into it, and pass over. One of our officers got his servant to carry him on his back. Our Colonel came riding to him, crying out 'Put him down, put him down', for he was very angry. We were well pleased at it. The French were keeping close behind us, and if the men did not keep up, they were sure to be taken prisoner. The roads were very bad, if they could be called roads. Many of us put on new shoes in the morning, and before night, had no shoes. Our marching was in the night as well as in the day. We had a blanket each of us to carry. But we made one blanket to serve two, and many of the men had none. I had a good comrade. He was abler to keep up with the Regiment than I was, and he carried the blanket. We came to what we called the Snow Mountains. We had a long day's march. It was 1st January, 1809. There were very few houses to be seen. Some of the men ran into them, but they soon came out. There were Spanish soldiers in them, sick, and some lying dead. We were now descending the mountains, and owing to the snow melting, the road was deep with mud and dirt. It was very dark. In going to one side, it was so deep that I could not get out. The Regiment was passing, and another coming up. To cry for help it was in vain. I made one effort after another, and to save myself from falling in, I had to throw down my firelock, and in this way I got out. I then got hold of my firelock, for it was not so deep down. But it was not easy to get my shoes, but I got them. I came off with my firelock over my shoulder, covered with mud, and my shoes in my hand. While I was standing, and not able to extricate myself, I could not help weeping, for I was not eighteen years of age.[5]

At Astorga Moore detached the Light Brigade under Craufurd and sent it on a southerly route to the coast to protect his flank. So while the main force threaded its way over the inhospitable mountains to Corunna, the Light Brigade headed for the small coastal port of Vigo. Neither route was easier than the other. Many fell by the wayside and perished, but it is a testimony to Moore's training of the light infantrymen at Shorncliffe that the losses of the new Rifle Corps were relatively small. The 95th, for example, lost only one sergeant, 13 riflemen and a bugler from starvation and exhaustion, while its losses in killed and wounded from rearguard actions amounted to 136.

During this retreat, as recorded by Rifleman Harris, Craufurd held a drumhead court martial for two would-be deserters—and a third rifleman, Dan Howens, who spoke his mind too freely in the General's hearing during the trial proceedings of the other two. For his insubordination, before the retreat was allowed to continue, Howens was awarded 300 lashes, the punishment being delivered on the spot by reliefs of buglers. Grim punishment indeed, for the buglers as well as Howens. Dan Howens' wife witnessed the punishment and carried her husband's equipment once the march resumed.

Wherever the retreating troops stopped to rest they found Spanish troops in possession of the only available accommodation. Wrote Sergeant Benjamin Miller of the Royal Artillery:

Frosty weather now came in . . . for we were getting on the mountains where the snow frequently lay all summer, which froze some of the men to death. Plague began among the Spanish Troops, but there was very few of them with us.

One town we passed through, we saw some Spanish soldiers carry some dead men into the yard. We looked in for curiosity and saw a large heap of dead bodies, froze together like lumps of dirt. Our officers soon ordered us away.[6]

The pursuing French were as hard pressed as the retreating British and used their cavalry to head the pursuit column. During one of the skirmishes with the 95th rearguard General Colbert, Commander of the French cavalry, was picked off by one of the Light Brigade's sharpshooters, who calmly reloaded his rifle and shot the young bugler who went to his general's aid. Then the nimble rifleman retired among his companions before the avenging French cavalrymen could reach him. Like the *tirailleurs* of the French Army, the British riflemen knew who were the important figures in the enemy ranks to put out of action.

At Vigo, the Light Brigade was removed by Royal Navy ships and taken to safety without too much molestation from the French. However, the fortunes of the main column under Moore were not as bright. At Corunna Moore was forced to fight before he could embark the survivors of the retreat. Struck by a cannonball in the shoulder, he died on the battlefield and was buried where he fell.

Major Napier, one of three Napier brothers and historian of the Peninsular War, was taken prisoner during the battle and saved from certain death by one Guibert, a French drummer. Wounded far in advance of his regiment, Napier was attacked for plunder by an Italian in the French service but managed to deflect the soldier's thrusting bayonet. 'Recovering in a moment, I regained my legs and saw the florid handsome young French drummer holding the arm of the dark Italian, who was in the act of repeating the blow.'[7] Quarter was given, but only after Napier had been relieved of his valuables. Helping him to the rear, Drummer Guibert defended the prisoner from a second murderous attack by his companions. Napoleon, to whom the story was related, always rewarded the generosity of his soldiers to the enemy. For his gallantry Guibert was awarded the cross of the Legion of Honour.

The shattered but victorious army embarked under cover of darkness to be shipped back to England. MacFarlane provided an illuminating account of the conditions of the survivors when they landed at Ramsgate.

> We were not long till we came in sight of Ramsgate. I left my old firelock with the sailors. But in preparing to leave the ship, I went to my knapsack to put on my new shoes that I got when I came to Corunna, but to my sad disappointment they were stolen away by some one. I had to keep on my old shoes without stockings. When I landed, the regiment was on parade ready to march off for Canterbury. We joined our company with the same appearance as we came from Corunna. We marched off, and it was not long till it came on very wet. I went forward as well as I could, but my old shoes would not keep on my feet. I had then to take them off. I did the best I could for some time but had to fall out of the ranks. A Corporal was ordered to go with me. The people were looking at the regiment passing, but when they saw me, I was looked upon as an object of pity. Well might they say, 'Here is a representative of what we have heard about Corunna retreat.' I was stopped; shoes and stockings brought to me, and I was putting them on, they were asking questions about me at the Corporal, for he was a countryman of their own. The English showed no small kindness to the soldiers that came from Corunna. When they came into the towns after marching, some of the people took them to their houses without billets. We came away, and I was very thankful for the kindness showed to me. My comrade and I was billeted in a public house. After getting our supper, the people that came in to drink were asking us questions about what we had come through, and what we had seen. But we were wearied with the journey, and my comrade was complaining of pain in the head and he wanted to go to bed.
>
> Next day we marched to Ashford, and this ended our journeying for a time. I said that my comrade was unwell, and when we came to Ashford, he was no better. He had to go into hospital, and it was not long till I heard that he was dead. A good number died of fever. Also our head surgeon Doctor Evans. He was much respected. For a short time, we got coffee for breakfast. We had not to get our knapsacks renewed, and it was well for them that lost theirs for they got £2.2.0. I should have let mine drop off my back, for it was not worth two shillings. After receiving what things I was in need of I was in debt about five pounds, but I received five pounds for my wound, and this paid my debt. In this place we were made a Light Infantry Regiment.[8]

The Peninsular expedition was in fact just another disaster to add to the list of military misadventures of the war with France. Many of the units which took part in that expedition were re-equipped and sent on the ill-fated Walcheren expedition. Within a few short weeks the men were dying in their hundreds from what was called Walcheren fever.

In the meantime the government decided to mount a major effort in Portugal under the command of Wellington, who had the services of General Beresford to command the Portuguese troops with British and Portuguese officers. The Peninsular War began in earnest with Wellington's arrival in Lisbon in late April 1809.

The Peninsular field army was assembled from far and wide. Throughout the war contingents arrived from Gibraltar, from other Mediterranean stations and from the West Indies. The 1/48th, a veteran battalion, arrived from Gibraltar almost 1,000-strong, including a healthy contingent of 22 drummers. Its sister battalion, the 2/48, arrived from Portsmouth 800-strong, together with 85 women, a hundred children—and a family of regimental orphans.[9] This is sure indication that, in spite of its reputation for severe discipline and a harsh life, the army's reputation for taking care of its own was firmly established and, therefore, as true for Wellington's army as it is today. Other regiments, too numerous to list, brought their families, sutlers and comple-ment of boys. One of these regiments, of course, was the 9th with Drummer James Wade in its ranks; the regiment had been on the Walcheren expedition.

It is impossible, indeed unnecessary for the purposes of this history, to describe the Peninsular war in detail. Of the numerous skirmishes, sieges and pitched battles fought and won by Wellington some stand out more sharply than others. However, to chronicle the history of the boy soldiers, there are some interesting incidents which portray them in sharp relief. Nor must we ignore the boys of the French Army who proved equally staunch in the face of their country's enemies.

French drummers played an equal—if not more important—part in battle tactics than their English counterparts, for the French had a distinctive manner of conducting an advance. Their columns advanced by solid blocks very similar to the Roman phalanx, many files wide and ranks deep. A drummer always led, beating a tattoo dubbed by the British soldiers 'Old Trousers'. Encouraged by the drummer, the French advanced, 'but as soon as the drummer fell'—together with the confusion caused by the galling fire of the extended two-line British counter-measure-—'the attackers retreated until their officers stopped them and began the same process over again'. This, of course, with a fresh drummer drawn from the rear reserve.

It is clear then that the French drummers had an unenviable position in French battle formations. Despatched with regularity when they were leading the advance, they shared the same fate as the other dead and wounded left on the field of battle. They were simply stripped and robbed of everything they possessed by the camp followers of either army as soon as those jackals could get on to the field, which was frequently while the contending armies were still hotly engaged.

The bravery of one French drummer at the siege of Tarifa by the French was compelling enough to be noted by Napier in his *Battles of the Peninsular*. Leading the forlorn hope, a young drummer marched alongside his commanding officer tapping out 'Old Trousers' amid the smoke and rattle of musketry fire. But only he and his commanding officer reached the breach unscathed, where the drummer stood, on a pile of rubble, beating out his 'rum-dum, rum-dum, rum-a-dum-a-dum-dum' within a few feet of the British defenders. His officer fell, wounded, and still he beat out his call. Not a single other survivor was on his feet. Moments later a British ball knocked him off his perch like a songbird blasted from the bough. The British defenders admired the boy's courage and this was probably the reason why no one would admit to the deed when questions were asked.

Even at this distance in time one is impressed by the bravery of these young soldiers. They were not always, however, brave and stalwart in battle. That sometimes they quaked, as happened during the French attack on Fort Matagora in 1811, is not surprising. Here the British defenders were in desperate straits. French gunners had the range to perfection, the walls were collapsing in half a dozen places and cannonballs were whistling about the place like carefree schoolboys. Mrs Retson, a sergeant's wife, was in a casement attending wounded men and desperately needed a bucket of water fetching from the well of the fort. She ordered a young drummer to bring the water, but he remained rooted where he stood, quivering with fright. Mrs Retson snatched the bucket from him and went herself. A shot cut the bucket cord from her hand. Undaunted, she drew water from the well and returned to the casement. Many of the women who moved with the armies in the field were brave and courageous and, as in the case of Mrs Retson, frequently demonstrated the meaning of courage to boy soldiers.[10]

In the whole record of the Peninsular War, however, there is no greater example of unflinching devotion to duty by boy soldiers as a group than that shown at the Battle of Albuera in 1810. A mixed force of 8,000 British and 10,000 Portuguese was commanded at Albuera by General Beresford, the British general apointed to command the Portuguese Army. Cut off from the main army, Beresford clashed with 24,000 French under Marshal Soult. During the preparatory manoeuvres to take up their battle positions, battalions of regiments were led on to the field by their bands of drums and dribbling fifes (drum and fife bands have long been known as 'the spit and dribbles'). The regimental bands then took up their positions either to the right or right-rear of their battalions to await further orders.

Albuera was a particularly long and bloody battle which, like Waterloo, dragged on all day. At times the British and Portuguese battalions were almost overwhelmed by the numerically superior French and, by all the canons of war, should have been defeated. When the conflict was over, the French having quitted the field, the British realised they had won a tremendous victory, but at enormous cost. The 3rd Foot was only able to muster three privates and a drummer; the 1/48th was, to the youngest drummer, wiped out; the 2/48th lost more than half its number, including all its drummers, except that seven of these were later discovered to have been taken prisoner by the retreating French; and a lieutenant of the 57th led the remanents of his battalion—170 out of an original 570 men. The band of the 57th was one of those stationed at the right of its battalion; there it stood fast all day under the command of the drum major. As one drummer after another fell or was sent off to replace fallen comrades of the line companies, the band diminished to a blob of half a dozen drummers and fifers. The picture they presented was later captured in the painting 'Fifes and Drums of the 57th', executed by Lady Butler many years later.

The day after the battle a drummer of one 57th company reported to the quartermaster for rations. 'How many men?' asked the quartermaster. 'No men, just me. I'm the only one left,' the drummer replied.[11]

The boy soldiers of Wellington's army died young or grew up quickly. They received the same rations as men—bread and a pound of beef a day—when rations were available. When the commissariat failed to bring up supplies, which was often the case, they survived as best they could, living on acorns or anything else they could scrounge. On the march if they lagged behind they fell prey to the bandits who infested the country or, during a retreat, an equally rapacious enemy. It was a hard and tough life for those who lacked the strength and stamina of their comrades. The life of a boy soldier, however, was not always grim and dismal. In winter quarters, especially during the period when the army retreated behind the lines of Torres Vedras and close to its supply port of Lisbon, they recovered from the exertions of hard campaigning and lived tolerably comfortable lives. There was a regular supply of food, fresh clothing, sport and entertainment to restore their spirits and help prepare them for the next season's fighting. Those who, like James Wade, reached their eighteenth birthday went on to man service, swapped drum, fife or bugle for musket and were replaced by fresh drafts of boys from Great Britain.

In contrast with those boy soldiers who served in the ranks, much has been written about boy soldier officers, yet this is no reason for ignoring them here. Of these boy officers it has been said that they 'inspired men twice their age and half their innocence'. For all the faults of the purchased commission system the boy soldier officers were, as a group, as important an element of the military machine as ranker elements. They grew up with their regiments and for the most part developed strong ties with the men they led.

At the Coa River at Almeida in 1810, during a skirmish with the French, Ensign Brown (later Sir George Brown), aged 16, was all for leaping over a wall to bag a couple of adventurous French skirmishers, but his sergeant, Robert MacQuade, pulled him down with the laconic comment: 'Sir, you're too young to be killed.' MacQuade went over himself, was hit by both marksmen and died immediately. He was only 24 himself.[12]

There were two categories of boy officer aspirants at this period. There were those, like Ensign Brown, whose families could afford to buy them a commission. Then there were those without financial means. Mostly, the latter were the sons of serving officers who lived in hope of being granted commissions without payment, following battle casualties among the commissioned ranks. There were many such youngster between the ages of 12 and 17, nor did they shun the fight when it came to a pitched battle, but would lay hold of a sword or musket and join the mêlée.

A catalogue of the names and ages upon enlistment of the young officers who joined the army and went to the Peninsula would make tedious reading. Only the more interesting of these are therefore cited, or those who figure later in this history. One of those worth mentioning in this latter category is Subaltern (later Reverend) G. R. Gleig of the 85th Foot who, when aged 17, began his service in the Peninsula in 1813. Wounded in the battle of the Nivelle, Gleig is a name to be remembered.

At the combat at Castrejan, when the opposing armies were groping through a dense early morning mist to make contact with each other, a dismounted cavalry officer came through the mist and smoke towards a line of British infantry formed up in battle order, waiting patiently for orders. The officer was holding his bared heart in place with a bloody handkerchief, for a shot had torn away one shoulder and part of his breast. Staggering past the infantry, he went to die in the arms of his son, a 14-year-old who had followed his father in hopes of obtaining a commission, for there was no money to buy one for him. One would like to hope he got one: his father had paid the highest price for his son.[13]

'Each man felt sure he sat between two friends,' (wrote Ensign (later Captain) Blakeney) 'wordly considerations beyond legitimate pleasures and professional ambitions, were banished from our thoughts. The field of glory was present to our view and equally open to all; none meanly envied the proud distinction which chance of war threw in the way of others. A fig for the friendship commenced at the age of sixteen or seventeen . . .' though he might just as well have truthfully said 'thirteen or fourteen'.[14]

Of such hardy, effervescent and courageous stuff were the boy soldiers of the Peninsular field army made. They shared with the hardened veterans the victorious advance into southern France when, suddenly and to everyone's intense surprise, Napoleon Bonaparte abdicated and went into exile on the Isle of Elba.

Elated as the victors were it was hard to realise that almost 20 years of continuing conflict with revolutionary France had suddenly come to an end. Wellington's army was shortly thereafter dispersed to the four corners of the earth. Some units were packed off to India, others to Mediterranean stations —Malta, Gibraltar, new possessions in the Aegean Islands—and others sent to reinforce the army engaged in Canada in the war with America.

As a consequence of this dispersal of the Peninsular Army the British government was hard pressed to muster sufficient troops the following year (1815) when Napoleon escaped from Elba and renewed hostilities. With astonishing rapidity he gathered his old army about him, put France on a war footing once more, and took to the field. With the lightning thrust of a rapier he struck north across the border with Belgium and attacked first the Prussian Army at Ligny in a bold attempt to separate the Prussians from Wellington's army. Having settled accounts, as he thought, with Marshal Blücher's Prussian army, Napoleon detached a large force under Marshal Ney to deliver a powerful left hook, while he with the main army moved to the French left to deliver a second decisive blow. Napoleon's strategem was sound. Once in position he would drive a firm wedge between the two opposing armies.

The first clash between Marshal Ney's corps and detachments of Wellington's army under the command of the young Prince of Orange occurred at Quatre Bras. Unfortunately for the French, Ney was negligent in following up his advantage of surprise. Some Brunswickers, Highland regiments and contingents of the Light Brigade in the vicinity of Quatre Bras rallied to the field to hold the French in check. During one of the cavalry charges against the highlanders a 15-year-old trumpeter of the 8th Cuirassiers mistook the Highlanders for women. He had never seen men in kilts before and in consternation cantered to his colonel to report 'Their continieres are firing at us, sir.'[15]

At the very time when the French should have been in hot pursuit of the enemy they ceased attacking and settled down to cook a meal. The 'pause that refreshes' was on this occasion a blunder of the first order, the greatest perhaps in a series of blunders on both sides that culminated in the Allied victory at Waterloo. This, however, was the situation in a nutshell during the period immediately preceding Waterloo.

Waterloo has probably been one of the most frequently dissected and analysed battles fought in the past 200 years. Even within the past decade or so there have appeared new accounts of this famous slugging match, told graphically and with feeling from different perspectives. Historians, it seems, have not tired of examining the contesting armies, generals, tactics used and the errors made. None, to my knowledge, have considered it from the viewpoint of the young soldiers who took part in it.

Some of the more well-known contestants owe their limelight to the accounts they later wrote, and on which historians have relied for piecing together the jigsaw puzzle of the battle. To name a few, there was William Leeke, who was a 17-year-old ensign; Sergeant Wheeler (the *Letters of Private Wheeler*); Sergeant Lawrence (ex-boy soldier); Rees Gronow (a boy ensign of the Peninsula field army); Sergeant Tom Morris (another ex-boy soldier); and Lord Albemarle (a mere youth at the time). In fact there were hundreds of boy soldiers on the field that day. Their presence was barely acknowledged in the plethora of literature which followed. What is more, these young soldiers, who ranged in age from 10 to 18 years, were hastily assembled because the veteran regiments of the Peninsular Campaign were, for the most part, dispersed overseas.

According to the 'Morning Report'[16] for 18 June 1815, there were, officially, 957 boy soldiers in the British contingent (67,000 all arms) of the Allied Army. Of the 957 some 36 were casualties of the Battle of Quatre Bras. That is, they were either killed, prisoners of the French, among the walking wounded or left wounded on the field (which meant they were as good as dead, for the French, in an age of medical incompetence, were even more inept than the British medical officers). Boy soldiers reported 'sick' on the morning report were those carried from the field of Quatre Bras wounded and, therefore, unfit to join their units. There was also a small number 'on command', meaning on official leave for one reason or another. The rest, a little more than 900, were 'present' and fit for duty.[17]

'Present' meant that they were ready to act as stretcher-bearers, to stand by the regimental colours, to play their regiments into their allotted positions on the field, to sound the advance, to order their battalions to form square, and to transmit the multitudinous commands of regimental officers throughout that long and gruelling contest. That they did is a foregone conclusion.

It would give a false impression to say that the almost 1,000 boy soldiers aged 10 to 18 constituted the upper limit of boys in the British contingent. There were many more than that figure baldly stated on the 'Morning Report', which takes no account of the 1811 order for the enlistment of boys which was still in force. The 14th Foot, for example, included 14 officers and 300 of its rank and file who were under 20 years of age. As Albemarle, who was one of the 14 officers, stated in his memoirs; 'These last, consisting principally of Bucking-hamshire lads fresh from the plough, were called at home "The Bucks", but their un-buckish appearance procured for them the nickname "Peasants". The battalion became known as "Colbert's Entire" '.[18] He continued:

Before the battle, when units were being selected for action or garrison duty, an inspecting general reviewing the battalion drawn up in square at Antwerp, exclaimed, 'Well, I never saw such a set of boys, both officers and men.' The Colonel of the regiment was upset and asked the general to modify his remarks. 'I called you boys,' the inspecting general repeated, 'and so you are; but I should have added I never saw so fine a set of boys, both officers and men.'

Still the general could not agree to declare the young lads fit for active service, and ordered the colonel to march them off for garrison duty. The colonel appealed to Wellington who reversed the order and the colonel gave the order, 'Fourteenth, TO THE FRONT, MARCH.'

Our men were . . . agreeably and usefully employed; they were quite at home with the 'Peasants' upon whom they were billeted, and clubbed their rations of bread, meat, and schnapps with the vegetables, cheese, butter and beet of their hosts. Whenever not on duty they were to be seen assisting the Boers and Boerrimen in their various labour. Before they left the canton-ment they had weeded the flax and the corn, and the potato crop of that year was entirely of their planting.[19]

It is clearly evident that a good number of the rank and file of other regiments on the field of Waterloo were also in their early and mid-teens. Shortly after the battle began a regiment of New Brunswickers, described in a number of accounts of the action as 'a boys' regiment', quitted the field. The 14th, posted at the right of the British line, spent the entire day under fire but not in the thick of the fight, which mostly was contained between Hougoumont and La Haye Sainte, the two farms forming part of the British line. This did not prevent the 14th sharing in the action. Again, Albemarle:

> We halted and formed square in the middle of the plain. As we were performing this movement, a bugler of the 51st who has been out with the skirmishers and had mistaken our square for his own, exclaimed, 'Here I am again, safe enough.' The words were scarcely out of his mouth when a round shot took off his head and spattered the whole battalion with his brains, the colours and ensigns in charge coming in for an extra share. A second shot carried off six of the men's bayonets; a third broke the breastbone of the lance sergeant . . . whose piteous cries were anything but encouraging to his youthful comrades. We were now ordered to lie down. Our men lay packed like herrings in a barrel.[20]

Thus from the 'Morning Report' for 18 June 1815, from the accounts of writers such as Lord Albemarle, and from the evidence already discussed, there were clearly a great number of boy soldiers in the battle of Waterloo, not just a few. My estimate of the number is that there cannot have been less than 4,000. If we allow, without direct evidence, that the Prussians, French, Dutch, New Brunswickers and others taking part had their own contingents of young soldiers, the estimate would be more than twice the number quoted.

The great war with France, which culminated in the Battle of Waterloo, was a high water mark in the organisation, development and achievement of the British Army. As a result of the groundwork laid by the Duke of York's reform group—which in turn stemmed from those enlightened commanders who had gone before, including Amherst, Wolfe, Bouquet and Abercromby—the army was better led, fed, housed and cared for than at any time in its history.

That the army stagnated for the next 40 years and, as a consequence, was totally unprepared for the next conflict when it came is a sad historical fact. The lessons of war were forgotten, the army estimates were cut back and control once more reverted to those with, as the years rolled by, diminishing military experience. The one bright light that shone fell on the care for, and treatment of, the army's boy soldiers. In this respect alone the British Army flourished, for its youngest element was provided with that essential foundation for fully developed adulthood: a structured education.

CHAPTER IX

SONS OF THE BRAVE

I N 1852, PRIVATES Bateman and Barry stole a muff from the regimental chapel and cut it to pieces. For this offence they collected 18 strokes of the birch each and four days in the black hole, followed by six days of extra drill. They were boys of the Duke of York's who, at that time, had the rank of private. They were both 13 years of age. Some few years later two 12-year-olds and an 11-year-old climbed on to the privy windows and indecently exposed themselves to the Commandant's servants. They were apprehended and confined to the black hole and there cooled their heels for four days on bread and water. In contrast to these misdemeanours and punishments, Private Cowell, aged 13, in 1857 stuck his fork into another boy's head and his punishment was to be denied a visit to the Crystal Palace.[1] These incidents, which are taken from the regimental punishment books, occurred during the years immediately following a dramatic change in the life of the Duke of York's. That change was the result of an upheaval in 1846; before then punishments were considerably more severe.

The intentions of the army authorities, as far as their young charges were concerned, were for the best. Their primary aim was for a structured educational system and in 1846 they became convinced that the methods then in use had such inherent weaknesses as to hardly constitute a system at all. To understand the prevailing practice it is necessary to retrace our steps to the beginning of the century.

The Royal Hibernian Military School (RHMS) was a flourishing institution long before the Duke of York's came into existence in 1803. At that time the emphasis, in both institutions, was on the spiritual enlightenment of the pupils as opposed to their secular education. Indeed, the original petition for the RHMS had stressed the need to '. . . preserve such objects from Popery, Beggary and Idleness, and to train them so as to become useful, industrious Protestant subjects . . .'[2] In 1802, on being shown plans for new school buildings for the RHMS, Wellington said, 'Take care what you are about; unless you base this on religion, you will produce only clever devils.'[3]

In 1800 Phoenix Park, in which the RHMS was sited, comprised 1,760 acres of mixed meadow and timbered land with 22 miles of roadway within its boundary walls. Originally, George III donated 3 acres of Phoenix Park to the school although the children were given use of a much larger acreage. The front of the main building of the school, an impressive three-storeyed building of brick and cut stone, faced south and commanded a magnificent view of the distant Wicklow Hills beyond Rathfarnham. The main building was flanked by two adjoining wings and from the west wing the ground fell sharply to the village of Chapelizod in the valley of the Liffey some little distance from the Hospital and outside the park wall. To the east, from the main gate, ran the Magazine Path, as it was known, which led to Magazine Fort. The Fort, the Chief Secretary of Ireland's Lodge, and the Viceregal Lodge could be seen from the school building, all lying in an arc 1,000 yards away. There were few other buildings in Phoenix Park at this time so that all was lush with the greens of grass and trees. The surface of the park was generally flat although the road which ran inside the boundary wall followed a seven-mile undulating course.

In the eighteenth century there was, between the school building and Magazine Fort, a stand of trees covering 15 acres. When cleared to provide the school with playing fields the area remained known as Fifteen Acres. Here also stood the old butt used by the gunners of Magazine Fort for gunnery practice as well as the young bucks of Dublin, three miles away, who settled their *affaires d'honneur* by duelling. The ground was chosen so that the combats could be seen from the Fort embrasures, by the officers who were forbidden to appear at such contests. The children of the RHMS, too, were afforded a grandstand view from the upper floors of the east wing.

As we have seen, during the Napoleonic Wars both the RHMS and the Duke of York's provided the army with a steady flow of boy soldier recruits. Despite the fact that they were technically orphanages and the children were under no obligation to join the army once they reached a suitable age (10 to 14 years), the institutions developed into military kindergartens. The military schools, it must be remembered, were financed, staffed and operated by the army and it was not unnatural, therefore, that colonels of regiments and the corps should come to regard them as seedling beds from which a sturdy stock was to be drawn. However, this was not a striking characteristic of the RHMS up to 1808 because, according to Hawkins, by 1800 some 2,274 children had been admitted (of whom roughly one-third were girls), yet only 200 boys had opted for enlistment into the army directly from the school.[4]

A new warrant was issued for the RHMS in 1808 and this was undoubtedly based on the success of the Duke of York's, for the new RHMS charter empowered the governors 'to place in the Regular Army as private soldiers, in such corps as from time to time His Majesty shall be pleased to appoint, but with their own free consent, the orphans and children of soldiers in Ireland, for ever.'[5] The phrase 'own free consent' occurs frequently in the annals of the military schools until well into the twentieth century and has to be interpreted with caution when applied to children. Free consent implies rational judgement—which children brought up in a closed military society would certainly lack. The attitude of the authorities may be summed up by ex-RHMS boy E. L. Souter, reminiscing in 1900 about his boyhood when he joined the school in 1880.

> About a fortnight after joining, the Commandant, Colonel Cotton, asked me at what trade of calling I would like to be trained; band, drums, tailors, shoemakers, carpenters or shirtmakers. He said that it was the practice to allow a boy to make his own choice, as a lad made better progress at the vocation of his own selection. I said I would like to be a tailor. The Colonel then pointed out the advantages of a musical education and the privileges enjoyed by bandsmen in the Army. The interview ended by the Colonel using his own discretion and sending me to Mr Bailey to be trained as a musician.[6]

The practice of channelling new boys into the bands seems to have been common to both establishments, for the military schools have produced an astonishing number of musicians (probably numbered in thousands) over the years; that is at least up until 1939 when a major shift in army policy occurred. By 1900 the RHMS had produced three Directors of Music, 30 bandmasters, 13 more were in training that year, and of course countless professional musicians. Billy 'Blowhard', the legendary trumpeter of the Rifle Brigade (95th Foot), who served for 52 years, was a RHMS boy. Not to be outdone, the Duke of York's produced Henry Lazarus, the internationally acclaimed clarinetist of the nineteenth century. His clarinet tutor is still used today. Thomas Sullivan, also a Duke of York's boy, went on to become Director of Music at Kneller Hall (the Army College of Music) where he raised his more famous son, Arthur, of Gilbert and Sullivan fame.

No one who studies the histories of these two schools can fail to recognise the parallel development of education they shared. The Duke of York's has been given undue credit for being the womb of the Royal Army Educational Corps and of army education. Much of the pioneer work was carried out at the RHMS until the time of its closure in 1924. Nevertheless, to describe the development of army education, it is necessary to concentrate on the history of the Duke of York's, the records of the RHMS having been destroyed in the London blitz of 1940–41.

As described by Schools Inspector Henry Moseley in 1846, the principal building of the Royal Military Asylum (later, as noted, the Duke of York's) contained in its central portion eight principal rooms, each of which was 86 × 34 ft, four of them being on the ground floor on either side of the vestibule and four others above. Five of these rooms were used as refectories, one as a music room and one for gymnastics. The four remaining rooms on the ground floor served the purpose of school rooms. They were lofty apartments having a double row of windows to provide ample ventilation. The wings of the building, five storeys in height, including the attics, were used as dormitories of which there were four in each storey together with apartments for a School Sergeant. Each dormitory was 35 × 19 ft and 10 ft high, each accommodating 24 boys, two sleeping in each bed. It will be noted that the Royal Military Asylum, Chelsea, was a similar construction to that of the RHMS, Dublin, except that it had two additional storeys.

Originally, the Duke of York's was a haven for the sons and daughters of the rank and file. (The sons of fallen or impoverished commissioned officers were admitted to the junior branch of the Royal Military College.) One curious clause in the Royal Warrant of the Duke of York's empowered 'Commissioners to have command and control of children born at the Royal Military Asylum and to make provision for the future disposal of the children.'[7] This clause suggests that the Duke of York and his wise counsellors deliberately provided for the possibility of illicit relationships between the male and female inmates of the institution and consequent issue of infants of the orphans. Two items reported in the Commandant's reports to the commissioners in the 1820s lend credence to the view that the wise men were correct in their predictions. First, it was discovered that boys and girls, unsupervised at night, were visiting one another's sleeping quarters. So in 1822 a formidable steel barrier was erected to separate the male and female dormitories. The following year the Commandant reported that '360 boys and 189 girls over 12 years were in the Asylum'.[8] This was a significant observation in an otherwise innocuous report. That same year the boys in the Southampton branch were transferred to Chelsea and the Chelsea girls were sent to Southampton. So much for that experiment in education.

From the very beginning of the institution's life Dr Bell's monitorial system of teaching was the accepted method used for educating the pupils, and he acted in an advisory capacity to ensure that his system was correctly enforced and to advise the commissioners on the results. In fact, the RHMS had employed monitors for the same purpose as early as the 1780s. Even so, the Duke of York's became an important establishment from which to develop and spread army education and was, therefore, closely watched by the authorities. There was, as we have shown, an enormous interest in the subject. Sergeant schoolmasters had been authorised for regimental establishments early in the century but the problem of instructing the schoolmasters was one conveniently solved by the existence of the Duke of York's. Why not, the commissioners reasoned, use the Asylum pupils for the purpose? They were trained to Bell's monitorial system, disciplined to the military life and, therefore, ideal recruits.

So it was that Corporals John Ducket and Patrick Doyle (aged 12 and 13) were 'approved by the Asylum Committee on 8 October 1811, to go to Portugal to assist in forming a school of the soldiers' children on Dr Bell's principles.'[9] Similar youthful emissaries were despatched to other corners of the Empire. Thomas Allcock and James McLeod were sent to Gibraltar in September 1815 to form a school and others to India, South Africa and the West Indies. In September 1817, Deputy Secretary at War William Merry received a letter requesting authority for 'two boys to go to Canada for the purpose of assisting the regimental schools in that Colony'.[10] The boy teachers were evidently sent because the bill for their passage and expenses amounted to £39.17.0 and Canada thereby was provided with its first 'publicly funded' schoolteachers. All of these young teachers it must be remembered were 12- and 13-year-olds.

So successful was the Duke of York's experiment that selected sergeant schoolmasters were sent to Chelsea for training. A report from the Commandant to Adjutant-General Harry Calvert in February 1812 advised that 22 sergeants had completed the teacher training course. Dr Bell later reported that 87 sergeant schoolmasters had graduated from the first two courses. Schoolmaster training ended in 1814, due no doubt to the cessation of hostilities with France.

It should not be imagined that all was sweetness and light at the Duke of York's. Life for the inmates had its darker side. The education process was conducted in one huge hall, with tiers and seats positioned against the outer walls for those children awaiting their turn for a dose of Dr Bell's physic. The sergeant monitors conducted their lessons on the open floor in competition with other monitors, also teaching. For children judged guilty of not paying sufficient attention to the instruction there was an iron cage suspended from the ceiling by a rope and pulley arrangement. In this contrivance an inattentive child would be confined, strung high in the hall like a monkey in a cage. Sergeants were permitted to administer the birch freely, without reference to higher authority, both in and out of the hall of learning. For other offences the children might be shackled to logs by their wrists for hours at a time. It is little wonder that boys and girls sought comfort in one another's company at night.

Such were the conditions that went hand in hand with the Bell monitorial system. They continued for many years until changes which brought about more humane treatment. However, it is easy to condemn such a system through twentieth-century eyes and despite this distasteful regimen of discipline the children survived.

Here we must reintroduce Ensign G. R. Gleig and others. Gleig joined the 85th Foot in his seventeenth year (1813), it will be recalled, and served in the Peninsular Field Army. In the postwar years he did well for himself by entering the Church and becoming an army chaplain. Whatever else one might say about him, the Reverend G. R. Gleig threw himself heart and soul into any task he undertook. He developed a flair for writing and soon had a prolific output. His *Life of the Duke of Wellington*, for example, is one of the better known biographies of the great commander. Indeed, Gleig became an intimate of Wellington during the Duke's later years, which in fact may have accounted for the clergyman's rapid rise in the ecclesiastical ranks of the British Army. It certainly did him no harm. Army chaplains had at that time joint responsibilities for the spiritual welfare of the troops and regimental education. In Gleig's case, though, his interest in army education seems to have occurred with dramatic suddenness and it was this interest, coupled with his characteristic energy and enthusiasm, which led to his being regarded as the father of army education and the Royal Army Educational Corps. The circumstances which led to his elevation to the pinnacle of command in this branch of the army are easily sketched.

Following the death of the Duke of York in 1827 conditions at the Duke of York's deteriorated rapidly, for the noble Duke, stern disciplinarian though he was, took a keen interest in the affairs of the institution and kept a restraining hand on the grosser excesses that might have been practised by the staff. Nearly a thousand children marched to St James's Palace to pay their last respects. Dressed in their scarlet uniforms, marching behind their massive band, and escorted by their nurses in red-lined black capes and bonnets, paced also by their sergeants and sergeant majors, they presented a memorable spectacle as reported by *The Times* of London. After this, punishments were more frequent, more severe, and life for the children became utterly miserable. In 1834, Gleig had been appointed chaplain to the Royal Pensioners Hospital and lived there in the chaplain's apartments for the next ten years. As the two institutions stood next door to each other he had ample opportunity to visit the school and to take an interest in its affairs. No record exists that he ever did. The only document prior to 1846 connecting Gleig with the school is the Commandant's report of 19 March 1845, item 11, noting the petition of Storekeeper Sergeant Beacock of the Royal Pensioners Hospital for admission of his son to the Asylum, accompanied by a certificate from the Rev. G. R. Gleig.[11]

The first adjutant of the school, Captain Lugard, died in 1843 after 39 years' service. He was followed to the grave a few months later by the Commandant, Lieutenant-Colonel James Williamson. Their places were taken by Captain Siborne as Adjutant and Lieutenant-Colonel A. Browne as Commandant. Siborne wrote his masterpiece *The Battle of Waterloo* when Adjutant of the School and his book became a standard reference work for later historians. Browne, on the other hand, had earlier served at Belem, Madras, where he might have come to know of the monitorial system as developed by Dr Bell, so it is quite probable that his appointment as the new Commandant was connected in some way with Belem. In any case, for the next few years the joint reign of these two men proved to be even worse than that which had formerly prevailed, as is indicated by Inspector H. Moseley's confidential report to the Privy Council.

The discipline is maintained under the direction of the Commandant and the Adjutant by the School Serjeants.

These men carry canes and are permitted to use them in respect of what are considered minor offences. Offences of a graver character are punished by flogging, by confinement in a cage or a black hole, by carrying a log chained to the person or by the drill.

The punishment of flogging is not inflicted except by the authority of the Commandant and in his presence.

A register of the punishments so inflicted has been kept since the appointment of Colonel Brown (sic) to that office.

I find by reference to this register that in the month which terminated with the 6th of April, 10 floggings of 12 stripes each were inflicted and 2 of 24 stripes and that in the preceding month of February there were infllicted 17 floggings each of 12 stripes.

It will afford your Lordship an opportunity to estimate that state of the discipline of which these facts afford the evidence if I inform you of the number of similar punishments inflicted in a twelvemonth in the Greenwich Schools.

I find that in the Lower School at Greenwich composed to 400 boys there were inflicted in the year 1844 only 21 such punishments and that in the whole School comprising the Nautical Upper and Lower Schools and containing 800 boys there were inflicted in that year 51 floggings. So that as many floggings were inflicted on 350 boys at Chelsea in the six weeks terminating with the 6th April last as upon the 400 boys of the Lower School at Greenwich in a whole twelvemonth. Or taking the whole of the Greenwich Schools the number of floggings inflicted on 800 boys in a year is one fourth of the number inflicted in the same time on 350 boys at Chelsea.

The punishments of the drill and the log are those most frequently resorted to. Six boys are on average daily under the punishment of the drill.[12]

To appreciate the events of 1846 we must leap to the year 1852 when an article written by Gleig and titled 'National Education' appeared in the *Edinburgh Review*. In this article Gleig claimed full credit for exposing the appalling conditions which existed at the Duke of York's under Browne and Sibourne. He reported that

Some time in the summer of 1846, two gentlemen met on the deck of a river steam-boat, which was plying its usual course from the Nine Elms Pier to Hungerford Market. One was . . . Mr Alexander Baring; the other was the Rev. G. R. Gleig, now Chaplain General of Her Majesty's Forces, and Inspector of Military Schools . . . A few days after the conversation . . . Mr Baring, then Paymaster General of the Forces, called upon Mr Gleig, and the two gentlemen proceded together to the Asylum [unannounced, he added][13]

Gleig was emphatic about the time of year and of his suspicions about the conditions in the institution. Alexander Baring, incidentally, was the father of Baring the Paymaster-General. However, contrary to what Gleig stated, he had nothing to do with initiating the investigation—as the records prove.

On 31 March 1846, the Paymaster-General wrote a letter to the Reverend E. Clarke, Chaplain of the Duke of York's, to introduce Dr Henry Moseley, a government inspector of schools. Moseley's confidential report on the conditions he found was dated 7 April 1846.[14] The report makes fascinating reading and is reproduced as Appendix A at the end of this book, followed by Gleig's article as Appendix B. The contradiction between these two reports is obvious. However, the Privy Council on Army Education acted with despatch on the

Moseley report. In June 1846, the Bishop of London was consulted on a suitable candidate for the newly-created appointment of Inspector-General of Military Schools. Gleig was offered the appointment and accepted it on July 1846, a good month before his reported meeting with Alexander Baring.

We might say that the appointment was secured for him by Wellington who, in early June, wrote a lengthy letter to Secretary at War Sidney Herbert in which he said, in support of appointing an Inspector-General of Military Schools:

> . . . it certainly appears to me that the best course to adopt under such circumstances would be to consult with the Lord Bishop of London, his Lordship being one of the ecclesiastical commissioners of our board and whose rank, character, high public station and employment must render him in all respects the most competent advisor in the selection of a person professing all the requisite qualifications for this office.[15]

Gleig was already Chaplain-General of the Army, having been appointed to that position in 1844 without losing his position as Chaplain to the Royal Pensioners Hospital. The new appointment added nicely to the plurality of his livings. Contrary to the impression given in his writings, Gleig was not himself the prime instigator of change but merely the servant chosen to orchestrate changes brought about by others. These changes were detailed in a series of directives, the most important being that signed by Herbert on 7 July 1846 which specified the pay, conditions of service and qualifications required of the new sergeant schoolmasters.[16]

We cannot overlook the extreme lengths to which the army commanders went to improve the facilities at the Duke of York's so that the institution might be transformed into a genuine teacher training centre. They took the unusual step of liquidating 'Army Prize Funds stock' (the army's share of prize money accumulated over the years), to provide funds for the new buildings and improvement of the old, thereby avoiding having to ask the government for construction capital. From prize fund sources they quickly raised £80,000 to underwrite the project. Here, then, was a clear measure of the army's charity and benevolence. Ageing and irascible they might be, but the most senior commanders of the army could not be accused of parsimony where the welfare of the rank and file and their young charges was concerned.

Within a few weeks of his taking up his new appointment, Gleig replaced both Commandant Browne and Adjutant Siborne. If any one person ought to have been fired that man was the Asylum's chaplain, The Reverend G. Clarke, for he was responsible for the education programme. One suspects, however, that there was something more to the hasty departure of these two officers than simple disagreement over what system of education was to be followed. Both Browne and Siborne had been on the half-pay list for some years before taking up their appointments at Chelsea and were therefore unlikely to jeopardise their comfortable positions by resisting a tide of opinion on the subject of education. However, it is likely that the new Inspector-General was intent on placing in those important positions men who would give him their unequivocal support.

Equally perplexing is why the august father of the RAEC should knowingly falsify the record in his article on national education just six years after the event of 1846. Gleig was only in his mid-fifties in 1852, a comparatively young and vigorous man of sound mind and body. He was also still a prolific writer (army education textbooks for many years after 1846 were almost exclusively written by him and, no doubt, provided him with a good income from royalties), so he cannot be excused for a slip of memory. Nevertheless, some years earlier he had been guilty of mixing fact and fiction to his own advantage. In an article for the *Gem Magazine*, published in October 1829, he had written an eye-witness account of the funeral of General Craufurd who was killed at the storming of Ciudad Rodrigo on 25 January 1812, an event which predated his own arrival in the Iberian peninsula by more than a year. (In his work *The Subaltern* he records that he 'embarked for the seat of war' in the summer of 1813.)

Brigadier Harry Shean, present Curator of the RAEC Museum, Beaconsfield, summed up this controversial nineteenth-century father of army education when he described him as 'an energetic, intelligent, highly-educated, dedicated opportunist.' But whatever the case may be concerning the motives of the first Inspector-General of Military Schools, Gleig certainly introduced sweeping changes into the curriculum of the Duke of York's for the purpose of training sergeant schoolmasters. The programme was an instant success and for years after many generations of army schoolmasters were instructed in their trade at the establishment.

In other respects change came slowly. The Guards regiments continued to mount a Guard at the school as they had done since it opened in 1803; the admission of girls was discontinued; at first the Spartan routine of daily life was only slightly modified; and some of the more severe disciplinary measures were abolished, notably the monkey cage and the logs. However, use of the black hole and flogging continued for many years.

The RHMS also underwent change in its system of education at about the same period, indicating that equal concern was directed at both institutions. If anything, the changes took place at the RHMS a little earlier than those at the Duke of York's, which leads one to believe that the Chelsea reforms stemmed from those which took place at the Dublin-based school. Colonel George R. C. Columb was appointed Commandant of the RHMS in 1845 and promptly set a committee the task of investigating the system of education then in use there.[17] As a result of that investigation, a Head Master, J. H. Gibbons, was appointed and remained in that post for the next 46 years. As the Columb Report was submitted to the Privy Council in late 1845, it is more than likely that this is what prompted school inspector Henry Moseley to visit the Duke of York's a few months later.

The same decision to discontinue the admission of female pupils to the

RHMS was taken as at its sister school. There were two interesting sidelights to this decision. Firstly, Councillor Drummond of the City of Dublin Council left £20,000 as an endowment for the daughters of soldiers and as a result the Drummond School came into existence in 1862. Secondly, in 1848, 21 girls of the RHMS 'volunteered' to emigrate to Australia.

Unfortunately, the entire records of the RHMS were destroyed during the London blitz in the Second World War. However, Commandant Columb's regime, despite his progressive views on education, was harsh and there is every reason to believe that the discipline at the RHMS was in every degree as severe as that imposed at the Duke of York's. Some sense of the conditions in which the RHMS children lived can be gathered from the Hawkins manuscript.

> It has been asserted against Colonel Columb that he never made any effort to lessen the harsh severities that were almost hourly inflicted upon the boys during the whole period of his command. It was left to every subordinate, however irascible his disposition, to punish promiscuously any boy in the School.[18]

Under the next Commandant, Colonel Cotton, the situation deteriorated to such an extent that by 1882 even these infant wards of the army refused to tolerate it any longer—they mutinied! Having rioted, they broke out of the school *en masse* and took to the Wicklow Hills to the south. Scattering far and wide around the countryside of Wicklow, these hardy sons of the brave put the authorities to vast trouble rounding them up, with the aid of the Irish Constabulary, and bringing them back under military escort in their twos and threes as deserters. When once more gathered together in their Phoenix Park quarters they would not behave and so a detachment of Scots Guards from Richmond Barracks, Dublin, was sent in to maintain order.[19] A court of inquiry was convened to investigate the mutiny (Hawkins's word, not the author's) and, as a consequence of its recommendations, the entire upper echelon of command was replaced. It was a victory for the children that would never be forgotten, even though the affair could not be counted as a battle honour worthy of being sewn on to the regimental colours.

One cannot emphasise too strongly the military character of these schools. They were infant regiments, no more and no less, with all the trappings, symbols, structured interior economy, code of discipline and punishments of a regular regiment of the line. They trooped their colours and laid the old ones to rest in their regimental chapels each time they were presented with new; they were organised into regimental companies with company sergeant majors and boy NCOs to maintain discipline; there were punishment parades and corporal punishment for those who broke the law; they were even subjected to that final indignity of military life: the regimental drumming out. Of the period under discussion there are no accounts of drumming out parades extant, although we do know that such parades were conducted. However, there are contemporary accounts, but these are best left for later chapters, when they will be quoted in detail.

It is obvious from what has so far been related that the simultaneous changes which occurred at the two schools in 1846 were limited solely to the restructuring of their education systems. A long time was to pass before any substantial improvement was effected in their disciplinary codes. For example, up to the early 1870s typical offences and misdemeanors for which children were flogged, confined to the black hole on bread and water, and given extra drill included: laughing and talking in the ranks, bed wetting, quitting the ranks, inattention on prayer parade, using foul language and disobedience. For these and like offences, boys were paraded before the adjutant or the commandant and formally charged. A few examples will suffice.

3 March 1852: Pte Vialls, aged 13. Trade, Shoemaker. Charged with breaking two awls and telling an infamous lie. Punishment: 18 cuts.
30 December 1852: Pte Ends Seta, aged 13. Charged with answering the Commandant in a disrespectful manner. Punishment: 6 cuts and 6 hours in the black hole.
31 December 1852: Pte Ends Seta. Charged with kicking and making a noise in the black hole, and being insolent and disrespectful to the sergeant major. (He threw his mug of water out of the hole and called the sergeant major a fat head.) Punishment: 18 cuts.[20]

1852 was the year in which Gleig's 'National Education' article appeared in the *Edinburgh Review*. Use of the black hole appears to have been discontinued in the early 1870s, for 1872 is the last year in which this form of punishment is recorded in the punishment records. Use of those twin instruments of retribution, the cane and birch, was maintained as the last resort of corporal punishment, although the authorities continued to make use of drumming out for extreme cases. Both cane and birch were 6 ft-long bamboo canes, the only difference being that the last two feet of the birch rod was sliced into strips. For administration of the cuts, or strokes, awarded a sergeant major gripped the offender's head between his legs, high in his crotch, pulled out the boy's shirt tails and took a firm grip on his trousers. With his feet set apart for balance and his posterior raised, the boy, doubled over, gripped his sergeant major's legs with his arms. Only then would the regimental sergeant major's rod be poised ready to whistle down the wind. Boys waiting for cuts were said to be 'standing by to receive boarders'.

Some lads invited the switch with unfailing regularity. For example, we read from the punishment register of the Duke of York's for 1887 that William Tart of E Company began filling his dismal 'crime' sheet from the age of ten and soon accumulated an impressive record, in the beginning mostly for wetting the bed. In 1888 he stood by to receive 106 boarders. Not unsurprisingly, it is noted that Boy Tart became increasingly disobedient over the years (with such misdemeanours as impertinence and answering back). No wonder; he was a marked man in more ways than one.

It may seem superfluous to note that the children of the military schools shared a common social background, yet it is important to stress this fact to show more clearly the positive benefits which accrued to them as a result of the educational reforms of 1846. In many respects—though not in the amount of punishment he received—Boy Tart represents the average boy who entered the Duke of York's during the last half of the nineteenth century. That is to say, he was ten years of age on joining; he had five brothers and sisters, ranging in age from 1 to 11 years; and his father was a long-serving soldier with a good conduct record. Boy Tart's father, Sergeant Edward Tart of the 105 Foot, spent more than half his 24 years in the army serving in India. The circumstances of his death are not known, but as he died at the regimental depot, Pontefract, Yorkshire, and was at the time on the permament depot staff, he probably died from natural causes. The 'petition' for William Tart's entry into the Duke of York's was submitted on behalf of Edward's widow by the battalion commanding officer.

Competition for entry varied, depending on the amount of fighting in which the army was engaged, but certain requirements were mandatory and generally it was not easy for a soldier or his widow to obtain a position for a son. All entrants had to have been born in wedlock; they had to be in sound physical and mental health; parents or guardians had to certify that the boy was not of dirty habits 'or in the habit of wetting the bed'; the father had to be, or have been, a regular serving soldier with a good conduct record; and, lastly, the petition, entitled *For A Soldier's Son*, had to be sponsored by the commanding officer of the unit in which the father either served or had served. In addition, there was the inevitable undertaking:

> . . . and if this application be granted, your petitioner hereby agrees that the said Boy shall remain in the School as long as the Commissioners thereof shall think fit, and to arrangements being made upon his arriving at a proper age, for his being placed in such employment, either as apprentice, servant, or otherwise as may be best suited to his capabilities, or—but that only with his own free consent—in the Army, in such branch as may be decided.[21]

Such were the conditions under which boys entered the military schools. Until about 1840 the chances of a boy rising through the ranks to obtain a commission, as did John Shipp in the early 1800s, were slim indeed. With the coming of the educational reforms their chances of doing so were considerably improved. This, it must be noted, was at a time when it was still more common than otherwise for commissions to be purchased. It was the higher standard of education that made the difference and this gave the boy soldiers a distinct advantage over their contemporaries entering the army direct from civilian life.

In the year 1900 there were an estimated 3,000 ex-military school boys serving in the army and of this number only 400 were private soldiers.[22] Between them the RHMS and the Duke of York's were able to boast of three major-generals, a handful of lieutenant-colonels and many lesser commissioned ranks. These particular boy soldiers were among the first rank and file soldiers to obtain commissions in large numbers.

While, then, we may feel sorrow for the suffering of the Batemans, Barrys and Tarts of the military schools from the thrashings they received at the hands of those set in dominion over them, they seem to have come to no real harm. On the contrary, as will be shown in later chapters in which letters and interviews are quoted, the evidence is that the majority thrived on the discipline they received. In the meantime we will leave the military school boys standing at ease while we take a look at some of those who served in India.

CHAPTER X
BADGIE WALLAHS

ONE SATURDAY NIGHT in the late autumn of 1890 four soldiers of the East Surrey Regiment were returning to Liffey Barracks through the streets of Dublin. Their Saturday passes were due to expire at 2000 hours but they had plenty of time, for it was yet only nine o'clock. The eldest one of the group was a 14-year-old and the youngest, Boy William E. Heard, was 12. Their studded boots clattered on the cobblestones and echoed eerily in the deserted streets, though the public houses were crowded enough. When they were not on a lighted part of the narrow streets the night was dark enough for them to see the sparks they struck from the cobbles with their steel-tipped heels.

Suddenly, in the dimly-lit lane ahead, one of them thought he saw shadowy forms darting for cover and in an instant the boy soldiers were alert for trouble. As Boy Heard later reported, stealth was out of the question, while retreat would have been unmanly. They therefore unbuckled their belts and wrapped them around their fists as they had been taught by the older soldiers. In the other hand they gripped their swagger canes tightly as one holds a sword, ready to use them as thrusting sticks. A few moments later they were set upon by half a dozen youths of their own age group. There was no provocation on either side, simply a natural animosity on the part of the Dublin youths and a love for the sport of soldier-bashing.

In the fight which followed, though outnumbered, the boys of the 31st Foot had the advantage with their heavy brass-buckled belts, swinging them with fury, striking heads and bodies with the buckles and lunging with their canes. It was a short, sharp brawl from which the Dublin youths fled, leaving one of their number prostrate on the cobbled street, his head bathed in blood. Uncertain as to whether their attacker was dead or merely unconscious, the young soldiers panicked and ran as fast as their legs would carry them to the barracks more than a mile away.

The corporal of the guard could see from their dishevelled state that they had been fighting and they did not deny what had taken place but answered his questions with frankness. He then called the duty officer, who ordered that they be placed in custody. The following morning the boys were paraded before the battalion commander, to whom each gave his own version of the incident.

Realising the seriousness of the situation, the commanding officer was in a quandary. Street fights between soldiers and civilians occurred frequently enough, but a death or serious injury was a grave matter which would not only reflect on the honour of the regiment but would almost certainly result in lengthy legal proceedings if brought to the attention of the civilian authorities. In 1890 Dublin was the capital city of the whole of Ireland and was also the centre of a growing antagonism to the British presence in the country.

For whatever motives, the commanding officer decided against making inquiries and chose instead to have the four boys confined while he placed the matter before the garrison commander. New regimental numbers, names and pay books were provided for them, suggesting that death or serious injury had been caused. Within a matter of days the boys were posted to new units, one each to a different overseas station. Boy Heard neither saw nor heard of his three companions again. He was sent to India and as punishment for his part in the affair was kept below deck for the entire voyage. The army authorities had again demonstrated ability to take care of their own.

Heard's subsequent history is interesting. He was posted to the Royal Artillery Depot at Peshawar where, in the officers' mess, he spent a year learning the trade of french polishing. At the age of 14 he was found to have an unusual talent for sketching and was sent to the North West Frontier (to the Khyber Pass, gateway to India from Afghanistan) to sketch gun positions. He took his discharge in Canada and joined the 25th Artillery Battery there as battery sergeant, serving in both world wars and retiring in 1947. He died at the age of 94.[1]

Boy soldiers were posted to India in their thousands over the period of the British presence, and although few reasons were as dramatic as that which led to Boy Heard's posting, nevertheless the accounts of some others who journeyed to India make fascinating reading. The incomparable John Shipp, whom we first met in 1797, was still only 15 when he arrived following a spell with his regiment in South Africa. Then there were John Cobbett and Alexander Alexander of the 91st Foot. Most wrote of the appalling conditions suffered during the long voyage to India and the attendant perils. Some, like Boy Clarke in 1839, survived the storms of the Atlantic, the treacherous Cape and the Indian Ocean, only to be shipwrecked on arrival—and that happened often enough.

. . . bump went the ship on a sand-bank, and we were wrecked at the mouth of the river Indus on 17th March, 1839.

We tried all night to get the ship off, but were unable to do so.

We fired guns of distress, and burnt blue lights all night, but not one of the country boats would come near us, and there we were sinking. We threw everything over to lighten the ship, but all to no purpose. Two of our men volunteered to take a boat on shore to see if they could get any relief. We tried to get ashore with the ship's boats, but they leaked, so we had to turn back. The men who went in the boat for help went up the river, and saw a bungalow and a flag staff. They ran up the river shouting. They thought they heard a noise, and found it was from two gun-boats going to Crutchee.

The Lieutenant had gone before them. The Captain said they were bound to come to assist us. They pressed all the country boats, and made them come and put in.

One gunboat came to the ship, and the other had to stay on the other side of the tide to pick us up at the beacon or land mark. We were at it all night . . . One boat went back to the ship, and the other put us in the native boats, and they put us on an island, and the next day we all got off. When the last lot left, they were up to the knees in water on the deck.[2]

John Holland, an ex-Hibernian, enlisted in the 91st Foot when it was stationed at Dublin in 1902. He was then 14 years old and he remembers:

Our turn came for India very early in 1903. We had a month's leave first, then 18 of us, five sergeants, five boys and eight men, left on the troopship *Sardinia*. The ship also had many warriors going to Sudan, Egypt and South Africa. The crew had plenty of cigarettes and chocolate for sale, but the price continually rose higher as the trip went along. There was Crown and Anchor for the gamblers. I tried the 'double your money and you are sure to win' game, but was sadly misled and lost what little I had. The Provost Sergeant tried in vain to stop the gambling.

We could get a good cup of coffee at night for a penny a mug. The lavatories were just an open space on deck. At Gibraltar where we dropped anchor the weather was clear and sunny. The Rock was a wonderful sight. It was here that a big basket of fruit was hauled on board (sent up to the deck by a hauling line thrown up by one of the bum boats), but someone stole it.

We reached Bombay at last and, as the harbour was so shallow, we were landed by barges. A short time later a few of us, all strangers to each other, lined up at a bar. I was last in the queue and because everyone said the one behind them was paying I was caught to pay it all. I remember seeing a few men on shore waiting to be shipped to Netley Hospital (Southampton), paralysed with VD. [John Holland here probably uses 'paralysed with VD' as a figure of speech even though some strains can lead to paralysis.] As there was then no cure they only got injections, which diminished the gums and showed the teeth to a disadvantage.[3]

He records that of the five boys who sailed to India as part of the 91st contingent 'one became a missionary, one eventually became the conductor of the BBC Scottish Orchestra, and one was sent home paralysed with VD. Whenever Lord Kitchener inspected a unit he always lectured against this complaint.'[4]

It is obvious from what Holland had to say that even with the coming of steam ships, conditions on board troopers at the turn of the century were primitive. They improved over the years, but troopships were never luxury liners. Trumpeter Joe Dobbs of the Royal Artillery was born and raised a true 'barrack rat' (the term used to describe children living in army quarters). In 1929, aged 16, Dobbs was posted to India for 6 years, travelling by troopship for three weeks by way of the Suez Canal.

> What an experience that was . . . It had to be seen to be believed. There were 8 other RA boys living on the mess deck; over 200 bodies, 16 to a mess table. Food was adequate, cocoa before getting into the hammock to sleep and what a palaver that was, and drawing it every evening. First in the queue meant in the hot climate you were allowed to sleep on deck. Returning it in the morning it had to be correctly folded or was thrown back at you. Washing bits of underwear and getting them dry meant watching them every second otherwise they were gone.[5]

Not all boy soldiers who served in India were shipped out from home stations. From the earliest days the British were in Imperial India (or what today comprises India, Pakistan and Bangladesh) there had come into existence a large European community of pensioned-off soldiers and their families, administrators, traders and employees of the Honourable East India Company. Both the East India Company's troops and those of the Crown were able to draw on the European community for boy recruits.

It is astonishing that the socio-military development in India should parallel that of the home army as closely as it did, even though the army in India did not always follow the lessons and ideas brought from England. We have already seen how Dr Bell's monitorial system, as developed in Madras, was exported to England for use in the Royal Military Asylum at Chelsea. In India, too, the officers expressed their concern for the orphaned sons of fallen British soldiers in practical ways. Sir Henry Lawrence established the first of four military asylums for military orphans. Sir John Lawrence founded another. These schools, which flourished until the partition of India following the Second World War, were an important source of boy recruits.

Lieutenant-Colonel J. MacKenzie-Rogan, one-time bandmaster of the Queen's Regiment and himself an ex-boy soldier who joined the 11th Foot at the age of 13, writes of his own recruiting expedition to the Sanawar Lawrence Military Asylum.

> Some nine or ten miles from Subathu is one of those excellent institutions founded by the late Sir John Lawrence for the orphan children of British soldiers . . . The Principal of the school, the Rev. H. Hildersley, received me very kindly and told me that there were about half a dozen boys who had just reached the age of fourteen and wanted to join the Army and follow in their fathers' steps.

I had a talk with the boys and explained to them the advantage they would gain by joining a regiment like The Queen's, in which the officers and in fact all ranks took a keen interest in the band. I was fortunate in getting the consent of six and a promise from others to join when they were old enough to enlist, and rode back to Subathu very pleased with the result of my visit.[6]

Boy H. W. Bancroft of the Bengal Horse Artillery was in a different category. He was the son of a serving soldier and in 1833, when aged nine, he enlisted in the Royal Artillery as a bugler. He later transferred to the Bengal Horse Artillery and, to join his new unit, in 1835 accompanied a column on a three-month-long march from the RA Depot at Dum Dum to Agra. He was then aged 12 and records in his memoirs that *en route* to Agra he saw several men flogged for petty offences.[7]

The East India Company Army also operated its own Artillery Cadet College along the lines of the Royal Military Academy, Woolwich. The cadets were extremely young (11 to 14) and the authorities evidently experienced the same problems of discipline and insubordination which plagued the RMA in the mid-eighteenth century. The troubles at the Cadet College at Baraset, not far from Calcutta, came to a head in 1809, for that year Captain Charles Stuart, of the 3rd Bengal Native Cavalry, was appointed to be Commandant of the College to restore order. An unknown author writing of the events in 1809, recorded:

At this College, which had been in existence but some six years, so slack was the discipline (before Captain Stuart took over the Command), so great the insubordination, so frequent the rioting and serious civil offences committed by the Cadets, that the place had become notorious throughout the length and breadth of Bengal; and the authorities had tardily begun to realize that this state of affairs could no longer continue.[8]

It is interesting to note that as late as the Second World War the Lawrence Schools were providing recruits for direct enlistment into the British Army. An ex-boy soldier, A. Dutton, who served an army apprenticeship at the Army Technical School, Chepstow, wrote:

A couple of weeks after my group had commenced service in January, 1940, we were joined by a number of sun-tanned boys in civilian clothes. They were from one of the Lawrence Schools in India and had come over in a wartime convoy, being delayed on route, hence the late enlistment. Most of them had spent all their lives in India to that date, their fathers either having opted for the Indian Army or having taken their discharges out there and from my own later experience in that country I would guess that the majority of boys from the Lawrence Schools had mothers who were of mixed Anglo-Indian parentage.[9]

It is unknown to what extent boy soldiers of Indian birth were recruited for units of the Indian Army, and when they first began to be taken on in strength. From what little evidence is available, however, one can surmise that boy soldiers were as common in the native Indian regiments as in the British Army. When Dutton finished his apprenticeship he was posted to India and seconded to the Madras Sappers and Miners.

The Madras Sappers and Miners were certainly recruiting boys as apprentice tradesmen in 1943–44 and when I first joined the corps, at the depot (Bangalore), I was for a very short time attached to the boys' Company as a Trade Instructor. Unfortunately, my contact was brief and I am unable to tell much about them, except to say how similar I found them to a bunch of British boy soldiers—same attitudes, same bearing and same pranks. The boys I was with were apprentice fitters; they were enlisted at the age of 15 and their training was similar to ours, extending over 2½ to 3 years. Most of the boy NCOs could speak some English, it was usual to find English more widely spoken amongst Southern Indian Units than in regiments from other parts of India, also a higher percentage of Christians, though the vast majority were, of course, Hindus.

The boys wore the same uniform as the men with the distinctive puggaree headwear of the Unit. Typical of the Indian Army of my day they were very regimental and very proud to be in the Army—it was always a good sight to see them on parade.[10]

From the foregoing accounts it is possible to get some idea of the circumstances in which boys were enlisted into the British and Indian armies.

We are also able to tell from contemporary accounts how the boy soldiers lived, worked, entertained and otherwise occupied themselves. With the exception of times when they were on active service and stores were in short supply, they were always well fed. Many did not think so, for most had voracious appetites. Writing of conditions in India during the 1920s and 30s, Dobbs reported:

Talk about being thrown in at the deep end! After 21 days, arriving in Bombay, I had to wait a few days before boarding a coastal tramp steamer. Then it was 3 days to Karachi sleeping on deck. Troop train then: 24 hours to Quetta, 6000 feet in the mountains. I there joined the only mechanised RA Regiment in India at that time. There was no welcome. I was just another body. It was pretty grim. Barracks made of mutty bricks, galvanised roofs, 12 to a room, bed, wooden box, bedding 6 blankets. In the centre a wooden table with two forms. During the winter it was really cold with 2 and 3 feet of snow, but never a shortage of coal. For washing purposes there was cold water all year round with a hot bath once a week in a tin tub. The six years I was in the unit the food was awful. Boys were allowed supper, except that there was little in the cookhouse to give. In all stations in India were the usual camp followers: char wallah, fruit wallah, egg wallah; the lot from whom you could buy to supplement rations, that is if anything was left from the 8/2d a week pay. I went to bed hungry every night.

All the RA regiments were timed by the call of the trumpet. Duty was a week about by the two boy buglers. In the winter during the night the trumpet would freeze, so before sounding reveille the trumpet had to be warmed by the cookhouse fire. One morning I remember I had to blow 'Get on parade' but not a note was heard. My trumpet had frozen again. The sergeant said, 'Trumpeter, now go round and tell them.' We had no long-eared monsters (horses) in our unit. We still had to sound the stable call

> 'Come to the stables all you men that are able
> Water your horses and give them some corn.
> Don't give too much or you will give them the horn.'

In the cantonment shorts or trousers were worn, but if the soldier wished to visit the city, coat, breeches and puttees, the lot had to be worn. In 1935 boys in the unit experienced the Quetta earthquake, and went into southern Afganistan with vehicles and guns. Ours was the first unit to cross the frontier with motorised vehicles and guns, in 1934, to a place called Charman. I was with it.

The Regiment had two Batteries, one in Quetta and one in Hyderabad Sind. They changed over every two years. I went to Hyderabad during my second year. Hyderabad, one hundred miles north of Karachi, in the Sind desert, spelled a complete change of climate from Quetta. (120 degrees in the shade, and no shade.)[11]

The movement of a massive armed column moving across India, protected by guns, flanking infantry and a rearguard of cavalry, and with the commissariat wagons and camp followers in the centre, must have been an impressive sight. From ex-Trumpeter Sidney Whitehouse, RA (retired Captain), came what must be the last description of a journey along the Grand Trunk Road.

I went to India at the end of 1921 and by the beginning of 1924 I was the Brigade Trumpeter of the 2nd Field Brigade. There were 2 Batteries in Lahore, 1 at Ferozepore and 1 at Jullundur. Preparations were in hand for a change of station. 2nd Field Bde were to move to Meerut to change with the 16th Field Bde who were to take over in Lahore.

When the organisation and packing was completed the advance party left one day in advance of the Battery. I was on loan to the 53rd Battery as the Major's trumpeter because the Colonel was not marching with the column. Each battery marched separately and 53rd moved off with 6 horse gun teams, 4 horse teams with the Firing battery wagons, G.S. wagons, Mess cart and spare horses etc.

Generally the line of March was down the Grand Trunk road and camping places were chosen daily by the advance party. Occasionally our stop was in the vicinity of a 'Dak' bungalow where the officers were able to take advantage of the facilities that the bungalow offered.

The advance party were responsible for the Camp site, for setting up cooking facilities, horse lines, latrines etc. Their main transport comprised bullock carts; then came the rear party whose job was to leave the camp site in good order and then follow on. The usual rate of progress was about 19/20 miles per day for 6 days the seventh being a rest day. The rest day was used for harness cleaning, shoeing where it was needed and for the men to do their washing, bathing and generally cleaning up. It was these rest days that the two 12 bore shotguns which the battery owned were in action but apart from a few birds—of the feathered variety—very little game was taken.

As a trumpeter, my main function was to see after the Major's horse and to my own. There were no calls blown at all during the march though I always wore the instruments. I was also used as a galloper to carry orders and messages down the column. I was also the Major's horse holder at all times.

Just before we reached Delhi it was learned that the G.O.C. in C. India had died and as we were on the spot we would be required to provide a six horse team and Gun Carriage to convey the coffin from Government House to the railway station. As a result of this order we had an extra rest day with spit and polish, grooming and a real buzz up for the subsection concerned.

This sad little interlude left us with two more days march to go before reaching Meerut where 2 batteries were to be stationed with one each an Agra and Bareilly.

The Battery had been on the road for 47 days and had travelled some 600 miles without any noticeable casualties.[12]

The subject of food is a recurring theme in letters and not everyone agrees with Dobbs on the question of constant hunger. MacKenzie-Rogan, for one, was satisfied with his lot. Writing of the fare provided to boy soldiers in 1867, he gives this menu:

Breakfast—a basin of tea or coffee and bread.
Dinner —(the noon-day meal):—alternate days—Soup, meat, potatoes and sometimes a second vegetable; baked dishes and roasts; sea-pie occasionally; plum-duff, suet pudding and treacle three times a week.
Tea —a basin of tea or coffee and bread.
Supper —provided by self from left-over meat. Soldiers brought their own butter and 'faggots'.[13]

Entertainment was never a problem where the boy soldiers were concerned. There were organised field sports, sightseeing trips, the native bazaars and all the wonders of the East, with fakirs, fire-eaters, snake-charmers and village craftsmen to watch. Despite the long marches, training and constant parades the boys devised the most devilish tricks and many were passed on from generation to generation in much the same way as younger children inherit from older children such games as 'tip the wicket' and 'jacks'. One of their most common pranks centred on tormenting the camp scavengers. Although more than one living correspondent has commented on the subject, John Shipp's published account is still the best description of this fiendish sport.

Those pelicans were extraordinary birds. The minute the dinner trumpet sounded flocks of them gathered round the barrack doors, waiting for anything the soldiers might throw them. No matter how many times they were tricked, they still came. Some of the more mischievous boys would tie two large bones together, with a length of string. One bird would pick up one bone, and another the other. Then, with the bones in their crops, they would soar round and round the barracks; pulling and tugging at one another, attended by a flock of crows and kites which would peck and harry them unmercifully. Sometimes, to add to the fun, a boy would tie a large piece of rag, or a paper kite, to a bone with a long piece of string. A pelican having swallowed the bone, would fly round with the rag or the kite trailing behind him, and hundreds of his own tribe after him as well, in hopes that he would throw up the bone, which these birds can do very easily. By and by, the whole crowd, whirling and squabbling, would be lost in the distance, but the same gentleman would be back again next day and probably with a bit of string still hanging from him.[14]

The literature, letters and official reports of soldiering in India provide a richer record of boy soldiers on active service than is to be found elsewhere, and it is an unusual luxury to be selective in portraying this side of the life of the 'badgie wallah' in India (derived from *baja wallah*, meaning music man). First, there is John Shipp's account of the investment of the fort at Dieg in 1804. He was then 16 years of age.

Shipp's regiment, the 22nd Foot, with three other regiments (the 27th, 33rd and 64th) became experimental boys' regiments in 1797. Because the 22nd had already seen service in South Africa against the Kaffirs and many in its ranks were still under age, it was still a battalion of young fighting cocks. The investment force spent two days taking up a position before the fort and digging in; then John Shipp was sent on a scouting expedition.

The night was dark as pitch, and bitterly cold. Secrecy was the great object of our mission, and we slowly approached the vicinity of the fort, steering our course towards a small village about eight hundred yards from the spot, where we halted under shelter from their guns. This village had been set on fire two days before, and its inmates compelled to take shelter in the fort. Small parties were dispatched in search of eligible ground for trenches, and within breaking distance. I was dispatched alone through the desolate village to see what was on the other side. I was yet but a novice in soldiering; and, believe me, reader, I had no great fancy for this job; but an order could not be disobeyed; so off I marched, my ears extended wide to catch the most distant sound.

I struck into a wide street, and, marching on tiptoe, passed two or three poor solitary bullocks, who were dying for want of food. These startled me for the moment, but not another creature could I see. I at one time thought I heard voices, and that I could see a blue light burning on the fort, from which I inferred that I was getting pretty close to it. Just as I had made up my mind that this must be the case, I distinctly heard a voice calling out 'Khon hie?' in English, 'Who is there?' I was riveted to the spot, and could not move till the words were repeated; when I stole behind one of the wings of a hut close on my right.

Soon afterwards I heard the same man say, 'Quoi tah mea ne deckah;' which is, 'I am sure I saw somebody.' Another voice answered, 'Guddah, Hogah;' which signifies, 'A jackass, I suppose;' for there were several wandering about. I fully agreed with the gentleman who spoke last . . . I resolved, therefore, to have a run for it, and off I bolted, up the same street through which I had come, when a whole volley of matchlocks was sent after me, but they did not attempt to follow—at least, as far as I know, for I did not stop to look behind me. I arrived safe at the division, not a little frightened; and I venture to say that I never ran so fast before in my life. This afterwards proved to be a strong cavalry piquet.[15]

Soon after this incident, Shipp was promoted and was well on the way to commissioned rank.

Bancroft, whom we have also met already, was on 'man service' when he took part in the First Sikh War of 1845–6, but was observant enough to take note of the punishment suffered by one of the young trumpeters in his battery, wounded during the battle of Moodkee in December 1845.

The trumpeter had five grapeshot wounds, all on his right side, from his ankle to his shoulder, his right leg was broken, and his horse shot under him, but it is pleasant to know that the riddled musician survived to enjoy a pension.[16]

Writing of his experience in the same Sikh Wars, a young soldier tells of the privation suffered by the troops from lack of water while they were on the march.

This was a very long day's march, over sandy deserts and plains. The water being short the horrors became past describing. We drew near to a well some time in the morning, and the confusion all round was fearful—the men rushing and pushing to get at it, some letting their caps fall into it, and some their bayonets; and I quite expected some of the men would go in . . . I was done up myself. Here my tongue was swollen, and mouth parched up; and I felt very weak. My brain seemed to be on fire, and my eyes as if they would jump out of my head. I felt as if I were done; but I made a rush at the water and got some. God knows what a relief I felt, as if I had lost a great load! When most of the throng was over, I filled a tin flask which I carried with me for that purpose; so did all others who had them. Our officers were as bad as the men. What thousands there are in England who do not know the value of a drop of water.[17]

Generally, casualties among the youngest soldiers went unnoticed, except by such as Bancroft who, an ex-rat himself, was probably more conscious of their lot than others might be.

With the outbreak in 1857 of the Sepoy Mutiny, which came to be called simply the Great Mutiny, much more notice was taken of the boy soldiers than ever before or since, and the reasons for this are not surprising. To begin with, the proportion of British soldiers to native soldiers in the country was very small. Consequently, during the few months when the mutineers had the upper hand they behaved with little regard for age, sex or station and slaughtered the Europeans with abandoned cruelty. Later, the vengeance visited upon the mutineers by the relieving British troops was equally atrocious. Patriotic writers, however, were selective in recording the events of the mutiny and chose those incidents which tended to heighten the cruelty of the mutineers—including their behaviour towards the unfortunate boy soldiers. Secondly, exceptional acts of bravery were undoubtedly performed by boy soldiers and more than one received the Victoria Cross.

Despite the popular misconception that the conflagration engulfed the entire Indian Empire, in fact the Great Mutiny was virtually confined to the Bengal section of the East India Company's 233,000-man army, and that in the territory of the Punjab. The actual outbreak occurred at Meerut, some 25 miles from Delhi, in early May 1857. Eighty-five Cavalry sepoys had refused to use the newly issued cartridges for the Minie rifle because it was said (and later verified) that the cartridges were greased with cow and pork fat and had to be bitten prior to loading. The cow was sacred to the Hindu; pigs were unclean to the Muslim. Imprisoned for refusing to use the cartridges, the cavalry sepoys were released by their comrades while the British were at church. The mutineers then killed most of the British garrison and fled to Delhi. From this incident the mutiny spread like fire in the treetops to other units of the Bengal Army.

A boy telegraphist in the telegraph office in Delhi was the first to raise the alarm, for the mutineers had won over the Delhi garrison and together began slaughtering Europeans in the city. 'We must leave the office,' telegraphist Brendish warned the Umballah operator. 'All bungalows on fire, burning down by sepoys of Meerut. They came in this morning . . . nine Europeans killed . . .'[18] Here the message abruptly ended and young Brendish, apparently, fell victim to the sepoys, for there were no survivors and Delhi became the rallying point for the mutineers.

The events at Meerut and Delhi occurred on 10 and 11 May 1857. Less than a month later it was the turn of the Allahabad garrison to suffer mutiny at the hands of the 9th Native Infantry. On the evening of the day this occurred, 6 June, eight newly-arrived boy ensigns not yet posted to their regiments were in the 9th Officers' Mess at dinner when the alarm bugle sounded. They turned out with the other officers and went to the parade square where all the Europeans were taken prisoner. According to the historian W. S. Fitchett, 'Seven had their throats cut like sheep.' The eighth, Ensign Arthur Cheek, aged 16, survived and hid for four days in a ravine but on the fifth day was re-captured and imprisoned with a Muslim sepoy turned Christian.

Soon after the Allahabad massacre, the garrison was retaken by a relieving force organised by Sir John Lawrence (later Lord Lawrence), the Chief Commissioner of the Punjab. Ensign Cheek was rescued by the Madras Fusiliers, but died of his wounds four days later, just 18 days after joining his regiment.[19]

During June and July the mutiny gathered strength. It might be thought that with abundant arms, ammunition and a vastly superior strength the mutineers could crush their opponents but, although leaders did emerge, they lacked the cohesion and discipline necessary to assure success. Nevertheless, they controlled Delhi and lesser centres for months. Lucknow was also largely in the hands of the mutineers, except that the Residency compound in the city was fortified and defended by a small garrison of British and loyal troops under the command of Sir Henry Lawrence, the brother of Sir John Lawrence. Henry Lawrence had had the foresight to provision the compound before trouble broke out and was therefore well prepared to withstand a siege.

Elsewhere, at Cawnpore, the British commander Sir Hugh Wheeler unwisely foresook a strong defensive position for a weak one in which, exposed to the fierce heat of summer and without water and other rudimentary supplies, his force held out for three weeks. Starvation and thirst forced him to surrender to Dandu Panth, the Rajah of Bitpur, under promise of safe conduct to Allahabad by boats provided by the mutineers. Boarding the boats, the unarmed soldiers were put to death and some 250 women and children returned under guard to Cawnpore where they were imprisoned. The day before General Sir Harry Havelock's relieving troops burst upon the city, the women and children were butchered and dumped into a well shaft. It is to Havelock's flying column, which provided the first relief of Lucknow, and a second column under Sir Colin Campbell, that we must turn for accounts of the boy soldier VCs won during the Great Mutiny.

In July 1857 Havelock assembled 2,500 men, mostly British, at Allahabad and set off along the Grand Trunk Road, fighting his way in a northwesterly direction, to relieve Lucknow. The march was a feat of dogged endurance carried out during the hottest season of the year. Marching and fighting all the way to Cawnpore, the column covered 126 miles in nine days, defeating Dandu Panth's (Nana Sahib) army at Fatehpur (12 July), Aong (15 July) and Cawnpore (16 July). It was the evidence of the massacre at Cawnpore which helped bring about the brutal reprisals wreaked by the British troops once they gained the upper hand and suppressed the mutiny. At Cawnpore, Havelock was forced to await the arrival of fresh supplies before he could continue his march to Lucknow, which he was not able to do until September. To reach the beleaguered garrison the relieving troops broke through a cordon of 60,000 besiegers (losing more than 500 men out of the original 2,500), merely to add to the strength of the defenders. This was because Havelock had the strength and momentum to break in but, encumbered as they were with women, children and the wounded, not to force a way out again.

Bugler Robert Hawthorne, aged 16, of the 52nd Foot, was in Havelock's column. On 14 September he accompanied an explosion party under Lieutenant Salkeld of the Royal Engineers who, in the act of placing the charge, fell wounded. Ignoring the danger of the exposed position in which the lieutenant lay, Hawthorne tended the officer's wound then dragged him to safety under constant fire, to finish the task of binding the wound. For this act he was recommended for, and received, a Victoria Cross.[20] We do not wish to diminish the bugler's bravery, but it has to be noted that he did no more than what many a soldier before and since has done, so we may well ask, why the high award? The probable explanation is that the award was then a recent one and the authorities were not, perhaps, as discriminating in granting awards as in more recent times.

In November 1857 a second relief column set out from Cawnpore under the command of General Campbell. The force included the 23rd Foot, the 53rd, 93rd and the 4th Rifle Regiment (the latter being Sikhs) as well as others and amounted in all to 5,000 men. On 14 November Campbell's men were in Lucknow, battling their way towards the compound through strong opposition. At a particularly large building known as the Secundrabagh, two 18-pounder cannons were brought up to effect a breach while troops of the 53rd, 93rd and 4th remained under cover in an adjacent lane. A breach was blown in the wall and the Sikhs raced the Highlanders to be first through the hole. This honour went to Sergeant Major Murray of the 93rd, but he was shot dead immediately after scrambling through. Surprisingly, because he was encumbered by his drum, a drummer of the 93rd was in the first rush. In his memoirs, Lord Roberts, who took part in this action, records that the drummer

> must have been one of the first to pass the grim boundary between life and death; for when I got in I found him just inside the breach, lying on his back, quite dead, a pretty, innocent-looking fair-haired lad, not more than fourteen years old.[21]

That boy soldiers were often prominent in the forefront of action is evident from the story of Bugler Ross, also of the 93rd. Earlier in the month, on 11 November, Ross had climbed to the summit of the domed Shah Nujeef building in the city with a lieutenant and a sergeant, to signal to those in the compound that they were on their way. To indicate their position Lieutenant

McBean put a Highland bonnet on the tip of the staff and waved the regimental colour. To draw the attention of the beleaguered garrison, Ross also blew the regimental call and the Residency answered by raising and lowering its flag. The trio descended, its mission accomplished, but Ross climbed the ladder a second time, alone. Holding on to the dome spire with one hand, he blew, it is said, the 'Cock of the North'. Ross was a 12-year-old.[22]

Bandboy George Monger of the 23rd Foot was yet another boy soldier of Campbell's column who earned a VC. He had what must have been the very lowest rank in the British Army, for his rank as Acting Drummer suggested that he had not yet mastered the instrument. Monger's act of bravery occurred on the breakout from the beleaguered city. Having made its way in, Campbell's force was considered sufficient, together with those already there, to break out and to provide the survivors with protection on the long road to safety.

On 18 November the column was delayed for a time by the mutineers, who were doing their level best to keep the British confined to the Residency compound. Caught in the open at an intersection, a corporal of the 82nd Foot fell wounded. Others in the vicinity scurried for safety, for the enemy musket fire was intense. There was little anyone could do to help the wounded man who, exposed to the cross fire, was trying with difficulty to move. Bandboy Monger then ran out and straddled himself over the corporal to protect him, and there the two stayed until something was done to clear the area.[23]

Finally, the third boy soldier VC was won later in November 1857 by Drummer Thomas Flynn of the 64th Foot. Flynn's age at the time is not known (put at 15 years by Special Collections Officer Coombs who says that his exact date of birth was not known), but he was certainly very young because his story came to the attention of Thomas Carter, a civil servant in London, who included it in his *Curiosities of War* published in 1860. Wounded in the fighting, Flynn charged the mutineers' guns and engaged in a hand-to-hand fight with two rebel artillerymen, in which he came out the victor.[24]

Which of the boy VCs of the Great Mutiny was the youngest is not known. None of their ages was recorded, although their stories are contained in Carter's *Curiosities of War*. The youngest soldier whose age is known when he earned a VC was hospital apprentice Apothecary Andrew Fitzgibbon, aged 15, who was attached to the 67th Foot. Although he was of the legions of boy soldiers born and bred in India, Fitzgibbon earned his award not in India but at Peking during the Second Opium War of 1856–60. Born in Bengal, son of Quartermaster-Sergeant Fitzgibbon of the Kumaon Battalion (late the Gurkha Rifles), Andrew Fitzgibbon joined the Bengal Medical Service and was sent with the 67th on the China expedition. He distinguished himself for extreme bravery by attending wounded under fire during the assault on the Summer Palace, 24 October 1860. Unusually, he was discharged from the army with ignominy during the Afghan War of 1878 for insubordination. However, when he died at Delhi on 7 May 1883, his cross was buried with him.[25]

The Great Mutiny was a time during which the battle exploits of the very youngest boys were observed and written about, as testified by the number of

VCs awarded to them. And it was not to be the last time they penetrated into the heat of the fighting, for they continued to be active combatants until well into the twentieth century. Even so, the beginning of another fundamental change in army policy concerning their activities can be detected well before the nineteenth century closed and it is interesting to note that the first evidence of this change in policy comes from the army in India and not, as one might have expected, from the Home Command.

This evidence is slight, but as one must look for even the smallest sign of change in the official attitude towards the use, training and employment of boy soldiers, it is worth noting. It appeared in 1885 on the occasion of the Third Burmese War which, though a brief one, came about as a result of Burmese interference with the British teak trade. In November 1885 an amphibious force travelled up the Irrawaddy River to attack Thibaw Min's capital, Ava. MacKenzie-Rogan of the Queens, who joined this expedition, recorded that 'Only the youngest boys in the regiment were prevented from going on active service.'[26] This is the first reference to an age limitation being placed on those who were permitted to accompany the force, but unfortunately he did not state what the lower age limit was. However, for reasons which will become evident when we touch on Kitchener's Sudan Campaign and, later, the Boer War, one would speculate that the lower age limit in 1885 was set at 14 years.

CHAPTER XI
HIGH-WATER MARK

THE BOER WAR (1899–1901) was not only the last great imperial war of the British Empire, it was also the last one in which boy soldiers served in the front line in the traditional roles they had filled for so many centuries. This is not to say that they never again saw active service. They did, on the North West Frontier of India, in the 'trouble spots' of the Middle East and in the First World War, but never again did they take part on so large and general a scale. It is also clear from extant records that very few were under the age of 14 years. Yet for the purposes of our study, the remarkable thing about the Boer War is that it is the only conflict where we can get a comprehensive picture of battle as seen through the eyes of observant young boys.

This hitherto little-known view of the war comes to light in a unique collection of letters printed in the limited circulation *Chronicle* of the Duke of York's School for the year 1900. The only copies of this journal are to be found in private collections and, for the extracts which form a large part of this chapter, I am indebted to Mr George Shorter, an ex-Dukie.

To appreciate the significance of these letters it is important to take note of the continuing contribution of the military schools to the ranks of the British Army. In the case of the Duke of York's, on 1 January 1900 there were 1,610 ex-Dukies actually serving their time, to say nothing of those who had fallen in battle or who had had their discharge. In this latter category there were many who proved to be extremely long-lived. One old boy, still sprite enough to appear at the 1899 annual reunion, was ex-Sergeant William Tuohy who, born in 1807, enlisted in the Royal Artillery in 1821. Tuohy developed a system of sword drill which became a standard drill of British cavalry and was expertly demonstrated for Bathsheba by Sergeant Troy in Thomas Hardy's *Far from the Madding Crowd*. Of the 1640 ex-Dukies in uniform in 1900, there were[1]

26 commissioned ranks
63 warrant officers, bandmasters and schoolmasters
571 NCOs

198 privates
258 bandsmen
266 trumpeters and drummers
258 boys

Had the records of the Royal Hibernians survived, a similar breakdown of those in service would have been available for that military school because the army monitors the careers of boys from the military schools extremely carefully and commanding officers were required to provide annual returns of such boys and soldiers in their units. Details provided in those returns included promotions and conduct reports. To say that these boys constituted the army's preferential stock is not stretching a point; that they provided the army with its NCO core is obvious. In short, the British Army operated its own family compact—and the military schools were part of it.

It is thanks to these reports, for example, that we know three ex-Dukies charged in the ranks of the 21st Lancers against the Dervishes at the Battle of Omdurman during Kitchener's Sudan Campaign in 1898; two survived. Of more significance to this history is the fact that another young trooper in that charge later rose to become a company sergeant major in the Duke of York's and served until the outbreak of the Second World War.

Writing of the immediate prewar period, 1938–39, one of the few ex-boy soldier correspondents (who wishes to remain anonymous) recalled his old sergeant major's bed-time stories.

Our Sergeant Major often came into the day room when we were having our nightly mug of cocoa before bed. He was a big man with a waxed moustache and you would never think he had ridden a horse in his life. If one of the boys said, 'Sarn't-major, tell us how you charged at Omdurman', he might gather about twenty or thirty of us around him in a circle and tell us the story, something like this.

'Well, lads, there we was in extended order, squadron by squadron, moving over the open plain. We was hot an' thirsty and the dust kicked up by the first rank was enough to make your eyeballs crawl. We didn't know till after what was ahead but all of a sudden, in a hollow, there was all them Dervishes, thousands and thousands of them. The Colonel says, trumpeter, sound the charge an' no mucking around or we're dead men.

'So down with our lances, arms at the ready and in we went, galloping like the devil was behind us and somehow we got through to the other side.'

If one of the boys questioned him about handling a lance and breaking it (which was a question often asked) he would say, 'Oh no, lad, it wasn't like that. You get it in, lift them past your saddle an' get it out when they're behind you.'[2]

Such tales of the old soldiers were the stuff on which the young ones were weaned. The army was a surrogate mother to them all, those with parents still living as well as the genuine orphans. All of these boys had fathers who were soldiers and a great many of them were simply following a family tradition, for soldiering is as firmly entrenched in the rank and file as in the officer class. There are many examples of soldier families from which to choose, but as we are dealing with the Boer War period we will cite the case of Sergeant Iddendens of the 14th Dragoons. The seven sons of the Iddendens family in 1900 were all in the army: the eldest, a sergeant in the 21st Battery, Royal Field Artillery, at Ladysmith (then under siege by the Boers); the second son, 21st Lancers; the third, 14th Dragoons in South Africa; the fourth, 1st Royal Dragoons; the fifth, 9th Field Battery in South Africa; the sixth, also in the 1st Royals; and the seventh, aged 15, in 14th Dragoons with an elder brother. So, with one exception, all were at the front.

Getting to South Africa, even with the arrival of the steamship, was still a hazardous journey at the turn of the century, but it had its compensations, especially for boys. Bugler William Mayham wrote

Just a few lines to let you know I arrived in South Africa after a pleasant voyage out on the *Kildonan Castle*, during which we saw Dolphins, Porpoises, Sharks, Whales, Swordfish and Flyingfish. We had it very calm in the Bay of Biscay. I was only ill the first day in the English Channel.

The food was excellent, Porridge, Coffee, Bread, Butter, and Jam for breakfast, and Tea and fresh Meat for dinner every day. The boys used to dine with the officers. There were only two of us. The other came from the Hibernian, and he and I used to have great talks about the old Schools. I am made a full bugler and have got my 2nd class certificate [of education] and am now sitting for my first. I go to School here every afternoon. I am stationed now at Wynberg Hospital, but when this reaches you I shall be with Lord Methuen's force at Modder River.

We are full up with wounded men and Boer wounded too. I have a chat to the Boers every morning; they speak English fluently and are very kind to me. We see plenty of Australians, Canadians, etc., every day coming in, and see the Ambulance trains from the Modder with wounded every week.[3]

Some were not as lucky at Mayham. Bugler A. J. Harper of the Royal Army Medical Corps wrote of the disaster that befell the ship at the journey's end.

We started from Liverpool in *Ismore* and after hanging about the coast of Wales for a week, we started on our journey to the Cape. After being on board for 30 days, she struck on the rocks in Hodge's Bay as I expect you heard. It was about half-past two in the morning. We all got ashore alright. We could see the land from the ship about a mile off. There were some Cape Dutch waiting for us. There was a village near by, and we stopped there for three days, when another ship came and took us to Cape Town, where we stopped nearly five weeks.

After stopping at Colesberg for three weeks or so, we joined Roberts at

Modder River, and went on his record march to Kimberly. From there we went to Paardeberg, and have been with General French ever since.[4]

He writes of coming across other boys during his travels.

I saw Ratcliffe at Naanwpoort on my way up to Modder River. At Orange River I saw Connolly, he is a Corporal. My brother who was at first monitor is out here in the West Riding Regt., I saw him at Bloemfontein. I also saw 'Nobby' Brennan in the same Regiment.[5]

Another of those who wrote of his journey to the Cape was Bugler R. J. Davies who was stationed at Gibraltar before being transferred to South Africa. He wrote from Stellenbosch on 9 February 1900.

We left Gibraltar for South Africa on November 20th in the SS 'Sicilian' and reached Cape Town on December 9th. There were about 250 Artillery on board, and I was surprised to meet Ledgerwood on board, in the 78th F. Battery. He was in my Company (C Coy) [at the Duke of York's] so we had our pranks to talk about. As for the voyage I can only say that we had fine weather, a decent boat, but very bad food. We landed at Cape Town but the 78th Field Battery went on to Port Elizabeth. After a few days we shifted on here, and here we have been for the last six weeks, much to our chagrin. At last they are going to shift us, and we are to proceed to Orange River. We don't know what force we join, but the general opinion is that it is Gatacre's. I also met another Company school chum up here—Sainty—who joined the School the same day that I did. He is in the 40th Company A.S.C. and proceeded to Modder River ten days ago.

We have had two or three incidents happen since we have been here. The population consists of loyal Dutch, and last Sunday week all the troops were called upon to put out a bush fire of three miles in extent, which some of the loyal Dutch ignited in the hope it would burn out the camp. Another time we had a night alarm, and then a bit of a railway smash on the line, but owing to the terrible speed at which the trains travel (about 12 miles an hour), no damage was done.[6]

The Boer War was a short, sharp and often bitter conflict, although there were frequent truces to permit the dead and wounded to be collected. When the war began in October 1899 the two independent Boer states of Transvaal and the Orange Free State united under President Kruger of Transvaal. The Boer Army of burghers invaded Natal and laid siege to three centres, Lady-smith, Pretoria and Mafeking. The British Army, commanded by a succession of incompetent generals, struck north from the Cape Colony to attack the Boers, to relieve the beleaguered towns, and to subdue the independent Boer states. This meant striking across the Modder River, a large subsidiary of the Orange River, and it was in the general area where the two great rivers flowed westward to the coast that most of the action between the contestants took place.

Unknown to the British, who were practically without cavalry support when General Buller marched north, the Boers were strongly entrenched on the Modder River when Buller's column approached it in November 1899. Drummer George Clayton, with the 71st Highlanders, wrote of this first major action.

We were first into action on November 28th, at Modder River. It was just before the battle that I met Monitor Hewitt [another ex-Dukie], who is in the 9th Lancers; he says they had it a bit rough being the only Cavalry Regiment up this side then. The battle was a bit stiff for us as we were in the kilt and our legs got burnt something awful as we lay there for a long time. All you could hear was the 'ping' of the bullets going by, and 'pass the word along for a stretcher', and 'pass the word along, they're flanking us on the left', but the most welcome was 'pass the word along to fix bayonets'. That's when the Boers shake a bit, as they don't relish the bayonet at all. I think they live up to the old motto—'He who fights and runs away'.

Our next fight was a bit worse. We formed up on Sunday, 10th December, and advanced a bit, but not far from camp when our Artillery started shelling them in a downpour of rain. We were told we could sleep till 12, midnight, which was something we weren't able to do, because of our wet clothes and the cold. At 12 we formed up ready to advance, and two men fired off their rifles by some carelessness. We were a few yards from the Boer trenches on the morning of the 11th, when the surprisers (ourselves) were surprised. We retired to camp the next day, the 12th. I expect you have read all about this battle of Magersfontein long ago.

It was after this battle we got the order to take no notice of two bugle calls, the 'Retire' and the 'Cease fire', which are on no conditions to be sounded, as we believe the Boers have used them themselves on different occasions.[7]

Drummer Rowe (unit unknown) was in the same action and was last seen marching with his battalion at Modder River, but was reported 'missing' after the action. (In the Boer War both the Hibernians and Dukies kept their eyes peeled for former companions and reported news of one another.) Subsequently his identity ticket was sent with others to the British by the Boers, from whom it was understood he had died of his wounds. He was later reported alive and well, though a prisoner.[8]

Among the many who died on active service during the war was Corporal A. G. Furnish of the Buffs in the 6th Division. Although not at that time on boy service, Furnish's letter, written a few days before his death, is of intrinsic interest for his description of the conditions under which the troops were fighting.

I received your welcome letter which came in the middle of the night, and I could not read it till the next day, when I had to read it while the bullets and shells were flying about, as we were having a very heavy fight. The two regiments that led lost terribly; my regiment lost 18 killed, 91 wounded, 10 missing. But the Boers fell into their own trap. They tried the white flag trick and one man beside me got up to see them and had his head blown off and I was covered with blood. We got right in amongst them and took about 400 prisoners.

Thank God I got through it all safe, but such sights I never saw in my life and never wish to see again. The Boers do bury their dead scandalously. We always have to re-bury them. We expect a big battle tomorrow (March 12th) as we are trying to get to Bloemfontein. Today is Sunday, and we have just finished a long march in the sun after a night in the cold without a blanket. It is very cold at night and just the reverse by day. So I must wait to finish this letter till we get to Bloemfontein as we are in a wilderness at present.

At last we have reached Bloemfontein and I must say it is a pretty place; the loyal Dutch and the English made a great fuss when we got here. They had Union Jacks flying and everyone had either a red white and blue bow on, or else a flag in their hats and even the natives had the same; all you could hear was how they had been treated by the Boers, but now they would get their rights.

I can tell you they had to pay for everything pretty stiff—sugar 2/6 a lb., tea 3/6, butter 2/6, bread 1/3 and 2/- a loaf, and other groceries as expensive. I shall be very glad to get home again as I am married and have two children. You must excuse this paper as we cannot get writing paper often and have sometimes to write on the ammunition paper off the packets when they are served out.[9]

Drummers Denbow and Rutter of the Argyll and Sutherland Highlanders were wounded and yet another, Corporal Shaul of the 71st Highlanders, won a Victoria Cross. George Clayton's brother, Thomas, who was also a drummer in the 71st Highlanders, wrote a letter on Christmas Day confirming much of what his brother had said.

You will wonder where I have been without writing to you. No doubt you have all heard of the fighting we have been doing since we came out here, at Modder River and Magersfontein. I tell you we have had to fight too, to make the Boers retire. We had about 15 hours of it at Modder River; in the burning hot sun and sand all day, and bare legs in the kilt. This was no joke I assure you. About 50 of our men had the sinews at the back of their legs burnt, and some of them are crippled for life, so the doctor told them.

I suppose you will hear of the fight long before you get this letter. I have only seen two Duke of York boys out here, not counting those in my own regiment. One of them is in the 9th Lancers, Hewitt who used to be drum-major in the School, and the other is in the Seaforth Highlanders, his name is Rowe. I saw him when we were going out to fight the Boers at Magersfontein but I could not speak to him. After the battle, when we retired to camp, I went to see him, but they told me he was missing.

You will have read of the killed and wounded at the two battles. Our two gymnastic instructors, Sergeant Smith and Corporal Mowatt, were killed and Adam Inglis in the drums. He used to come up to the school sometimes. All the Dukies in this regiment are all right except Kirton. We have here Cox, my brother, and myself. George Meredith's brother is here and is quite safe. It is very hot now and the sand burns our feet.[10]

Those in the thick of it, for all the danger, were the envy of those who were not. Drummer John Hammond, stationed with the Royal Berkshire Regiment on the Isle of Wight, reported his disappointment because his battalion was not destined for the South Africa front and hoped for action elsewhere.

Well, in the first place, I am very happy in my regiment. I have been appointed effective drummer and now I clear 9½d a day pay which I think very good for a boy of 15, don't you?

All my regiment feel it keenly at not being sent to the war in South Africa. I think it a shame, as the 1st Royal Berks distinguished themselves at Tofrek, on the 22nd March, 1885, and were made a royal regiment on the field of battle. I am sure we should give a good account of ourselves in South Africa if we only had the chance to go. As it is, they are bringing the Royal Sussex Regiment from Malta preparatory to sending them to South Africa, and sending us to Malta to linger in obscurity.

We have one consolation, however. There is a rumour that the Abyssinians intend overrunning the Soudan, so if we are at Malta we may have a chance at them. I am sure Menelik will find the men he can't lick in my regiment.

Thomsett is getting on very well. He is also an effective drummer. All our old boys are getting on famously. We are going to have our photo taken in Khaki and I will send you one as soon as I can.

Well, I think this is all now. I hope my next letter will be from the front, either South Africa or Abyssinia, Kruger or Menelik, it don't matter which.[11]

Through the early months of 1900 the fighting became intense and the British were far from gaining the upper hand. The new high-powered rifles with smokeless cartridges in the hands of skilled Boer guerrillas spread the battlefields over much wider areas. This required a new style of fighting and different tactics from those used in the past. But the British generals were not up to it and those statues and monuments erected to their memory after the war are better now regarded as monuments to their blunders: Magersfontein, Colenso and other, equally costly, failures.

Drummer William Ratcliffe, who joined his regiment, the 1st Suffolks, shortly before it moved to the front, testifies to the ferocity of the fighting and skill of the Boers.

I am writing to give you a brief account of the disaster which befell our regiment on the 6th January near Colesburg. We were called up about midnight on the night of the 5th and fell in, in 'quarter column' as follows, A, B, C & H Companies. There was some bother in finding our places, but after that we moved off taking the line between two of our own picquets and they did not know we had passed them, so that will show you how quiet we went.

When at last we halted, the Colonel told us that no man was to fire a shot and that no bugles were to sound, while the pass-word was to be the same as at Gibraltar, 'Steady the old 12th!' After that we marched on again in column of route as follows, H, C, A and B Companies. We went about 100 yards further and halted, when the order was given to 'fix bayonets,' two or three at a time so as not to make a noise.

We advanced to the bottom of Pink Hill which we were to attack, but failed, as you know. We advanced—but very slowly till we got to the brow of the hill and then halted, while the scouts advanced to find the enemy. They returned and reported that they had found a trench about 50 yards over the brow of the hill, but it was deserted. But the Boers were too artful for us, they had another trench which they occupied behind the empty one.

The Colonel called the officers to him to tell them how they were to manoeuvre their companies: when the Boer sentry discovered us and fired a shot which we took for their signal. Then we had to keep low as they all let fly, and must have fired a whole magazine at us during the next ten minutes. We all lay quiet, which was the best plan, during this time. We were quarter columns and as thick as bees, but my Company being in the rear we did not hear much of what was said by the Colonel, but anyhow the front Company (H) got the order to charge, which they did, and all the front rank went down with the exception of one man.

The Colonel, seeing this, gave the order to retire, and then fell. We retired to the bottom of the hill to wait further orders, but all the officers remained on the hill when four of them were killed, 7 taken prisoners, and 1 wounded, besides 28 men killed, 75 prisoners, and 20 wounded who returned to camp.[12]

Many of these boys excelled themselves in what proved to be a new and very mobile kind of warfare. Characteristically, those who performed outstanding acts of bravery said nothing of their exploits in their letters and their conduct came to light only in the correspondence of others. Trumpeter Price of the 6th Inniskilling Dragoons was one such case. Writing from Modder Farm on 29 January 1900, Corporal John Macken reported in a letter:

Our first attack on the Boers was made on New Year's Day, about 2.30 a.m., and by all accounts we gave them a very good New Year's gift. There are, or rather were, four old boys up here with my regiment, but I am sorry to say one has met his death. It was like this, my squadron was on picquet, and during the night the Boers had managed to work round our flank and occupy some hills a few hundred yards from us.

In the morning my troop was ordered out to water horses. We had hardly left cover when we heard a rifle report. We looked at one another not knowing the meaning of it, but we had not long to wait before a perfect hail of lead poured into us from the hills. We collected ourselves and lined the hills waiting for the arrival of the infantry and artillery. All of a sudden we were ordered out to draw the Boer fire while the infantry rushed the hills. This plan turned out a success. One could see the Boers flying in all directions, at the same time being pursued by nineteen men of this regiment.

It was in this pursuit that one of the old boys got killed. I did not see him myself, but learnt later that he had been shot through the head. Poor chap! I felt very sorry, he being my old school-mate. His name was Corporal Patterson, and his School number A1. Another old boy named Price, greatly distinguished himself. Our squadron officer had his horse shot under him and was left almost on his last resources, when Price galloped up and brought our officer and himself safely out of fire on one horse. No doubt he will be recommended for this, at any rate let's hope so![13]

In a national weekly newspaper in January 1900 there appeared a story from a reporter at the front of the battle of Colenso. The report concerned the bravery of a young trumpeter of the 66th Field Artillery Battery who galloped away to bring up more ammunition. The battery was running out and Trumpeter Frank Wilde succeeded in his mission but, the correspondent noted, 'fell a victim to the bullets of the enemy'. Trumpeter Wilde, however, wrote a slight correction.

Just a few lines to let you know we are getting on with the war and driving the enemy back. We have taken Colenso and crossed the Tugela which is a very fine river, but the town is a complete ruin. The Boers have blown up the Railway Bridge, not leaving one stone on another. We have been over the old Battlefield where so many of our comrades are buried, and we saw a lot of our horses with their harness on but no flesh on their bones. We saw human remains also, something dreadful to see.

We have captured one of their strongest positions; it was a hard fight for our men. Did you read that bit in the newspaper last January, in a letter from a soldier to his people? It was telling how our ammunition was running short and I rode after an ammunition waggon and fetched it up to the guns while the bullets were flying round me. The man in writing to his people said 'the trumpeter received his death wound,'—but, thank God, I wasn't hit at all.[14]

A short time later Wilde wrote again.

You have heard by this time that we have relieved Ladysmith. It was a very hard fight indeed, and there were a lot killed. The besieged troops were very glad to see us come in. They had been living on horseflesh and biscuits. The stench of the place was something awful. We are beating the Boers all over the shop, and everyone expects the war to be over soon.

Yesterday we had a big hail storm, the hail stones were as big as eggs; they came right through the tents. Some men who happened to be out in it got black eyes and big bumps on their heads. One native got killed. All the horses broke their ropes and ran for their lives, cutting themselves all over. It took us all day to find them. I never heard such a noise in all my life. Luckily the storm came on in the daytime. If it had come in the night we might have thought it was the Boers.[15]

Bugler John Craig of the 25th Company, Royal Engineers, was in Ladysmith during the siege and wrote a long letter the following July describing the subsequent movements of the company as part of General Buller's column. He wrote:

After the siege until the 16th May I did very little but eat and drink, trying to recoup my strength, which I must admit I did to my entire satisfaction. On the aforesaid date we received orders to pack up and proceed to Modder Spruit, and arrived there at 10 p.m., and then to bed. It was my first experience at bivouacking, as we had no time to pitch our tents.[16]

There follows a detailed account of the company's movements via Sundays River, Waterskloof, Kalibas, Ingagane, Iukuba Spruit and Utrecht. Then, following an action at Laing's Nek, he continues

A good many prisoners were taken in the capture of Wacherstroom, among them some women and children who were at once released. This place was captured by a Battery and some Mounted Infantry after a short skirmish, and a few men wounded. During the advance our Company has made drifts for the guns and transport to get through, as well as preparing the water supply. After a fortnight's stay we made a move for our present camp which is in rather an outlandish place, even for northern Natal. The only things on view, apart from the scenery, are a few Boer dwellings, which I can assure you are not very artistic.

My first ramble was to visit a spot where the 60th Rifles are buried who fell in the Battle of Ingogo, on the 8th February 1881. A major, now in camp with the KRRs who fought with the 60th in the above fight, gave a lecture some few days ago on various points of interest during the battle.[17]

Before we move on to some boy soldiers hospitalised with wounds, yet another interesting letter from Trumpeter Frank Wilde is worth quoting. Even at 14 he writes with the understanding of a veteran soldier. It is without malice or rancour and, furthermore, betrays frank admiration for the fighting qualities of the enemy.

We have been out here about nine months, and are about tired of it. We went through the Battle of Colenso, where I am sorry to say my Battery lost four guns, and the 14th Battery lost six. It was an awful fight, and we were within 300 yards of the enemy's rifles; our men were getting mown down. It was a dreadful sight. All our officers got shot down, and the gunners stood to their guns till all our ammunition was gone.

Trumpeter Aggas was taken prisoner, but he got away by pretending he was wounded in the leg, and a gunner carried him into camp. I had a few narrow escapes, but I never got wounded. We have been in a lot of engagements, but none as bad as Colenso. Many a time since I have been on active service I have thought how I should like those good dinners that I used to leave on the dining hall table. Four biscuits is not much to do about twenty miles a day on, and sleeping on the open veldt.

This war should have been over three months ago, only the Boers have been a bit smarter than we thought. I will be jolly glad when it is all over, and will give you all a look up when I come home.[18]

Wilde was later recommended for his bravery during the battle of Colenso but, apart from correcting the error about his untimely death, made no mention of the incident in his letters.

Among the many boys wounded in battle, Thomas E. Trump and George A. Yearsley, of the Essex Regiment, wrote a joint letter. Neither was a drummer nor trumpeter but both held the rank of Boy Soldier. Describing the frequent get-togethers of ex-Hibs and old Dukies, they wrote

During our short stay at Modder River previous to our advance on Bloemfontein under 'Bobs', [Lord Roberts] many of us congregated together and spent a most sociable evening around a camp-fire, but we all expect that by the time this reaches you many of them may be killed or wounded in different engagements whilst trying to avenge previous defeats inflicted on us by the Boers.[19]

There followed a list of boys in hospital with them and a note of their wounds—arms, elbows, shoulders and legs shattered by bullets and other forms of enemy action. Like many a soldier lying wounded in a hospital bed, Boy Yearsley turned poet. In memory of a charge by the Essex and Welsh Regiments at Driefontein on 10 March 1900, he wrote

Three cheers for the noble Brigadier
Of the gallant eighteenth Brigade,
Who stormed the trenches at Driefontain,
When their splendid charge was made.

Who cared they that bullets came down like rain,
And shells in the mid'st of them crashed,
With bayonets fixed and a ringing cheer,
Right into the foe they dashed.

A hand to hand fight and the kopjes were cleared,
And the Boers were falling back,
Naught could withstand that resistless force
Of the brilliantly planned attack.

The Essex and Welsh their laurels gained,
And nobly they bore the brunt,
And even where hottest the battle raged,
Presented a dauntless front.

What though their ranks are sorely thinned?
Their comrades who died that day
Have earned their glory, won their fame,
Which never will pass away!

Although these lines were written by a boy barely into his teens there is a flavour about them which captures the gallantry and dash of the Boer War period, one that was to be reflected in the *Boy's Own*-type papers published over the next 30–40 years. Lieutenant-Colonel Baden-Powell, who became the hero of Mafeking and in whose lap the international Scouting movement was born,[20] organised the boys and girls of Mafeking, but it has to be remembered that for hundreds of young boys like Yearsley the battle was only too real.

The spirit of the age was not only manifest in the reality of the war by the placing of boy soldiers into the battleline but is reflected in the music, poetry and literature of the age. At the same time, while there is no direct evidence to support a change of policy about the use of boys in the front line, it is obvious that someone, somewhere, between 1900 and 1914, thought about it, because never again were they employed on a large scale in general action.

Many of the hymns sung in the church militant, though written with strong military metaphor, have been taken in a too literal sense by the unliterary; 'Onward Christian Soldiers', 'Soldiers of Christ Arise' and 'Fight the Good Fight' are examples which readily come to mind. Such hymns, whether chosen for the purpose of inspiring soldiers to do battle or simply for their stirring words and melodies, were for generations the standard choice of hymns at garrison church services. Similarly, generations of boys of the Duke of York's School have been inspired by the school hymn 'Sons of the Brave', written by the Reverend G. H. Andrews, the School Chaplain, in 1900.

Oh Lord, The Banner floateth o'er us,
   Beneath its folds we stand and sing;
In Majesty go Thou before us,
   Our Saviour Christ! Our Captain-King!
Sons of the Brave! our hearts now hail Thee—
   Bravest of all! and cry to thee:
Oh Lord, make us Thy faithful soldiers,
   And lead us on—to Victory![21]

CHAPTER XII
JOHNNY CANUCK

THE PRESENCE OF Australian and Canadian troops in South Africa during the Boer War was something new to the pattern of Britain's imperial wars. Contingents of the Indian Army had been used in actions outside India from time to time, but as directed by the British government. The arrival of Australians and Canadians was different, for they came of their own volition, willingly and without coercion. The arrival of Dominion troops impressed Bugler Mayham, who noted in a letter home 'We see plenty of Australians and Canadians every day coming in',[1] a sight which must have convinced him and others of the rightness of the British cause.

In its attitude to boy soldiers Canada, more than any other dominion in the Commonwealth, based the interior economy of its national army on the British model and one does not have to look far to explain why. Unlike Australia and New Zealand, which developed into autonomous states relatively free from the threat of external aggression, Canada had always had to cope with both the possibility and the reality of invasion. Under French rule this was from the British and, under British dominion, from the United States of America which, from the earliest days of nationhood, cast covetous eyes over the entire continent of North America. This state of affairs continued until well into the second half of the nineteenth century, after which time US strategy for territorial expansion became more benign and expressed itself in a striving for economic domination. Today Canada is proud of having the longest undefended border in the world, but it must be remembered that this boast is of comparatively recent origin.

We have seen to what extent the American Revolutionary Army made use of boy soldiers during the 1776–83 war. It made use of them as much from necessity as from a desire to follow British tradition, for the fledgling country remained desperately short of manpower throughout its struggle for independence and therefore took what it could get. Similarly, at a time long before Canada could be said to have an army of its own, the precedent for enlisting boy soldiers had been set. This was during the post-revolutionary war period, from about 1785 to the War of 1812, when the United States began flexing its muscles.

The development of an independent Canadian Army occurred over a long period, from about 1800 when locally-raised militia units were first formed, until 1900 when the country could truly be said to have an army of its own. During that same period the strength of the protective force provided by the British Army gradually diminished until it dwindled away to nothing. During that long transition period spanning almost, but not quite, 100 years the enlistment of boys came to be accepted as a perfectly natural practice.

If we are to pinpoint dates, places and occasions for the creation of an all-Canadian military formation, we must begin near the turn of the nineteenth century. With Europe about to be plunged into turmoil again as a result of the French Revolution of 1792, the United States, whose leaders maintained close ties with France, was perceived by the British to pose a real threat to the Canadian nation. In 1793 Sir John Wentworth, the Lieutenant-Governor of Nova Scotia, proposed to Adjutant-General Sir Henry Dundas that a provincial force would be better than militia for the defence of the territory. The following year, after the declaration of war with France, Dundas instructed the provincial governors to 'take necessary steps for raising and forming from among inhabitants . . . a corps not exceeding 600 men, to be divided into six companies, with the usual establishment of commissioned and non-commissioned officers.'[2]

The Governors of Newfoundland, Nova Scotia and New Brunswick had a large number of half-pay loyalist officers on whom to draw to form militia regiments. In 1799 the Royal Nova Scotia Regiment and the New Brunswick Regiment were raised to the rank of fencible regiments, meaning that they were available for general service in Canada rather than being limited to the defence of the provinces in which they were raised. The Peace of Amiens in 1802 brought about the disbandment of these regiments but they were re-created the following year and placed on the regular establishment of the British Army as fencible regiments along with the Royal Newfoundland Fencibles.

In 1810 the New Brunswick Regiment was alone approved as a regiment of the British line, a singular achievement for a force raised entirely overseas. This distinction it shared with the 60th Foot (the Royal Americans) and the 40th (also raised in New England). Writing to Sir Martin Hunter, a veteran of Bunker Hill and Colonel of the New Brunswick Regiment, Colonel Torrens stated: 'His Majesty has accordingly been pleased to approve of the New Brunswick Fencibles being made a Regiment of the line and numbered 104th Foot.'[3]

The muster rolls of the regiment are highly illuminating, not simply for the number of boy soldiers who served in it but also for the mix of national origins of those in its ranks. French Canadians constituted more than half of the regiment's strength; English, Welsh, Scots, Irish and a sprinkling of Hessians and Brunswickers made up the remainder. The 104th was only in existence for seven years, being disbanded in 1817 (the number was later assigned to another regiment), but 168 names recorded on the muster rolls were acknowledged as being drummers, buglers or, simply, boy soldiers, although many of those who enlisted as privates began their service as early as 15 years of age. Of the 168 boys on the rolls, 19 deserted (as compared with more than 200 on man service), 13 died of natural causes, 4 were killed in action, and 4 were taken prisoner during the war of 1812. About 40 of those who began as boy soldiers were promoted to the senior non-commissioned ranks. This record may be taken as typical of the experience of all three regiments raised in Canada at this period.

In 1813 the 104th achieved an astonishing feat of endurance by marching from New Brunswick to Quebec and on to the Niagara peninsula in the depth of the icy Canadian winter. The families and boy soldiers of the regiment, however, did not take part in the march, but waited in New Brunswick until the coming of spring, when they rejoined the regiment by water transport.[4]

The history of the Canadian Army is outside the scope of this book, except insofar as its boy soldiers are concerned. Nevertheless, as militia units of cavalry, infantry and artillery came to form part of the regular military establishment, or Permanent Force as the Canadian Regular Army is known, the use of boy soldiers became a firmly established practice. They were taken on strength as young as ten years of age until at least 1968, when the Canadian Army ceased to take underage soldiers altogether.

Canada had enough troubles along her border with the United States to require the nation to keep troops in readiness for any eventuality. For this reason it is no wonder that until recently the nation developed with a strong consciousness of the need for military defence. The War of 1812, the Irish-inspired troubles of the 1850s and 1860s, and the Riel Rebellion of 1887, kept both the regulars and militia on the alert. When fighting did break out, Canada's boy soldiers were as involved in action as were the men.

For the first time in its history, it was the Boer War which provided the country with the opportunity to give an account of its military abilities overseas. The 2nd Royal Canadian Regiment, which included a company of the Queen's Canadian Rifles, played a prominent part in the surrender of General Cronje's Boers at Pardeberg and the action was portrayed in the painting 'Dawn of Majuba Day' in which the regiment's 14-year-old bugler forms the focal point. The painting now hangs in the Royal Canadian Military Institute, Toronto.

The Boer War was for the Canadian Army, as for the British, the last war in which general use was made of boy soldiers on active service. At the same time, it was not the last occasion on which the country's youth went into action. Another opportunity came with the outbreak of the First World War in 1914.

Canadians from all walks of life flocked to join the armed forces and the volunteers included thousands of the underaged. Many are the cases of boys who, truthfully stating their age to the recruiting sergeants, were told to take a walk around the block to reconsider—in other words, to falsify their age. No great effort was made to weed out the youngsters and hundreds of volunteers who served were, by our definition, boys. There were also the *bona fide* boy soldiers of the regular army who, in the early days of the war, were shipped to France and went to the front with their regiments.

Here again it is necessary to differentiate between those who enlisted as boy soldiers and those who lied to get into uniform. Because those in the latter category qualify as boy soldiers, although they were doing a man's job, we are justified in discussing their experience. Among the many youths who, by reason of their physical development, could not possibly be mistaken for adults, there is the unusual case of Robert Clarence Thompson of Picton, Ontario, who was barely 13 years old when he first enlisted. 'He wore short pants when he went to the collegiate,' his brother Earl recalled, 'and borrowed long pants to enlist. He was in 33 days until my father got the authorities to release him.'[5] In March 1916, when barely 14, Robert enlisted again, and was sent overseas. After six months' training he was sent to France and fought at the Battle of Vimy, but the authorities discovered his true age and returned him to Canada for discharge from the army. Like many a boy before and since, Thompson was stubborn and within a month of his discharge he was back in uniform. When the Halifax disaster occurred on 16 December 1917, in which an ammunition ship blew up and demolished the town with a huge loss of life, Thompson was in the relief battalion which was rushed from Toronto to help the survivors and restore order. Whether at Halifax or elsewhere, Thompson proved himself a good soldier and was quickly promoted through the ranks to sergeant major. In this rank, aged 15, he led his company at the Battle of Mons and was in his sixteenth year when the armistice was signed on 11 November 1918.[6]

There were many boys of Thompson's stamp, not all of them Canadians. Some, like Frederick Ives Lord, were Americans who crossed the border, in both world wars, to serve the Allied cause. Lord, born in 1900, first joined the 3rd Texas Infantry when he was 16, but was found out and given an honourable discharge. He then doctored his birth certificate and successfully enlisted in the Royal Canadian Flying Corps to be trained as a pilot. Intelligent, sharp-witted and brave, Lord was credited with downing nine enemy aircraft before being shot down himself over the British lines and wounded. He was awarded the DFC and given command of a flight. He won a bar to his DFC while piloting an RE8 machine in an attack on the Pinega River, Russia, where he went with the Allied Expeditionary Force in the wake of the Russian Revolution.[7]

The cases of Lord and Thompson are among the few recorded in official and unofficial papers, but they are by no means unique. Warrant Officer R. E. Henley of British Columbia also fought at the Battle of Vimy, and was just 13 years old when he enlisted. He tells his own story.

I never met any of the boys in the boys' battalion in England—(the Canadians had so many boys they formed them into boys' battalions) although my commanding officer had orders to send all underage soldiers back to England (from the front), but this was never carried out . . . I had no desire to be returned to England as I had heard through the usual latrine gossip that close order drill was one of the main subjects in the Boys' Battalion.

I originally enlisted in 1915 but caught pneumonia in England and when they caught up with my age I was sent back to Canada. I again enlisted and went overseas as a trumpeter. At Ross Barracks in Shorncliffe, the cavalry barracks, I put my name on a volunteer list to transfer to infantry and, to my surprise, I was transferred to the Quebec Reserve Battalion. On completion of training I went on draft to the 42nd Battalion RWC, arriving in time for Vimy. I was a rifle grenadier and a Lewis gunner in the battalion. I was wounded twice and evacuated, ill with bronchitis and chest trouble, from Mons two days after the armistice was signed . . .

In training I thoroughly enjoyed the service. In France I was scared and stayed scared all the time. A scared soldier lives longer. I also learned never to volunteer for anything. I had good NCOs who were mostly married men with families of their own. If I strayed too far out of line I would soon be brought to account. In the main, discipline was mostly swift and just. The officers and NCOs made men's lives miserable but that didn't last too long in France and Belgium.[8]

Henley was demobilised at 17, but served again when he enlisted in 1939 for the Second World War and, on being demobilised for the second time, joined the militia.

Bill Taylor was another boy who found himself in the Flanders mud. It was cold in no-man's-land, perishingly cold, and he had become soaked to the skin the moment he crawled out of the trench. Attached to one ankle was a cord which was played out as he wriggled his way forward. Somewhere out there in the inky blackness, when his companion had found a suitable spot, the two-man patrol would use a simple system of jerks on the line to communicate information to those in the trench. In places, the width of no-man's-land was less than 50 yards so it was important to have early warning of the approach of raiding parties. Once in position and accustomed to the darkness they could make out the slightest movement within a radius of 30 to 50 feet. Two pairs of eyes were better than one. Lying close to his companion, waiting and watching in the small hours of the night, Taylor came as close to another human being as he had ever been.

He was a small, wiry lad who, having been an orphan as far back as he could remember, was by nature a loner. He remembered being sent to Canada from London in 1908. He was one of a large party of charity children from the Dr Stephenson Orphanage and, like many of those waifs, he had no idea of where or when he was born. One thing was certain: he was still a child when war broke out.

He had been working as a farm labourer then—boys became farm labourers, girls were farmed out as domestic servants. In November 1914 he was in the Toronto Exhibition Grounds, watching the 20th Battalion being put through its paces. A guard, taking him for a new recruit, directed him to the medical station. That very same day he became a soldier bold in the 20th Battalion.

The following September (1915) the battalion went to France where it was thrown into the trenches, much the same as a non-swimmer might be thrown into the deep end of the pool and there left to sink or swim. Taylor swam, many perished. For the next three years the battalion was continuously at the front, either in the trenches or immediately to the rear, resting. Loos, Ypres, Passchendaele, the Somme were all names and places with which the unit became intimately familiar; Taylor too. He remembers the early days when there was a certain amount of fraternisation with the enemy and of how they used to shout to one another across no-man's-land. For three days, on and off, he conversed with a German soldier who had been born and raised in Toronto and who had at one time worked in the King Edward Hotel. He answered the call to return to Germany to fight for a fatherland he had never seen. His brother chose the opposite side.

Crawling into the middle of no-man's-land became a regular outing for Taylor. It required nerves of steel, a keen eye and acute hearing. Besides, 'It was a hell of a lot better than trying to save your face from a rat,' he said. Taylor was wounded in 1917 and spent a long time in a hospital in Britain before being returned to his unit, fit for duty. He arrived there just in time for the signing of the armistice, and was still in his teens when he returned to Canada, but he felt years older.[9]

Evidence of the flood of Canadian boy soldier recruits during the 1914–18 conflict is to be found in the formation of those already mentioned boys' battalions and reserve units to which boys discovered at the front were returned. This happened only at the whim of the unit officers, for it is clear that hundreds of cases of discovery were purposely ignored.

One who served in a reserve battalion was Walter Beck, who was posted to the First Depot Battalion of the Nova Scotia Regiment when he enlisted, aged 15. Beck was shipped to Britain, to the regiment's 17th Reserve Battalion, then stationed at Aldershot. He recalls little of the discipline he experienced, except to note that it seemed to him severe, for 'the imperial NCOs used to scare the hell out of me',[10] he reported. (British Army rank and file were known to the Dominion soldiers as imperial troops.) He has hazy recollections of witnessing a drumming out parade when stationed at Aldershot, but remembers enough to provide the essential details.

Regarding the drumming out, you know it is so long ago it may have been a general court-martial. I think it was at Aldershot in England. The drums were used and the man in question was a young officer. They ripped off his rank insignia and other decorations and he stood there a buck private. I do not remember what he was charged with or any other details, but, as a boy of fifteen, to me it was scarey. I thought they might shoot him, but they just dismissed the battalion and he stood there alone on the parade square. It was very touching.[11]

These boys who enlisted in the boys' and reserve battalions were in addition to the normal complement of acknowledged boy soldiers in the Canadian Army. Many of the regular boy soldiers were sent overseas with their units, as Trumpeter Henley testifies, but stopped from going to the front later in the war. Their presence in the Permanent Force, once the army returned to its peacetime establishment, was assured, but the number of openings available presented a problem to other young boys who wanted to join. There was, however, a way of getting into the regular army.

First they joined a militia unit and then transferred to the Permanent Force as soon as a vacancy occurred. Major John E. Malone was typical of those who entered the army by this route.

I joined the Canadian Machine Gun Corps in February 1936, in Ottawa, at the age of 16. The CMGC was disbanded in 1937 and I was transferred, as a boy, to the Princess Louise Dragoon Guards. Then, in 1938, I joined the Royal Canadian Dragoons as a trooper.[12]

One of the most interesting of the boy soldiers in this category who joined between the wars was Captain C. Earl Cloutier, a product of Canada's two main cultural streams, the French and the English, and whose family followed the military tradition. His is the only known case on record, after John Shipp, of a boy soldier who rose twice to commissioned rank, having passed each time through the lower ranks.

At the age of 14 I enlisted as a signaller in the 1st Canadian Field Battery and later transferred to the 15th. (Both units were permanent active militia batteries.) At the age of 16 I was enlisted as a boy into the Royal Canadian Regiment.

Boy soldiering was the most memorable and certainly the highlight of my career in the Canadian Army. The discipline was very stiff but we had thorough training in the hands of expertly-qualified NCOs, some of whom had come from the British Army to serve in Canada. The calibre of these prewar NCOs and officers has not been duplicated since.

Flogging and birch caning were but rumours that drifted in from British sources. I never had experience of this (corporal punishment). As the RSM of the regiment was once heard to say, 'These boys will one day be men and may very well outrank those that would have them caned today.' As to drumming out, we were briefed and practised in the drill. Though it was something frequently talked about I never had the misfortune of having to witness such an event.[13]

Boy soldiers of the pre-Second World War era were trained in the use of small arms and rifle drill as were the men, but had the additional duties of serving as buglers. They received half the adult soldier's pay, or 50¢ a day, paid at the rate of $7.50 twice monthly. Summing up the education he received as a boy, Cloutier said, 'The litany for boys during my day was military law and King's Rules and Regulations for Canada; we could recite them backwards.'[14]

It would be impractical to quote all the letters received from Canadian ex-boy soldiers, so I have chosen those which help give a picture of the life they led, the training they received, their treatment and something of how they themselves felt about their experience.

Captain Edward W. Farmer, who served with Cloutier in the Royal Canadian Regiment as a boy, gave his opinion of service conditions in 1938.

As a boy of 15 years of age I must say that at no time was I afraid or worried or depressed. Boy soldiers were highly respected by all ranks, and God help anyone who did not acknowledge this fact. They did not baby us in any manner whatever, but were fair and helped us in any way they could through our initial training. I personally feel, as I'm sure all other ex-boy soldiers do, that it was wonderful training and a terrific way of life. I would go through it again if that were possible and would highly recommend it to every young boy.[15]

Unlike boys in the British Army, who tended to be segregated from the men, Canadian boy soldiers took their place in the ranks alongside the men and were not set apart from them until the onset of the Second World War. Similarly, they were subject to the same discipline and duties, but with the added requirement of having to obey orders from privates, who were of senior rank. Farmer, who happened to be the last Permanent Force boy soldier to join the Royal Canadian Regiment, once refused to obey a senior private's 'request' to help clean mess tables. He was charged and sentenced to 4 days CB (confined to barracks), with fatigues and extra parades.

Breaches of the unwritten code of behaviour among boy soldiers were dealt with by means of kangaroo courts, run by the boys themselves. Those found guilty of breaking the code (theft from a comrade, for example) were severely punished. It was not uncommon for a culprit to be subjected to group scrubbing in a cold shower. (Kangaroo courts appear to have been fairly common among all boy soldiers and will be dealt with in more detail later.) Farmer reports that 'although I was disposed not to approve [of such courts] I really believe they did curb some problems we had with new recruits.'

By the time Farmer was 16 he had been promoted to the rank of boy sergeant. There then came to him the strangest detail to fall to the lot of any boy soldier.

I was called off the square and told to report to the CO. He, in turn, told me to report to Brigadier MacDonald at headquarters. The Brigadier lectured me on the importance of being punctual for parade and being back in the barracks at 1600 hours without fail. He had me worried sick and then ordered me to report to the Squadron Armouries for a very special detail. No end of questioning could persuade him to tell me why. Special indeed! I found myself the sergeant instructor for the newly-formed CWAC (Canadian Women's Auxiliary Corps), 150 very beautiful girls and me only 16. As it happened it was a most gratifying job as I found that you can train women parade square drill and many other basic training programmes in half the time it takes to teach men.[16]

There are few surviving boy soldiers of prewar vintage, for the obvious reason that they were among the first to be sent on active service as soon as they reached man service age, but some while still boys. The fall of France, Hong Kong and Singapore, and those operations so costly to the lives of Canadian soldiers—Dieppe, North Africa, Italy and the invasion of Europe—took their toll. Canadian records are even more sparse on the subject of boy soldiers than those maintained by the British Army. Until ex-Boy Soldier Donald M. Fowler reported his record, the impression was that the Canadian Army had a longstanding age restriction of 14 years for enlistment. Fowler, however, enlisted in the Princess of Wales's Regiment in 1936, aged 11.

In June 1940, aged 14, I joined the Stormont Dundas and Glengarry Highlanders, going overseas in July 1941. I returned to Canada in July 1945, having served in the U.K., Normandy, Belgium, Holland and Germany, and took my discharge in 1945 before my 20th birthday.[17]

His brother, Karl, also began his boy service at the age of 11. He joined the Royal Canadian Ordnance Corps, but got no further than Newfoundland in the Second World War. Said Fowler: 'I have since learned that in the First World War there were a number of 11-year-olds in the Canadian Regular Army and, I believe, one or two made it to the trenches in 1914–18.' This is not unlikely, for some as young in the British Army units went to the front line during the early period of the First World War.

From Professor R. G. Roy of the University of Victoria, British Columbia, we learn something of the conditions of boy service. He enlisted in the Cape Breton Highlanders in September 1936 with the rank and pay of a boy. There were two other boys in the regiment, all serving in the signal platoon. Roy described what life was like for them.

I mentioned that our pay was 70¢ a day [boy soldier pay in 1936 was 50¢ a day, but was increased to 70¢ a day in 1939]—not terribly much but it is remarkable what one could buy with 70¢ in 1939. About the only unique thing about being a boy soldier was that we didn't have to do guard duty. We did everything else—on the ranges, foot drill, arms drill, route marches, the whole business and routine of basic training.

We shared quarters, meals and everything else with the others in the platoon—that is, the older men. They accepted us without any condescention and we got along exceptionally well together. I must say that in our innocence we were sometimes surprised at their sexual activity, shall I say—and by that I mean out of barracks, not in—but I suppose one has to learn the facts of life and for us it was [in] a barrack room.

As far as discipline was concerned there was really no problem. I was once put on a charge by a sergeant who didn't like my effort at PT instruction. The charge—'Conduct to the prejudice of good order and military discipline in that he did not shave before coming on parade.' Naturally, I didn't have anything to shave so he was perfectly right. The company commander gave me a couple of days CB and that was that.[18]

The experience of such boy soldiers as Fowler who went overseas was clearly an exception to the general rule, for the authorities, evidently conscious of what had happened during the First World War, promptly gathered all young soldiers into special units. Those from units in central Canada were posted to Wolseley Barracks, London, Ontario, where some 500 were formed into a Boys' Battalion. Two other centres were located, one in the Maritime Provinces and the other in western Canada. Assuming that the strengths of the three centres were equal (no records have been located to show how many boys were in the service), Canada must have had about 1,500 boy soldiers in its regular army at the outbreak of the war.

Strict measures were enforced to ensure that underage soldiers did not slip past the recruiting desks as they had in the First World War, and although some may have done so, no reports have been received from ex-Rats who did. However, as one enterprising Canadian boy discovered, the easiest way of getting nearer the action was to travel to Britain and join the British Army. In this respect, Dahn D. Higley (who later became a Chief Superintendent of the Ontario Provincial Police) had something in common with Thompson and Lord. In 1938, aged 15, Higley enlisted in the Kent Regiment (a non-permanent militia unit), but as a man, not a boy. Suspecting that he would not be permitted to serve if war came, or would at best be kept in Canada, he travelled to Britain at his own expense in 1939 and enlisted in the Royal Corps of Signals as an apprentice tradesman. At that time apprentices were taken into the British Army between the ages of 13 and 14, but an exception was made in Higley's case because he was from overseas.

In 1942, Canada's Deputy Commander of the General Staff (DCGS) submitted a proposal for the formation of Young Soldiers' Battalions, five in number, for Canada's active army.[19] These were to be reserve battalions for recruits aged 16 to 19, to serve the same purpose they had served in the First World War. Then, to satisfy a growing need for skilled tradesmen, the Adjutant-General submitted a brief to the Privy Council in November 1942, 'for the purpose of obtaining authority to permit the enlistment of boys, who would undergo trades training.'[20] As a result, the Canadian Technical Training Corps

(CTTC) came into existence in June 1943 for the purposes of training electricians, machinists, mechanics, clerks, draughtsmen and surveyors.

Brigadier-General W. J. Yost was among the large number of boys who began their military careers in the CTTC during the Second World War. Yost joined in circumstances not unlike those of the Thompson-Lord-Higley group. In the Merchant Navy, aged 16, he falsified his age in order to join the air force, but failed the colour test for pilot training. He next enlisted in the army, at which point the authorities caught up with him and quickly transferred him to the CTTC and, after training, posted him into the Signal Corps.

There was no change in pay for boy soldiers throughout the war in the Canadian Army; it remained constant at 70¢ a day. WO I Larry Phipps, a CTTC entrant, dwelt at length on the schemes of conniving superiors for whittling away the boy soldier's meagre pay. In his account there are echoes of the complaints voiced by John Shipp so long ago. Having already noted some deductions, he goes on

> The little we received as our due was cut further because of lost or damaged kit. Kit inspections were often conducted in our absence. When we returned there was always something missing so we'd have to pay for replacements as well as getting extra duties for deficiencies. As soon as we were paid we had to contribute to the barrack fund through the platoon officer. The platoon officer, we were told, was responsible for the condition of the barracks; hence the need for us to contribute! We were always being assessed for damages which never occurred and so lost our contribution.[21]

Phipps, however, like Shipp, accepted this with philosophical resignation.

> These lessons were expensive, but we had no feeling of injustice and accepted it as part of our new way of life. It did a lot to meld us into two camps and to promote a feeling that it was 'us' against 'them'.[22]

The trades for which new entrants opted were chosen on economic grounds, based on the monetary return they could expect. A driver mechanic earned 25¢ a day extra pay, while a clerk earned 50¢ in addition to his normal pay. No one mentioned that a mechanic could advance to 75¢ a day extra, whereas a clerk's pay was fixed at the beginning rate of 50¢ more. The truth, according to Phipps, was that there was a need for clerks in the army, not mechanics, so a slight deception was practised. 'Looking back,' he said, 'we were either a trusting lot—or really dumb.'

There are striking similarities in the attitudes of Shipp and Phipps, despite the century or more that separates these two ex-boy soldiers. Whether dwelling on the care and feeding of boy soldiers or conveying the sense of unity boys derived from the platoon and company system, Phipps maintains a balance between the ludicrous and the poignant.

Meals were a strange arrangement in my view. We were like locusts devouring everything in sight. There was never enough food for all of us, but quite enough for ten out of the sixteen [the platoon strength], perhaps in the hope that some of us would not be hungry. This was certainly wishful thinking on their part [the authorities] as we were seldom filled at mealtimes. What little money we had left went on snacks at the dry canteen.[23]

After basic training they were sent on field exercises, but the subject of food remained the dominant concern of their lives. The last in the line-up always went short. Added to this the food served to them was indiscriminately mixed when doled into their mess tins: soup poured on to their pudding; chocolate syrup on the mashed potatoes. A boy had to be careful what he presented for filling. Phipps wrote:

I usually chose to have soup in my enamel mug, the main course in the larger mess tin, bread and dessert in the smaller one. Having soup in the mug gave me my share of all the food available with the probability of being able to get tea or coffee afterwards, though with soup flavour to it. It seemed better to have an off-flavoured beverage than a gravy-flavoured dessert, though better dessert with gravy than none at all. I was never able to get out of the habit of eating my meals in a civilised sequence; others just had the food heaped on and began at the top, no matter what it was.[24]

Soon after the apprentice training scheme was instituted the enlistment age was raised from 16 to 17 years, then a little later to 17½. All recruits were officially boy soldiers and remained so until their eighteenth birthday. The CTTC continued until 1945 when, having served its purpose, the Corps was phased out of existence. While it lasted, many thousands of Canadian youths passed through the scheme to become skilled tradesmen.

Other units of the Canadian Army continued taking boys between the ages of 14 and 18 for service in the traditional roles discharged by boy soldiers, as clerks and musicians. However, although the CTTC was abolished in 1945 it was found necessary to introduce a modified 'soldier apprentice plan'[25] in 1952 because the army found that it could not do without a reliable source of skilled tradesmen after all. Those tradesmen who were trained under the old wartime scheme were getting near the end of their time by the early 1950s and there was no solid base in Canadian industry from which to draw skilled tradesmen. Indeed, Canadian industry had traditionally relied on Europe as a source of skilled labour and consequently neglected to develop a structured apprenticeship programme of its own. This is still largely the case today. The army's new scheme, begun in the early 1950s, effectively produced the same results as the CTTC scheme had done previously.

From 1952 on the apprentice soldiers were known not by the traditional military epithet of 'Rats' but as 'the little green monsters', from the green bands worn on their shoulders to distinguish them from the men. The average annual intake of boys into the army under the new scheme, from 1952 until 1968, was 400. They served in the Artillery, Engineers, Signals, Service and Ordnance corps in trades ranging from clerk to radio technician. In addition, an average of 100 boys annually enlisted in military bands as musicians.

Concerning the mix of English-speaking and French-speaking youths enlisting in the Canadian Army, it is to be noted that, according to the records, Francophones constituted roughly 25 per cent of the junior soldiers.

In 1968, as a result of the Hellyer reforms (named after the minister who engineered the restructuring of the Canadian Armed Forces), the enlistment of boy soldiers was discontinued, so bringing to an end both a tradition and practice which Canada had inherited from the British Army in the very earliest days of its nationhood.

Senior Warrant Officer Richard Morgan was among the last batch of boy soldiers to enlist before the Hellyer reforms took effect, and his response to the survey of Canadian boy soldiers serves as a fitting endpiece to this chapter, for he candidly reveals opinions which have the ring of truth about them. Writing of his reasons for enlisting, he testifies:

The reason I joined the apprentice scheme was quite simple. I was soon to be expelled from high school; homelife was intolerable; and I was in trouble with the local police. No one would hire a kid like that but the army so I joined. In my case it was a worthwhile experience because I have a grip on life today and am still in the forces. However, had I expected to obtain everything that I was told would be mine on completion of apprentice training then I would have been a dismal failure.

Beside my picture in our [high school] graduation book was a statement of future outlook. It stated 'most likely to be an alcoholic'. This proved true and was obviously evident that that time.

I was promised 2 years of complete high school, senior NCO training, full trade qualifications. None of this materialised. I did, however, get an education in life and reality.[26]

On military discipline, he writes

Discipline in our time was often unrealistic, harsh and it certainly eliminated any human rights one might have thought he had. Mass punishment was the norm. Charges were easily obtained and a service tribunal [by then in force] was frequent. Normally 14 days CB and a $25 fine was standard for any minor offence such as lint on a uniform. While on CB extra work and drill was carried out daily. The drill was given by a drill instructor at double time with [the offender wearing] greatcoat, battle order and carrying a weapon. Often we were taken to a small indoor range with the heat on and double-marked time for an hour.

On one occasion I was given the choice of running up and down a huge ash pile or being punched out by the instructor.[27]

Morgan's report is certainly out of the normal run of replies received in the survey, but what he offered on the negative side of boy soldier life serves the point he makes later—and this in agreement with the vast majority of respondents—that the experience taught him self-discipline and gave him a purpose in life.

Since the first truly Canadian permanent force regiment, the 104th Foot, was formed in 1810 boy soldiers have been a feature of the Canadian Army. Having lived and worked and marched and died, both on and off the battlefield, they have formed part of the strong and vibrant military ethos which has characterised Canadian life since the French first created New France. Contemporary social attitudes in Canada militate against the use of boy soldiers. However, should another conflict occur, enterprising Canadian youths will find new ways of inveigling their way into uniform.

CHAPTER XIII
EASY GRACE DOWN UNDER

IN THE AUSTRALIAN *Bulletin* dated 23 May 1912, there is a cartoon showing a burly army instructor twirling a cane before a puny 12-year-old holding a rifle as tall as himself. 'You 'aven't got a proper command over your rifle, m'lad,' says the instructor. 'You want to 'andle it same as I 'andle this cane!' The cartoon, appropriately, is entitled 'Easy Grace'.[1]

Of the many letters and reports received from respondents in Australia there were relatively few from ex-boy soldiers of the Australian Army. While this fact does not rule out the existence of Australian ex-Rats (indeed, Australia has a thriving apprenticeship programme for young soldiers), it tends to confirm the impression that the country has no strong tradition as regards the enlistment of boys. As mentioned at the beginning of the last chapter, there have been few compelling historical reasons for Australia to encourage its underage male citizens to get into uniform.

However, this was not always the case, for there was a time just before the 1914–18 war when an Act of Parliament, passed under a Labour government, imposed compulsory military training on all males between the ages of 12 and 18 years. The nation demonstrated by this Act and public acceptance of the scheme that, given the right circumstances, the country had the will to train boys for military service. In fact, Australia actually conscripted its youth on a scale that far exceeded anything Great Britain or Canada were prepared to do. This chapter deals principally with that 'Boy Conscription' Act of 1911–15.

Until the turn of the nineteenth century Australia had relied on the Royal Navy for defence against potential aggressors. That no aggressors had appeared on Australia's doorstep was beside the point. From the time that the last British soldiers left Australia in 1870 the only soldiers in the country were unpaid part-time volunteers, taught and trained by officers and NCOs seconded from the imperial army. A volunteer force from Australia had been sent to New Zealand during the last of the Maori Wars of the nineteenth century, but it was the Boer War which awakened the nation to a sense of the need for military preparedness. The 16,500-man volunteer force sent to South Africa in 1900 marked the beginning of the Australian regular army.

Shortly after the Boer War the country became conscious of the possibility that others might be interested in the vast Island Dominion. No one was quite sure which world power posed a threat to Australian national security. J. H. Chinner, a private citizen interested in the country's military preparedness and one-time mayor of Unley, feared as early as the 1880s that tsarist Russia was the main threat; George MacKay, of Bellingen River, NSW, voiced his fear of the Japanese; yet others thought China might send armed colonists south to establish a bridgehead in the Northern Territories. Apart from the appearance of some Japanese fishing craft off Thursday Island, there was little evidence of a threat to national security from any quarter.

Be this as it may, the seeds of concern had been sown, fear fed on rumour, and increasing numbers of public figures expressed themselves on the subject. The Defence Act of 1903 was undoubtedly the result of this growing public awareness. The Act provided for the compulsory enlistment, in the event of national emergency, of all Australian males between the ages of 18 and 45, in five categories. The Australian National Defence League came into existence during the early years of the twentieth century and any patriotic Australian could become a member upon payment of one guinea. Branches sprang up everywhere so that by 1909 there was sufficient popular support for the government to introduce and amend the Defence Act which, effectively, brought about the creation of a permanent army of 1,500 men, to be backed up by 17,000 militia and 5,000 volunteers.[2]

On 1 January 1911 the compulsory elements of the Defence Act (1903–10) came into force, to provide for the registration and training of the nation's youthful males. Twelve- and 13-year-old boys were to become the junior element while the 14–17-year-olds were to be the seniors in the scheme.

Some 155,000 boys in both categories registered for national training in 1911, but of these only 59 per cent (approximately 92,500) were selected as suitable for instruction as young soldiers.[3] These youths were cadets and not boy soldiers by our definition. Nevertheless, in view of the compulsory character of the Defence Act and the subsequent declaration of war with Germany in 1914, when many thousands of those enlisted in the cadet scheme went overseas, consideration is justified.

The Australia cadet movement went back to 1859 when there was concern about French aspirations in the Pacific. All cadets were volunteers at school. By 1906 they numbered 13,000 and, by 1909, the total had increased to 23,600. By 1910, the year compulsory registration for cadet training was legislated, the voluntary system produced 10,500 senior cadets and 24,000 juniors. This was a solid base on which to build the compulsory training of the country's youth.[4]

As noted in John Barrett's book *Falling In* (1979), the scheme was not without opponents. There was in fact considerable opposition from the Quakers, the Australian Freedom League, trade unions and various Church groups. Some youths were sent to prison for refusing to don a uniform and submit to military training. In June 1914 Tom Roberts, a 16-year-old Quaker and conscientious objector, was sentenced to three weeks' detention at Fort Queenscliff and given an additional week of solitary confinement by the army. Generally, however, opposition to the Act was small in relation to the vast majority who accepted it.

Of one result of the Boy Conscription Act of 1910 we can be certain. By August 1914 the country had a substantial army of trained men and thousands volunteered for service overseas. That many thousands who volunteered and went were underage is unquestionable. Confirmation of this came from Lieutenant-Colonel I. H. Edwardson of the Australian Army when he wrote:

> Certainly in World War I and World War II, many underaged boys falsified their ages to enlist (as did numerous overage recruits). I personally know of one who was 16 who served in Malaya at the start of World War II, was captured by the Japanese, escaped from Singapore only to be recaptured near the Thai border.[5]

The compulsory training of boys in Australia was discontinued in 1929, but the accompanying table covering the period 1911 to 1915 is a record of the boys selected for instruction during those years. The table takes no account of about 50,000 junior cadets, and is confined to senior cadets, compulsory trainees in the citizen force and several thousand trainees with the navy.[6]

Numbers registered and undergoing compulsory training

	1911	1912	1914	1914	1915
Number registered in training areas ('000s)	155	184	221	252	286
Number training ('000s)	92	110	131	142	161

The situation remained the same in the Australian Army with regard to underage soldiers until 1948. Other than the cadet scheme there were no boy soldiers before that year. With the demobilisation of the war veterans, but with the continuing need to maintain a standing permanent force, the military authorities found themselves faced with the same shortage of skilled tradesmen that the Canadian Army experienced with the disbandment of the CTTC in the Dominion. The Australian Army then introduced an apprentice training programme for boys in the age range 15 to 17. This was patterned on the British and Canadian systems.

Roy Thompson of North Adelaide was in the first group of boys to enlist under the programme. He writes:

> In 1948 the Army Apprentices School was formed. I was in the first intake of 63 boys and enlisted as a fitter and turner. Boys were aged between 15 and

17. The conditions were three years at AAS followed by one year in an Army workshop for qualification. This was followed by five years as a soldier/ tradesman. Because the theoretical training could be concentrated, the education department accepted the reduction in time.

The system has since been altered to two years at AAS followed by two years in an Army workshop. I have renewed my interest because my son has recently completed his two years.[7]

Australia's apprentice training programme is still in force and, because it was begun some few years before the enlistment of boys into the Canadian Army was discontinued, it may be said to be carrying on where Canada left off.

CHAPTER XIV
A4 SOLDIERS

THE STORY OF boy soldiers in the twentieth century can be conveniently split into three distinct but overlapping periods. These are first, from 1900 to the late 1930s; second, from the early 1920s to the 1950s; and third, post-Second World War to the present. The first of these periods forms the subject of this and the chapter following. Drawing on a substantial number of reports from ex-boy soldiers who served during the first 40 years of the century, a lively and sometimes intimate picture of boy soldier life can be sketched. These reports focus on education, discipline, punishment, recreation, messing, training, pay and behaviour.

On the whole, the boys who enlisted during the early years of the century continued to serve as musicians, but the emphasis was on bugling and the duties of regimental trumpeters; drummers were less evident. From 1860 on the early function of the drummers to signal orders at the company and regimental level had been supplanted by bugle and trumpet calls. Boys with trades training as tailors, bootmakers, saddlers, armourers and clerks were more in evidence. Increasing emphasis was placed on the education of young soldiers, a compulsory requirement being that the possession of army certificates of education was tied into promotion. Medically they were in a category known as A4 which signified that they were 'fit [for active service], but under age'.

The A4 classification was one of series beginning with, A1 meaning 'fit for active service', which has come to be accepted in the English language as synonymous with 'first-class health' or, simply, 'excellence'. Boy soldiers, by definition, could not be classified as A1. A2 meant 'fit in one month' and A3 'fit in a few months'. These ratings were post-Boer War classifications not brought into general use until the outbreak of the First World War.

Many changes in army life and organisation were instituted following the Boer War. This was not surprising, for the 1899–1902 conflict in South Africa was nothing for British arms to boast about, as most historians agree. The reforms, spearheaded by Lord Haldane, put new life into the army and ensured that Britain had an efficient, highly-trained professional force to put into the field when war with Germany broke out in August 1914.

There is no evidence that the military schools were directly affected by the Haldane reforms, but certain changes did occur. The Duke of York's School at Chelsea was moved to new premises built for it on the cliffs of Dover and has remained there ever since. In addition, a third military school was created. The idea of building a third military school for the sons of Scottish soldiers was first proposed in 1901, when an appeal for funds was launched. The Scottish Highland Brigade suffered severely during the war in South Africa, but whether it was this fact or simply a desire on the part of officers of Scottish regiments that Scotland should possess such a school is not known. In any case, it was the issue of a Royal Warrant in 1905 that assured the existence of the new institution.

On a site obtained near the village of Dunblane, premises were developed, the buildings constructed, and Queen Victoria School (QVS) opened its gates in 1909 to 270 sons of Scottish soldiers. All other conditions for the acceptance of pupils were identical to those governing the acceptance of boys in the other two schools. The Royal Hibernian Military School remained where it had always been, at Phoenix Park, Dublin, and there it stayed until it was closed in 1924. Thus for a few years, at the beginning of the century, there were three military schools staffed, financed and operated by the British Army. To find out how underage soldiers reacted upon joining the army and how they accepted the life, we cannot do better than cite the experience of John Holland, whom we first met in Chapter X when he went to India. He joined the 2/91 Argyll and Sutherland Highlanders in the summer of 1902, aged 14, direct from the RHMS, and was sent to Ballykinlar Camp, County Down, where, he records, there were transient troops from many units quartered in tents by the seashore.

There were about 20 of us in a tent which was equipped with a small rail along the centre for equipment. We had our own canteen and plenty of food; a pound of meat, a loaf of bread, vegetables and soup every day. After eating we washed our canteens and cooking dishes with sand at the shore. We boys were paid 4½ a day, less ½d a day for washing shirts, etc., which were washed by a soldier's wife. We were contented and happy. There was a lot of talk about flogging but to us [of the Hibernians] it seemed in the past. However, the band was different. A sergeant home from Africa was a terror and used his walking cane for caning.

Food was cheap in the canteen: ½d for buns and cakes; 1d for a fried herring; 1d for a large apple pie. For our cleaning kit we could buy Rosemary soap for 1d; boot blacking, button polish and white Blanco for straps was also very cheap. Eggs, butter and bread were to be had at a Soldiers' Home.[1]

Boy soldier training was not highly organised. Boys generally marched with the men, paraded, and joined the regiment on manoeuvres. All boy entrants before the First World War were in the same category as John Holland. They were clearly young soldiers, musicians and in trades training (John Holland was a tailor), but with the outbreak of the Great War another category of underage soldier came into existence, made up of those who, like their Commonwealth army contemporaries, enlisted to serve in the ranks of adult soldiers.

One respondent, A. H. Dall, who willingly told of his experience, objected to the term 'boy soldier' because, he said, they were in all respects adult soldiers even though underage. Recruits of his class, he pointed out, were A4 soldiers.

From August 1909 to August 1913, I lived with my parents at the No 4 Depot RGA at Great Yarmouth, Norfolk. My father had just left the Royal Artillery as a Master Gunner, after 22 years service, and had taken a position as Canteen Manager. We lived in the barracks. The Depot trained recruits as gunners and also trained trumpeters for the RHA, RFA and RGA.

I was a boy soldier, but only in respect of the fact that enlisting 10 December 1915 at Colchester, into the Essex Regt., I was 'on draft' for the Dardanelles after two months training, but was prevented from going by my father, after very forceful agitation from my mother. I was then just 15 years 10 months old, and a marksman to boot. This resulted in my being sent to join the Machine Gun Corps at Grantham in Lincolnshire on 16 February 1916. However, I did manage to evade my mother and finally found myself with the 21st Brigade Machine Gun Company, 30th Division, in the first week of the battle of the Somme [July 1916], between Bernafay Wood and Ginchy.

I managed to survive and hide my age for some weeks before the fateful letter arrived informing my CO that I was only 16 years old. I won't repeat what he said before he sent me, a very proud boy, 'down the line' to Camiens, near Étaples where I found myself just one of several hundred such lads of ranks ranging from Private to CSM and CQMS. Just the MGC had a permanent reservation for sixteen places each night on the 2100 hours boat from Boulogne to Dover. Within a month or two there were over 400 of us inflicting our boyish pranks (or nuisances!) upon the already overworked training and organising staff.[2]

We have already taken note of the enormous number of boy recruits taken from orphanages. The practice first began during the Napoleonic Wars; it happened in India and continued no doubt throughout the long history of boy soldiering. The First World War was no different because orphans, either through their own efforts to enlist or by succumbing to the blandishments of the recruiters, continued to accept the King's shilling. Frank W. Ebdon, an orphan from the Shirley School Orphanage, Croydon, was escorted to London by his bandmaster (an ex-musician of the Royal Rifle Brigade) and there attested for the RRB. Having passed his medical and been graded A4, Frank went by train and ferry to the Isle of Sheppey to join his unit as a musician. With him were five other recruits from the Shirley School.

> In the beginning it seemed very strict because we were always under supervision and seldom on our own. Everything we did was so different from what we were used to—'Boy, do this; boy, do that!'—from the life in the orphanage. Yes, it seemed a harsh and cruel life for a lad of 15, but with good discipline, regular hours and ample food it soon became natural.[3]

He remembers being caned 'good and hard' by the Provost Sergeant in the yard of the Quarter Guard building for being absent from retreat parade, but had become used to it.

> In the orphanage, to be caned or held over the gym horse and caned happened frequently. I was 16 at the time. This retreat parade was performed twice a week on the parade square. It took nearly one hour because we had to play several marches after sounding 'Retreat'. Cigarettes and matches were found in my pockets which, as you know, was a no no.[4]

Of his time in the QVS, Councillor Joseph J. Watson, one-time mayor of Dover Town, had this to say:

> Being an orphan at age of 5 and having to live in an orphanage until I was old enough to reach the required age of 8½ years to qualify for admission to the QVS Royal Military, I found to be a very harsh 3½ years and I found a bonded sympathy for people like Oliver Twist who also faced these problems, although only in books.
>   My entrance to the QVS was a wonderful experience and probably the turning point in my future years as a soldier, councillor and Town Mayor of Dover.[5]

Life of course was very strict and discipline was moulded on the military lines with every member of the staff regular soldiers. Fred Burgess joined the Royal Field Artillery and was sent to Ireland where he saw boy service during the 1916 Rebellion:

> There was a certain amount of tension and we only went into the town in groups of four or more and we all made sure we had our jack knives with us. During the Rebellion, the senior boys were called on for duty as roving picquets around the barracks. Most of the men who were sent into Dublin seemed to look on the whole affair as a joke. They had more trouble with looters and drunkards than with the so-called rebels. About a hundred prisoners were brought back to Athlone; they were just the scum. All in all, I enjoyed my service there. There were several ex-Duke of York's boys in the section, and one or two from the Hibernians.[6]

References to ex-Dukies and old Hibs (now joined by the QVs) occur again and again in the correspondence of ex-boy soldiers who had no other connection with the military school boys but as comrades on boy service. It is therefore no accident that the lives and experiences of the military school boys form an important part of this narrative. John M. Waters is representative of the more than 3,500 such boys who enlisted during the First World War or shortly thereafter. He had joined the RHMS as an 8-year-old before the war, upon the death of his soldier father, and later joined the RAMC as a bugler. He records that there were 410 boys in the RHMS in his day, divided into six companies. Once a year there was a Trooping of the Colours ceremony, held on 15 acres. The four nine-pounder guns used for gunnery instruction were paraded at the same time and were almost as important a feature of the parade as the regimental colours.

Waters was first posted to the Queen Alexandra Hospital, Aldershot, where the unit, in common with the rest of the army, was governed by the sound of the bugle, despite the fact that it was responsible for operating a hospital.

Daily I used to blow the bugle calls, including those for 'officers dress' and 'officers mess'. On one occasion the Mess President, a major, dashed down the stairs on hearing my call, shouting 'Bugler, that was bloody awful, bloody awful! I shall certainly tell the colonel about you.' I wondered what more he expected for 7/6 a week.[7]

Bugle calls remained an important part of military life until the late 1930s and while bugles are still blown they are no longer used to the same degree as during the first half of the century. Captain Henry Corke, an ex-Dukie who enlisted for regular boy service in 1921 in the Royal Engineers at Chatham, provided an excellent description of army life by the bugle.

Reveille was blown at 0600 hours in the summer months and at 0630 in the winter. Defaulters paraded a quarter of an hour after reveille, in full marching order and at the call of the bugle. Breakfast followed shortly after when, again to the sound of the bugle's clarion call, everyone paraded and marched to the cookhouse. Within an hour the main morning parade took place. For this, a sustained 'G' was blown five minutes before parade time, followed by the 'Fall in' which brought all troops on to the parade square at the same time! Another call summoned the sick to sick parade and yet another for 'Orderly Room'. This was held at 1000 hours if there were any disciplinary cases to be heard by the CO (Saturdays and Sundays excepted).

At Brompton Barracks, the bugle heralded the start and finish of recruit drill and training sessions; mail distribution once a day; fire alarms and fire drills. The first appearance of the CO, at 0900 hours, was recognised by the duty bugler, when all personnel on or near the square were brought to attention until dismissed by the CO with a 'Carry on, please!' The duty bugler was also in attendance when the main guard was called out by the sentry on post for every call made officially on its services. In fact, the bugler was used to communicate every instruction of a general nature. There was a call for everything we did. After the 'Tea' call at, say, 1630–1700 hours, the main defaulters parade of the day was held when all those on jankers (defaulter's punishment) paraded in full marching order. There was 'officers dress' and 'officers mess' at 2000 hours followed by the 'First Post' at 2130 hours and 'Last Post' at 2200 hours. The main guard turned out and stood with arms presented for the duration of the playing of the Last Post. Lights out ended the normal round of calls for the day.

At Brompton, it was the practice for the orderly officer to inspect the main guard at odd times during the silent hours so there was little or no respite for the duty bugler. It was a very long and busy day on main guard duty, for a bugler more than anyone. Erring buglers found guilty of misdemeanours were given additional duty with the main guard.

Thus, it was not until one looked back upon one's recruit days in Chatham that one realised how busy buglers really were and how much the establishment depended upon their efficiency for the running of the unit.[8]

Boy soldier training was no sinecure. Some enjoyed it, some did not. Many wrote of funny experiences and odd things happening which stuck fast in their memories. One wrote of the weekly pay parade when the boys lined up in alphabetical order and of the CSM shouting to one boy 'Phillips! Phillips, why aren't you with the Fs?' John Waters, the ex-Hib, told of an occasion on parade at Aldershot:

The Commandant of the depot told me to lift my foot up so he could feel it and, turning to my company commander, said, 'Is that an army foot?' 'Yes, Colonel,' he replied. 'His foot is like that every day on every occasion, rain or hail.' The Colonel shook his head in disbelief, but I have to say that it gave me very good service and out-wore many a boot.[9]

Numerous were the testimonies from ex-trumpeters of mounted units, of the pleasures enjoyed by the ownership of a horse. In what other circumstances would a lad be given charge of his own horse, short of being of a family wealthy enough to run its own stables? One of the most compelling submissions came from ex-Trumpeter Roy Julian who, on completion of his training in 1929, was posted to the 2nd Light Brigade RA. He was 15 then and quite small for his age, being less than five feet in height and weighing not more than 87 pounds (his squad officer thought he would have made a fine jockey).

His first horse was a pony of 15 hands named Sally with whom he became firm friends. The early 1930s were the last years before mechanisation took over, and when a unit was sent overseas it took its horses with it. The 2nd Light Brigade, a pack-mule artillery unit (Kipling wrote his famous poem *Screw-Guns* about the pack-mule mountain artillery), was sent to Egypt in 1930 and of this experience Julian wrote:

Sally was my pride and joy. I was totally responsible for her, for grooming, exercising, and her general well-being. She was a great friend to me and I've never forgotten our wonderful times together in spite of having many other horses during my time in the Army.

We had three 7-pounder guns and, because we used pack mules, our gunners had to march. HQ personnel were mounted and missed the slogging miles of marching over the desert. I remember a particular practice camp. We went by road from Jelmleh to Mena, a distance of 20 miles. My Section Commander decided to walk and that his trumpeter, myself, would do likewise. So, with our two horses, we had a tiresome journey, but eventually arrived safe and sound.

What of my trumpeting days and years? Looking back I can honestly say that I enjoyed them. Beginning at Bulford [Barracks], opening the window of a barrack room in winter and sounding reveille—it was freezing outside; on to Egypt to see the Pyramids and climbing them for the first time; being lost in the desert on manoeuvres and having to rely on my faithful friend Peggy to get me back to our battery lines. These are just a few of the things I remember and which lead me to say that my years as a trumpeter prepared me for the strenuous years ahead in the army, during peace and war.[10]

Forty years later Trumpeter Julian retired, a major. Major C. E. Corke, MBE, was another of the trumpeter types.

A boy took on more responsibility after he had left the depot and was given a horse and harness to look after. His duty in the field was as horse holder attendant, either to the battery commander or to the battery captain.

There was a marked contrast in the discipline in the Boys Depot and that found in the service unit which one joined on first appointment as Trumpeter. In the depot one had to call everyone with a stripe or more on his arm 'Sir'.[11]

Ben Benford, whose father before him as well as his two brothers served as boy soldiers, enlisted in the RRA in 1938. He thought that boy service could be sometimes harsh and cruel.

The one thing that I and most other boys hated more than anything was the numerous kit inspections. These could be as many as four and five in an evening. Usually we had the trumpet major come and inspect us. I swear to this day that it was the one duty they revelled in. I've seen a TM literally sling a boy's kit all over the floor and tell him that he would be back in an hour to inspect again, threatening that if the kit was not up to his requirements he would spend time on 'the hill'. The 'hill' was a punishment. It involved doubling up and down a steep concrete hill about 1 in 6, stretching for about 70 feet, dressed in full kit with a knapsack full of bricks. Take it from me, it was a killer. I recently saw a film called 'The Hill', based on the same punishment, except that it was located in a detention camp somewhere in the Middle East. Anyway, that hill was only half as bad as the one we doubled up and down.

I can remember so many instances of what one could call sadistic behaviour by one or more of the trumpet majors. My own experience of this type of brutality occurred the time we were first allowed out of camp after completing our compulsory training (3 months), during which we were confined to barracks. I was returning to barracks dressed in my breeches, puttees and spur and, as I passed through the main gate I heard a voice boom out 'Boy! Come here.'

I turned and saw the most hated TM in the depot. I doubled over to him (one doubled everywhere) and stood to attention to give my number, name and rank. He questioned me as to where I'd been that evening and asked if I had at any time had a conversation with a girl, which I had as a matter of fact. Realising that it was possible he had seen me I admitted the fact. He ordered me to strip to the waist and then searched my clothes. After what seemed an eternity, he ordered me to get dressed and to 'Get the hell out of here'.

At the door of the guard room he called me back and stood there, looking at me with a sadistic smile on his face. He removed my peaked cap and that is when I began to shake like the dickens because inside the cap I had hidden a packet of Woodbines with three cigarettes. Ordering the two gunners on guard duty out of the room, he made me chew two of the cigarettes. There's no need to tell you what happened next. I was as sick as I've ever been, but at least I didn't go on report, otherwise that would have meant six of the best.

Another time we were in the stables doing our sounding practice under the same TM. We had to sound the calls as instructed and when my turn came he told me to blow 'Boots and saddles'. I thought I'd done quite well, but he told me to repeat it. I had only blown a few notes when he rammed the mouthpiece of the trumpet down my throat. Luckily no teeth were broken, but he split my lip and that, he said, was for triple tonguing, which was not permitted.

Even after three months I found it hard to get into the swing of things. Many a night I heard one or two of the boys crying their hearts out. We later learned that some of them got their parents to get them out and I often wished in those early days I could have done the same thing except that I could imagine what my father would have said, him having been a boy soldier himself.

Reflecting on those months at Woolwich, I would say that I doubt very much if boys today would have stuck it. I left Woolwich a full-blown trumpeter and was posted to Hereford. Looking back on my introduction to army life I would say that it was bloody hard but, at the same time, I believe it stood me in good stead later.[12]

(Benford's father, a veteran soldier, died in a Japanese prison camp. His brother, imprisoned in the same camp, was later shipped to Japan, survived the sinking of the POW transports by American submarines, and returned to Britain after the Second World War.)

To detail the messing, living conditions and training of boy soldiers prior to 1939 would require a volume alone. However, from a selection of detailed accounts, it is possible to give a picture indicative of the whole boy soldier experience.

First Don Luckett, who joined the mounted arm of the Royal Engineers at Aldershot in 1934, aged 14.

The first few weeks after joining were the most trying weeks I had ever known. The barrack room looked so bare; all the beds at that time were of the two-piece slide-in type (a MacDonald bed) which could be made up in what was known as 'arm-chair' fashion. One biscuit, or small mattress, was laid with a blanket wrapped neatly round it to form the seat. The remaining two biscuits were stood upright, wrapped in another blanket. The remaining blanket, plus a bolster and two sheets, was neatly folded behind the upright biscuits with a clean hand towel on top. The nap of the blankets had to be brushed one way! The beds were of iron slatted construction. When made up for the daytime they were lined up either side of the room in two long lines that were ruler straight.

The floor was hand-scrubbed white. Two small electric lights hung from the ceiling and sported the regulation green shade, whilst two six-feet-long scrubbed trestle tables with four forms to sit on completed the furniture. A cast iron coal box stood at one end of the room with sides gleaming mirror-like from the black lead polish we applied. A round coal bin had a can ashbin upturned on top of the coal. This bin or tub was likewise shone with black lead and the rim or edge burnished until it beamed. The brooms and dry scrubbers stood rigid and scrubbed white in one corner. Over each bed there was a wall-mounted green locker with each boy's kit neatly displayed therein. The equipment with which we were issued was hung underneath the locker on three pegs in a set fashion and woe betide any lad whose kit or bed space didn't come up to the required standard, for it meant a severe dressing down by the trumpet major, followed by extra fatigues such as scrubbing, kit layouts or some fiendish task he dreamed up for us.

Kit was issued within a few days of joining and it meant several trips to the regimental tailor who made 'things fit'. I well remember the two pairs of boots I received. They were brownish green in colour and covered in a thick layer of grease. I was assured that the grease would eventually come out (but it never did) and that once I'd bought the stain to turn them black I would eventually get the high mirror-like gloss that was needed in those days. I tried everything that was suggested, from walking in horse manure to rubbing them with raw potatoes and immersing them in hot water—this last idea to the chagrin of the chap in charge of the bath house. I even tried pissing on them, but for all these fancy remedies those boots remained full of grease, dull and unwilling ever to turn black despite the application of several bottles of dye bought out of the meagre pay we received each Friday. I eventually outgrew them several months later and the new ones were more amenable to spit and polish so that no longer was I the outcast because of dull, greasy boots.[13]

John Bradley, a Duke of York's boy, enlisted in the RASC in 1938 and he wrote of the all-too-familiar experience of military school boys who joined regular units.

My warrant was made out to North Camp Station, which is three miles from Buller Barracks (transport was arranged for new arrivals at Aldershot Town Station). I come out of the station with quite a large suitcase holding all my worldly goods and see a large figure in uniform and ask the way to Buller Barracks, having made the boob of saying, 'Excuse me, sir, can you tell me the way to B.B.?' This was to a lance corp MP who said, 'You don't call me "sir"; you call me "corporal" and B.B. is a three-mile walk and there ain't no bus.'

    I duly walked the three miles and reported to the guard room at Buller Barracks a little the worse for wear, only to be greeted by the Provost Sergeant asking 'What the bloody hell are you?' (me being in full Dukie khaki plus great coat with, as I thought, everything bulled to the eyebrows plus full corporal's stripes). Like a twit, I said, 'Have you never seen somebody from the Duke of York's Royal Military School before, sarn't?' Well, you should have heard the reply. What it meant was that a little piece of dirt like me did not talk to the Provost Sergeant of the Royal Army Service Corps like that. After that we never did get on, but he sent me, with one of his corporals, to the Boys' Pit (as he called it) where I duly reported to the Trumpet Major who was the senior NCO in charge of the boys.[14]

John Thompson enlisted in the Royal Tank Corps in 1934.

I joined . . . in August 1934 and travelled on my own from Newcastle-on-Tyne to Bovington Camp, in Dorset. Never having travelled further than twenty miles from my home, I found this journey very worrying. I arrived at Bovington in the evening and reported to the guard room and from there was taken to the dining room for a meal. This consisted of fatty bacon and potatoes and although I was very hungry I could hardly eat it. However, after a couple of weeks at Bovington I did not turn up my nose at anything I was given to eat.

    Next day I had the normal inspection, short haircut and issue of kit. My civilian clothes were packed up and sent home, as wearing civilian clothes was not allowed. The first few weeks were spent trying to get my kit into some sort of presentable shape. The boots were very greasy and hard work was required, spitting and polishing to get a shine. Trousers were put between two pieces of cardboard or plywood and placed under the bed mattress and laid on at night to get a good crease. I soon got used to lying on a hard bed.

We had kit inspection regularly, but the purpose of the inspection seemed to be to see if everything was laid out neatly and in line and not for serviceability. Items of kit were made to look square by inserting pieces of carboard. While at Bovington, I was admitted into the hospital with tonsillitis. This was not a pleasant experience, as the treatment in those days was to paint the throat with iodine with a long brush. Also, daily I had to polish the floors and brass fittings and then make sure I was in bed ready for the M.O.'s daily rounds.[15]

Cyril Rawlinson, yet another ex-Dukie, attested for the Scots Guards in 1931 and eventually rose to the rank of Drum Major.

When I joined the Scots Guards there must have been about 13 boys including two boy tailors. The remainder were drummers, flute players and pipers. As a matter of interest, the flute and pipe band had quite a few members from the Dukies and QVS, Dunblane.

In those days we had to pay for all our uniforms. We received an allowance for this which was less than adequate. I remember that a drummer's red tunic cost £8 in 1935. We couldn't wear them in the rain. A tailor boy would turn a pair of blue trousers inside out, including the red stripe down the side, and make them look brand new for 2/6. They were excellent tailors.

Life in the Guards was excellent provided one kept his nose clean. Smartness was essential: body cleanliness a must (we had to sign the bath book at least once a week). I was fortunate because I could play the flute, beat the drum and read music when I joined on my fifteenth birthday whereas other boys could not. I was only 5'3" and favoured because of this.

If you became a marksman you wore cross guns on your arm and for these ex-boys were always welcome in the butts, armed with a pencil and bits of adhesive paper on each finger. The paper covered all the outers while the pencil gave the right number of bulls wanted. Result—you became a marksman and got more pay.[16]

The small amount of pay boys received was by no means standard throughout the service. Whatever a boy was paid depended on his stoppages and the whim of his officers, who would hold a certain amount back for when the boy soldier went on leave. It was therefore important for a lad to increase his earnings above the basic rate. Becoming a marksman was one way; education was another.

Schooling in my time was taught by a sergeant from the Regiment concerned [in the Guards] and probably the same for all infantry. Education was a must. The certificates were the 3rd, 2nd and 1st. Extra pay was granted for the 2nd class. If the instructor liked one a 2nd class certificate could be obtained by a small bribe. The class was usually given the same problems about a month before the exams and, on occasions, an exam. paper would be accidentally left on the table.[17]

Joe Dobbs of the Royal Artillery said that being a 'barrack rat' gave him a great advantage when he enlisted in 1929.

I made good progress and was made a Boy Lance Bombadier in my squad. We were responsible for the discipline of the squad, marching them to riding school, education and the sports field. For duties performed we received an extra 2/6 a month. Most of that was lent to other boys, with interest. Fortunately we were not found out otherwise, it was no Boy Lance Bombadier and six of the best.[18]

Don Luckett wrote about pay in 1935:

Upon entry a boy's pay was six shillings and five pence per week. When a boy had passed his second class certificate of education, and received his cross trumpets as a fully-fledged trumpeter, he then received another shilling a week, bringing his pay to 7/5 a week. From the basic 6/5 a boy actually received 4/-. The balance went to his credit and, on passing the required tests and getting the extra shilling, the same amount was credited as the basic pay—2/5. Either way, it wasn't very much at all as regards pocket money once one had brought items such as boot polish, Blanco, metal polish, and stamps to write home. Most boys were flat broke by Saturday evening at the latest, pay parade being mid-day on a Friday. So it was that we were always in a 'hard up' state.[19]

John Bradley writes of his 1935 experiences:

Pay, the biggest laugh of all, was 11d a day, of which we were allowed to draw 2/- a week for the first six months. The rest was credited to us. Once we had passed out from Aldershot we were rich because we could draw 5/- a week. After the first year clothing allowance was paid for kit replacements and if you looked after your kit it was possible to make a small profit on this. Also, pay was increased to 1/1d a day.
    Once we reached the two-year stage and put up our first Good Conduct badge the pay was increased to 1/3 a day. (By this time the war had started and new drivers joining were paid 2/- a day.) When I was promoted to full corporal on my eighteenth birthday I was the local millionaire, my pay going to 6/3 a day. It was also discovered that I should have started my man service when I was seventeen and a half, so I got six month's back pay as a private.[20]

All in all, though boys moaned about the pittance they received and the sometimes tough treatment they had at the hands of some NCOs, they looked upon the life they led as a good experience. Ben Benford wondered what boys of today would have thought of his boy service and suggested they would not 'put up with it'. Major Phil Marrison of the RASC (1934) wrote:

> I would not have missed being a boy soldier for anything. I am sure I cursed about it quite a lot of the time, but looking back I am convinced my code of conduct for life was formed during my 3½ years boy service. In all, it was an unforgettable experience, with mostly happy memories.[21]

Henry Corke summed up the general feeling expressed by many when he wrote:

> Looking back on my service career, I feel proud of having served in the Corps (Royal Engineers) over a quarter of a century. Being born in the 12th Field Company and nurtured in its traditions, I don't think I would have been happy following any other profession. To this day my best pals are those who served with me in uniform, and the majority served with me on boy service.[22]

Of more concern to the A4 soldiers than the pay they received, their training or living conditions was their food and, to some extent, the discipline. These two subjects, along with comment on their behaviour, form the subject of the next chapter.

CHAPTER XV
HARD TACK AND DISCIPLINE

Food was the most frequently discussed subject in the A4 soldiers' correspondence. They never could get enough and sometimes went to extreme lengths to satisfy their appetites, as some of the extracts quoted here indicate. John Thompson, it will be recalled, found his first meal of fatty bacon and potatoes inedible but soon got over his squeamishness. John Bradley of the RASC, describing the early 1920s, was able to write more optimistically.

> Regarding food, need I say more than if the RASC couldn't feed itself then the Army would have been a poor place. At that time the Army School of Cookery was run by the RASC and all of our cooks had to attend courses regularly. As always, some cooks were better than others, but not so bad as to ruin the first-class food with which they were supplied. In my view we were very well fed, but many of the places we had as mess halls and kitchens were in barracks which were pre-Victorian and, consequently, were cold, cheerless places, very difficult to keep clean. Once the war started it was hard to maintain the same standards as we had prewar, as most of the kitchens had to feed twice as many people as they were designed for, so if you had a good cook you treated him like royalty.[1]

What sort of food was provided during the between-the-wars period? Major Bill Davidson, who enlisted in the RRA in 1934, at Woolwich, has provided us with a typical menu from that period.[2] TB & M is tea, bread and margarine, and on some days, it will be noted, there was no margarine, and on other days no supper. The obvious conclusion to draw from it is that the heavy meals of the day were breakfast and the noon meal, which was known as dinner. The evening meal, taken at seven to eight o'clock at night, was called supper. Also, despite what some ex-boy soldiers wrote, the food appeared to be substantial.

Royal Artillery Menu at Woolwich, 1934

	Breakfast	Dinner	Tea	Supper
Sunday	Liver & onions Tea & bread	Roast beef potatoes, greens Rice pudding	TB & M Cake	Cocoa & biscuits
Monday	Bacon & mash TB & M	Boiled meat, potatoes, baked beans Stewed fruit & custard	TB & M	Cocoa & biscuits
Tuesday	Rissoles & gravy TB & M	Brown stew potatoes, peas Currant roll	TB & M Fish paste	Cocoa & biscuits
Wednesday	Sausage & mash TB & M	Roast, potatoes, cabbage, Yorkshire pudding	TB & M	Cocoa & biscuits
Thursday	Bacon & egg Tea & bread	Meat pie, potatoes, tea	TB & M cheese	—
Friday	Shepherd's pie TB & M	Stew, potatoes, peas	TB & M	—
Saturday	Soused herring TB & M	Hot pot, potatoes, peas	TB & M	—

For meals, [wrote Joe Dobbs] we were issued with an enamel mug and plate which were very durable and withstood rough handling although the enamel sometimes chipped, being maintained at the expense of the individual.[3]

Don Luckett of the Sappers had a low opinion of army food.

The food wasn't very good. It was always very plain, usually badly cooked, and tasted awful. It was a case of eating it all though, as we were always so hungry! We had breakfast, a mid-day meal, and tea around 4.30–5 pm. As there were no suppers there we had slices of bread or whatever else we could get hold of (steal!), to be devoured later in the barrack room although this was strictly forbidden. Many times we baked potatoes in the fire and ate our fill of them of an evening, ears on the alert for any authority that might happen along.[4]

Luckett was in the mounted squadron of the Royal Engineers. Like all boys working with horses, a great part of their day was spent cleaning stables, grooming the horses and feeding them. This helped solve the problem of their own demand for food.

It so happened that once a week the horses were given a feed of bran mash. Every Friday evening it fell to the lot of two boys to light the copper and make the feed for all the horses. I think we had about fifty at that time. Our own tea those Friday evenings consisted of a thing called a faggot, a kind of inglorious rissole, dished up with gravy, but so vile that not many ate them, so when the bran mash was made we used to eat quite a lot of it ourselves. It tasted like fresh brown bread and was delicious.[5]

Cyril Rawlinson and his companions in the Scots Guards resorted to other methods to satisfy their appetites.

Three of us broke in the messroom one night. I pinched a loaf, another a gallon pot of jam, and the third a big lump of butter. We saw the police sergeant coming so we climbed out of the window, ran back to our barrack room and stuffed our loot into our kitbags (where we kept our underwear, etc.). We climbed into bed and were sleeping like angels when the police sergeant came into our room. Of course, he knew it was us but turned a blind eye when our answers were obviously 'No, we've been in bed since eight pm.' After he had gone we went straight to our kitbags to pull out our loot. The air was blue when the boy with the jam pulled out the pot. He had put the jar in his kitbag upside down with no stopper on it and everything was covered with the stuff.[6]

In 1923 Joe Dobbs was among a party of boys from Woolwich taken by train to the Great Exhibition at Wembley.

On the return journey there was a prolonged and unexpected stop at Dartford, where some of the more venturesome boys jumped out on to the platform. There was a stack of kippers on the platform awaiting shipment. How those crates were smuggled out of Chatham Station and brought back to barracks forever remained a mystery, but as we had only been issued with bully beef sandwiches of 'doorstep' proportions, and few had the necessary cash to buy the cooked mid-day meal so necessary to healthy, growing boys full of vim and vigour, we were ravenously hungry by tea time.
    In the early evening the fish were cooked over the barrack room fires in their own juice on barrack room coal shovels. The smell of fish pervaded the rooms for days afterwards. I cannot recall any disciplinary action being taken, mainly, I suppose, because no one wanted to be involved. Moreover, there was no proof that the disappearance of crates of kippers from Dartford Station could be apportioned to the boys.[7]

Given the circumstances and opportunity, these boy soldiers could take as good care of themselves and survive as boys of generations past had done—and would do in the future, as the reports of boys of the following generations prove. They could give a good account of themselves when the need arose and although there was no longer opportunity for active service except, perhaps, on India's North West Frontier or in parts of the Middle East, there were other opportunities to demonstrate bravery. Henry Corke recalled the rescue at sea, off Gosport in 1921, by boys of the 22nd Fortress Company.

Boy Hayward reported a boat capsised off Fort Monckton in heavy seas. With a full crew of boys from the fort, CSM Giddy launched a galley. Manned by Giddy, two boy lance corporals, Marsh and Eagle, and boys Leach, Lovell, Smith and Dovey, the galley plunged through the billowing waves. About a mile off the shore two lads and a man (who was unconscious) were picked up. CSM Giddy tried to resuscitate the man by artificial respiration but that effort proved unavailing. The two lads were saved. The participants in the rescue each received a certificate from the Royal National Lifeboat Institution for their bravery.[8]

Lieutenant Rambahadur Limbu, VC, who first enlisted in the Gurkha Rifles in 1944, aged 15, wrote that he was in for no more than a few weeks when he deserted. Wandering around Nepal for the next two years, he often wished he could re-enlist, but concluded

I could not go back to the recruiting depot again to join the army. They would not accept a deserter. Even if they did and found out later that I had been enlisted as a boy soldier but deserted it after a few days, they could certainly arrest me and put me into jail. I could not take that risk. To become a soldier, therefore, was out of the question for me.[9]

Commenting on this admission, however, Lieutenant-Colonel H. C. S. Gregory of the Gurkha Welfare Trust pointed out:

Rambahadur Limbu's desertion could, I believe, be described as a technical rather than a real desertion. The boy was still at the recruiting centre, had not been put into uniform and had not started his training. In those years and in that part of the world it was not uncommon for young men and boys newly recruited and awaiting the move to the Training Depot in Malaya, to be overcome with homesickness and to slip away into the hills. A very serious view was not taken of 'desertion' in these circumstances.[10]

In spite of his fears, Limbu did re-enlist and went undetected. He won his Victoria Cross on 21 November 1965, in Sarawak, when a Lance Corporal in the 10th Princess Mary's Own Gurkha Rifles.

If there were opportunities to excel in other fields than those of active service, there was that other side of the coin, the discipline and punishment meted out to them. Benford wrote of pack drill on the hill at Woolwich; Joe Dobbs also made reference to the same punishment, except that in his day it was known as Paradise Hill.

Flogging was all but abolished in the 1870s as a result of the Cardwell reforms, although the term must be qualified as far as boy soldiers were concerned. Even for those on man service the threat of this form of field punishment was still on the books in the First World War and the *Field Service Pocket Book* for 1914 provided for up to 30 lashes to be administered by the provost-marshal to those below NCO rank for breaches of military discipline on active service in India.

For boy soldiers, flogging by birch and rod (but not the cat) was both officially and unofficially administered until well into the Second World War. The rod (cane) is still given in the military schools, though rarely these days and only under the most strict control, much the same as in state schools.

Flogging was not the only method of punishment. There was defaulters parade, given as so many days CB (confined to barracks and commonly called jankers); the rod or cane; military detention (the glasshouse); and, surprisingly though increasingly rare, discharge by drumming out. Boys were commonly given 7/6—that is, 7 days CB and 6 strokes of the rod or birch across the bare backside. As a last resort, however, in the majority of cases, the worst offenders were quietly discharged without ceremony.

John Holland reported that after his return from India in 1914 he had a personal experience of this type.

Men who were unsuitable were given their civilian clothes back and told to leave at the gate. When I was corporal in command of the guard at Fort George, Inverness-shire, late one afternoon, Sergeant-Major Kerr, strict but a real gentleman, called for me at the guard room and said, 'Corporal Holland, take Mr —— from the prisoner's room. Take him fifty yards from the gate and let him go. The prisoner, a deserter, had on only a ragged shirt and trousers, the same in which he had given himself up two weeks earlier. Fort George is in a lonely and desolate place. He asked me for sixpence for a cup of tea. I gave him sixpence and watched him go. It was dark and cold and the place was isolated, with the sea on one side and scrubland on the other. Then I reported to the sergeant who was still waiting in the guard room.[11]

Frank Ebdon remembers being caned 'good and hard' by the Provost Sergeant during the First World War. Leslie Robinson, on boy service with the Royal Horse Artillery in the 1920s, recalled a birching in 1928.

Henry Corke told what happened to a thief during his time as a boy bugler at Chatham.

A curious incident occurred just after I enlisted in 1921 and it concerned a boy who was being discharged through his bad character. He had served several periods of detention for misdemeanours and especially for stealing. Things got so bad at the last that the bulk of the boys would have been only too pleased to lynch the culprit, especially those who had lost kit or personal belongings at his hand. For his own safety on his last night he was lodged in the company store under the personal care of the company storeman, a kindly corporal who had a soft spot for most boys and, generously, even bought a cooked supper for the delinquent. You can imagine his chagrin the next morning to discover that he, too, had been robbed, of a pair of civilian plain-toed boots which ORs were permitted to wear with their walking-out dress. By that time, however, having been escorted to the train, the culprit was well on his way.[12]

Derek S. Scholfield recalls some of the instructors and their punishments in his boyhood as a trumpeter trainee in the RRA.

Instructors were often without feeling, and were instrumental in provoking bully boys to take action against other boys. An example; once when being inspected on Church Parade, the Inspecting Officer checked me for having metal polish stains in the bell of my trumpet and bugle. What happened after the Parade was over and officers had been dismissed, was for the Squad Sergeant to rebuke me yet again, and to say in a loud voice, 'When I was a boy, if anyone had been checked for leaving metal polish on his instruments, he was thrown into the horse trough.' Yes, you know the answer, I was propelled at the double by the bully boys and into the horse trough.

Another case comes to mind. After returning from gym, we were running late. I was last in changing and, being made the scapegoat, harassed to the point of breaking. In the end I cracked and threw my trumpet and bugle to the ground. I was in the act of throwing a drum at the Instructor, but was stopped in time. In looking back after all these years I feel the Instructor realised what happened, so the end of the story is that he awarded my punishment there and then on the spot. It was to scrub the outside metal stairway with toothbrushes that night. Where the toothbrushes came from I know not, but I will never forget the night as it poured with rain and two Instructors took it in turn to watch that I carried out my punishment.

On another occasion ten of us were in the disused stables to practise our trumpet and bugle calls. We were on our way back to the barrack room, coming by way of a short cut, when we saw coat hangers beside a broken side of the old gun store. We picked them up, divided them between us and used them to hang up our greatcoats and tunics. The next thing we knew was that the barrack room was searched and all ten of us were on a charge after spending almost the day in the guard room. The punishment was a flogging, each boy got 10 lashes of the riding whip. This punishment was meted out by the Battery Sergeant Major, Sammy Rushton, in presence of the Battery Commander, Major Barker, RHA.

I had almost deserted from the Regiment but was too frightened as I had seen the brutal handling of about twenty boys who under cover of darkness, left the barracks during the Coronation of 1937 as they had had enough of army life.

The funny thing that followed, was that whilst weeding a piece of rough ground as part of my punishment, I was asked by a driver what I had done to get punished. I told him and he went to the Guard Room and the next thing we are told was that this soldier had owned up to breaking into the store and that we were not responsible; that in fact he had backed a mess cart into the store, and had then gone on leave without reporting the event. The result was we all were given late passes for a month and the charge sheet was destroyed.[13]

The punishment of jankers was too often given, and mild enough, to merit long discussion. Bill Davidson, however, was one who experienced jankers for an innocuous 'offence' and finished up in the glasshouse. Military prison for boy soldiers was the most dreaded of all places.

I enlisted in July 1934 and in the October of that year ran into trouble, receiving three extra drill parades for some minor offence. Whilst on these I was charged with being late on parade for a kit inspection in the barrack room. I had nipped along to the ablutions to splash water on my hair to stick it down and got back just as the NCO and inspecting officer arrived at the barrack room door. As I was obviously not standing by my bed I was late for parade and received five days CB when I appeared before my OC the following day.

CB included amongst other activities reporting to the guard room for fatigues within minutes of reveilie being sounded. One did the normal day's work then paraded behind the guard at six in the evening to do pack drill which was followed by more fatigues, usually in the cookhouse. Sunday was easier. One reported every hour (or half an hour, I'm not sure) in a different kit. Full dress and breeches, puttees, spurs etc. and then fatigue dress and, by alternating, one was kept active and usefully employed.

Returning to the barrack room exhausted after fatigues, I crawled into bed. Shortly afterwards a duty lance bombardier came into the room and told me to get out of bed and clean my top kit—that is, the folded great-coat buttons, boots and webbing brasses which were on the shelves above my bed. It was not very long before lights out, the last post having been sounded, and I'd had enough and argued. Obviously he did not like Scots and I finished up in the guard room.

Next day I was seen by my OC and remanded for the commanding officer who sentenced me to ten days' detention in the military detention barracks at Aldershot. I was 14 years old.

I packed my kit and was escorted by a bombadier and gunner, taken by train from Woolwich via London to Ash Vale to the glasshouse where I was subjected to all the stupid, mindless, petty so-called activities the staff ordered prisoners to do. I shovelled sand from one dump to another. I polished endless tea buckets only to see them dumped back into a water tank. I polished buttons and folded and unfolded blankets and I couldn't help wondering what it was all in aid of because it began only because I wanted to look smart when I stood beside my kit.

My pay was affected of course. I lost that, but as I only got eleven pence a day it wasn't much to lose. We were only allowed to draw 3 shillings a week in any case. One or two other boys were sent to detention that year by the moron we had as a CO. Eventually a parent heard about it and, I believe, took it up with his MP and this type of punishment stopped.[14]

The ultimate disgrace was still ignominious discharge by drumming out of the regiment. In the heyday of this ceremony the prisoner was led on to parade before the regiment by the most junior drummer. After being stripped of all badges of rank, buttons, decorations and accoutrements the prisoner was taken to the gate to the 'Rogues March' and literally kicked out by the drummer. Questioned on this subject, many respondents flatly denied that a drumming out had been held since the Boer War at least. Despite this popular denial there are enough eye-witness accounts to substantiate the fact that they did occur from time to time in the first half of this century. The last known such parade was held in Halifax, Yorkshire, during the Second World War. Fred Burgess, earlier quoted, who served in the Great War and later transferred to the RAF, recalled a drumming out at Cranwell in 1920 or 1921 (he could not be certain of the year).

The prisoner was a corporal in the RAF Service Police, found guilty by court-martial of stealing service kit from a comrade and sentenced to be reduced to the ranks, discharged with ignominy, to be drummed out of the RAF, and to serve 9 months in a civilian prison.

All available officers, NCOs and airmen were marched on to the parade ground where they formed three sides of a square. The fourth side was formed by the station band, with drummers forming the front rank with muffled drums.

The prisoner and escort were marched to a central position in front of the band and behind the station warrant officer and station commander. The parade was then called to attention and the station commander read out the prisoner's number, rank, name, offence and the sentence.

The station warrant officer then faced the prisoner and cut off his corporal's chevrons and shoulder badges, removed his cap badge, and then cut off his buttons and belt buckles. These were all dropped to the ground and ceremoniously heeled into the asphalt.

The prisoner was then marched off to the guard room to a slow, single beat played by the drummers. The parade was then dismissed.[15]

Burgess remembers the drumming out very well. He was impressed by the ceremony of the parade, but had no compassion for the prisoner because stealing from a comrade was looked upon as one of the worst crimes in the service.

Cyril Rawlinson was a drummer in the Duke of York's when a drumming out took place there in the late 1920s.

I was a drummer boy and we did a continual roll until the boy had passed through the gate. Quite an emotional experience. I cannot explain how I felt; it was terrible for all the drummers, and we were emotionally upset for the remainder of the day. It took a lot of the go out of us. Not a pleasant experience.[16]

The last parade of this kind at the Duke of York's occurred in the early summer of 1939. By chance, two witnesses testified to this incident. The case involved three boy NCOs charged with homosexual behaviour with younger boys. One of these younger boys, Jim Hassel, described his involvement in the affair.

I was dragged out of bed to the Prefect Sergeant's room; myself and a fellow named Kelly and someone else. They [the authorities] didn't catch me but they did one of the others. I thought after going through the ordeal quite a bit that it was normal. Anyway, we all ended up in front of the commandant, Colonel W. A. T. Bowley,* and had to tell what happened. The three who took us got drummed out and I was one of the three kids who had to give evidence.[17]

The other witness, earlier noted in Chapter IX when describing how he and his fellows were weaned on tales of the Battle of Omdurman, attended the parade and described much the same scenario as that given by Fred Burgess.

Lastly, T. G. Stephens, who enlisted in the Royal Engineers and attended the School of Military Engineering, Chatham, had this to say.

The drumming out occurred when I was at Halifax during the war. The whole battalion was paraded on the four sides of the square. The sapper to be drummed out was escorted on to the centre of the square by military police, the CO then read out the sentence and stripped the buttons and badges from his uniform—he was then marched off. I believe the crime was that he repeatedly swallowed objects when on posting for overseas, thus preventing the posting by being admitted to hospital. I think the last thing he swallowed was a teaspoon.[18]

*Prior to his appointment as Commandant of the Duke of York's Colonel W. A. T. Bowley commanded The Royal Warwickshire Regiment. He handed over command of his late battalion to Montgomery.

Despite what might be thought of the life boy soldiers led from the foregoing description of summary punishments, none of the respondents felt in the least downtrodden by their experience of military life. On the contrary, they felt they had a reasonable measure of freedom and at times got up to no end of devilry, of which the following accounts are a sampling.

Bill Davidson of the Royal Artillery:

I recall the capers involved in 'pawning' kit. Ted Horsfall, a friend of mine, was the pawn king. One of the lads would get round the back, heave the parcel over the wall on a signal and I'd get the parcel and deliver it to Ted. I was a very good runner and no military policeman in Woolwich would catch me. Ted did the actual pawning and took the biggest risk as he could be easily caught going into or coming out from the pawnship. Tickets were kept hanging on black threads in the ventilators as it was a crime to be in possession of one. We each got one penny for our efforts.[19]

George Shorter, an ex-Dukie, told of an incident at Inkerman Barracks during his boy service in 1933.

One Saturday, Sergeant Marks, the duty sergeant, lay down for his after-noon kip, and he had faithfully done his duty at the wet canteen. Marks had a magnificent moustache, waxed to proud perfection. Young boys of the regiment crept into the orderly room and performed silent surgery on the sleeping sergeant.

When he awoke he stretched himself, adjusted his dress and stepped outside to survey the deserted roads and barrack blocks for victims to terrorise. When he grandly twisted his moustache he discovered he had only one spike and he bellowed like a trumpeting elephant. 'Those bloody, bloody boys!' Of course, we all heard, but no one dare go near the wounded elephant.[20]

Luckett of the RE Mounted Depot, writing of his life as a trumpeter, said that once a boy passed his trumpeter's test the world was his oyster, because

Boys were always in great demand for different functions such as officers' guest night when a dozen of us blew some fanfares for the benefit of the officers and their guests. We were in demand for Remembrance Sunday, regimental dinners, sports days and funerals. One such funeral we attended was the cremation of the author of the Bulldog Drummond books, whose nom de plume was 'Sapper'. The writer in fact was Lieutenant-Colonel Cyril McNeile.

One tale I must tell concerns a gaffe I made once as orderly trumpeter. The wet bar or beer canteen for other ranks used to close at 9.30 pm upon the sounding of the first post, blown in the coal yard opposite the canteen. As orderly trumpeter I marched out very smartly and sounded a real good 'First

Post', even giving myself a pat on the back for sounding off so well! But imagine my horror when I got back to the guard room to find the RSM ready to blow a gasket and many of the old sweats demanding to know 'What's up?' I had blown First Post half an hour early! Looking back, I was lucky not to have been lynched for depriving the boozers of half an hour's drinking time. As it was, I got an extra Saturday guard duty for my error. I never made that mistake again![21]

The temperance movement, which had been launched in the 1850s to combat excessive drunkenness in the army, was on the wane but still active in the 1920s when boys of the Royal Engineers, Chatham, were compelled to attend meetings. Henry Corke reported on this subject.

An infrequent evening diversion was compulsory attendance [at a meeting] to listen to a speaker representing the Royal Army Temperance Association, when we were encouraged to sign one or two pledges, 'A' as a total abstainer or 'B' as a moderate drinker. Meetings were held in the NAAFI hut and, I believe, a cup of tea was provided as bait to sign one of the two pledges. Membership for the first two years was free but continued membership entailed an annual subscription for which service jewels (or medals) were awarded every two years without payment.

A regular subscriber could amass quite a few jewels (which were about the size of the normal miniature medal) throughout life but there was little or no chance of wearing them except at subsequent RATA meetings and their appeal lost itself in time as they were of no value, either as an award or intrinsically. The intentions of RATA were good when drunkenness was rife amongst members of the armed forces.

Incidentally, this Association just outlived the 1939–45 war, when it was finally disbanded with a membership of about half a dozen keen and zealous men who tried hard to keep something active and to guide servicemen (and women) on a sober path. Luckily the whole character of the armed forces has changed for the better in the last fifty years and drunkenness is not as pronounced as it was at one time.[22]

Little is known of the behaviour of boys of the Queen Victoria's School, Dunblane. As for the Royal Hibernians, the school was disbanded in 1924 and those boys remaining were sent to the Duke of York's. Apparently, Dukies were in the habit of fighting pitched battles, the first four companies invariably arranging themselves against the other four. The strange feature about these battles is that the boys, though never taught the tactics of Wellington's close-order formation, formed themselves undirected into companies, which suggests that they had something of their soldier fathers in their blood.

Jim Hassel remembers a furious snow battle fought in this manner in the winter of 1938–9, when matters got out of hand until brought to order by the arrival of the RSM. Said Hassel, 'We had to run around the school perimeter for that, until RSM Jones said stop. That was to teach us a lesson.'[23]

In London in the Scots Guard of the 1930s, a more serious activity was taught to a couple of boys by an old soldier. Cyril Rawlinson recalls:

An old soldier took two boys out of barracks and taught them the art of pinching anything from private cars. Result—one boy finished up in the police station for trying to get a fur coat out of a car, but it turned out to be a large black dog![24]

The majority of the A4 boys who served in the 1920s and 30s were to become senior NCOs and commissioned officers during the Second World War, which is testimony enough to the sound training they received as youngsters. As noted by Henry Corke in his correspondence, one of the boy lance-corporals who took part in the rescue at sea off Fort Monckton in 1921, Boy Lance-Corporal Eagle, reached the rank of Lieutenant-Colonel. Bill Davidson wrote:

I recall Boy Apprentice Carpenter ('36 entry) retiring as a major-general and colonel commandant. Apprentice Hughes retired as a brigadier; David Turner out of my term and Wally Woodly, both colonels; Alf Baker, Dennis French, Mervyn Dix and Don Stewart all made lieutenant-colonel. Out of my term of 44 apprentices I am unable to account for four of them today, but, excluding those, 40 per cent of the term were commissioned and at least another 25 per cent made warrant officer.[25]

Davidson reached the rank of major before retiring in 1972, having served 38 years of army life.

These A4 soldiers were the last of a particular breed of boy soldier because, beginning in the 1920s, the authorities recognised the need for a different kind of adult soldier. Drummers, trumpeters and buglers, while still needed in military bands, had had their day. The army had become mechanised and skilled tradesmen were in high demand. Therefore the army, as never before, geared itself for the appearance of the apprentice tradesman.

CHAPTER XVI
JACK'S LUMP

W HEN JOHN HOLLAND joined the Argyll and Sutherland Highlanders in
1902 he was credited with the trade of tailor on his attestation papers.
Similarly, Frank Ebdon on enlistment into the Rifle Brigade in 1916 was
recorded as being a bootmaker, even though he was to become a bugler.
Indeed, before 1939, most boy soldier recruits were credited with a 'trade
occupation' on their enlistment documents: farrier, cooper, blacksmith, tailor,
bootmaker, harness maker. As most of them were 14-year-olds it is hardly
likely they could be considered to be skilled artisans and, without previous
experience in their trade, once they joined their regiment or corps they were
instructed in some skill other than soldiering. For as much as 50 years before
1900, battalions of the line and corps such as the Royal Engineers, the cavalry
and Royal Regiment of Artillery had each developed their own trade training
programme, in much the same way that education was introduced into
Wellington's Peninsular Army.

In 1849, for example, a general order was issued in the Corps of Royal
Engineers requiring that all boys enlisted as buglers be trained as masons or
bricklayers.[1] During the 1914–18 war some buglers were selected for training
as architectural draughtsmen and, in 1919, the 22nd Fortress Company (an
earlier disbanded unit) was reintroduced as a Boys Company and, for the first
time, boy entrants were required to sit an examination to qualify for acceptance
into the Corps. With the introduction of tank warfare and the increased use of
mechanised transport during the First World War, the need for skilled
tradesmen became increasingly evident. To satisfy that need the first apprentice training school devoted entirely to the technical education of boy soldiers
was opened in 1924. This was the Army Technical School (ATS) at Beachley
Camp, Chepstow, from which the Royal Army Ordnance Corps was to be
supplied with the fitters, mechanics, armourers and electricians it needed.
(The abbreviation ATS was to cause the apprentice tradesmen a great deal of
embarrassment during the Second World War after the women's Auxiliary
Territorial Service came into existence.) Beachley Camp was formerly a

prisoner-of-war camp, a fact not entirely lost on succeeding generations of apprentice tradesmen, as A/T E. Anthony Dutton, who joined the ATS in 1940 as an apprentice fitter, noted:

> When I was at Beachley Camp it was a bare, hutted place surrounded on three sides by water, a spur of land where the River Wye joins the River Severn. It had been a German POW camp during the 1914–18 war and had not changed very much from those days.[2]

In 1924 the new technical training school opened its gates to 1,000 boys between the ages of 14 and 15 and maintained that strength for the next 20 years.

Whereas many apprentices in private industry may have spent their first six months ambling back and forth in the workshop, loaded down with billy cans of tea for thirsty machinists, the army tackled its task with characteristic efficiency. Apprentices were not to be employed as carriers of tea cans, but were to begin a concentrated apprenticeship as soon as they could settle into their new life.

Upon joining every A/T, regardless of his elected trade, was issued with a block of steel sawn from bar stock. His first task was to remove the greasy mill scale from one face of the block with hammer and chisel. For a 14-year-old boy this was no easy task. He soon dulled the chisel's cutting edge, bruised his knuckles when his hammer head missed the tool, and found the steel to be unyielding. His instructors made it look all too easy. To a cacophony of ringing metal, rows of new apprentices belaboured their lumps of steel for weeks on end. When one face was chiselled flat he worked mightily with a bastard file to make the surface smooth and flat. The second face was worked and shaped to be square to the first and so on until all six faces were smooth, silver bright and square one to the other. A hole was then drilled into the block with a ratchet drill and opened up into a square hole by means of file and hacksaw. Next a brass block was shaped to fit into the hole and the gaps between brass and steel checked by eye and feeler gauges to ensure the squareness of fit. The entire process, of rendering a greasy block of steel and hunk of brass into a gleaming work of metal art, took up to three months, by which time the A/T was expected to have acquired the feel of metal: the softness of brass, the hardness of steel. To thousands of apprentices over the years this first piece of steel came to be known as 'Jack's lump'.

Only after completion of this basic fitting course did the apprentices take separate paths to become vehicle mechanics, armourers, electricians and fitters. In addition, they attended school for their certificates of army education. The course of training developed at Chepstow, which covered a period of three years, was followed by other corps but not on so grand a scale.

T. G. Stephens of the Royal Engineers, who began his service in 1929 at the age of 14, reported:

I joined the army as a boy in December 1929 as the result of a national examination which, I think, was held every six months. I entered as an apprentice architectural draughtsman. This was my choice, but the trade you got depended on your position in the examination.[3]

He joined the Boys Company at Chatham, 120-strong and made up of 60 to 70 A/Ts, the rest being buglers. They worked at their trades during the day and went to school until 8 o'clock at night. Life in those days, he said, was hard but not harsh or cruel.

What we all found tough was washing in cold water, especially in winter. The wash basins were in the barrack block but there was no heating or hot water. The bath house was next to the WCs and here there was hot water. Dirtiness was not tolerated and if any boy was found to be dirty then 'barrackroom law' took hand and the culprit was scrubbed in a bath of cold water. I only knew of this happening on two occasions.[4]

From 1930 on the training programmes instituted by arms of the service to satisfy the need for skilled tradesmen proliferated. Some corps were more ambitious than others but whatever branch of military service one considers there was some form of apprentice training established so that, clearly, a transition from employment of boys as musicians to tradesmen can be found to be under way.

John Bradley, the ex-Dukie who ran foul of the provost sergeant at Buller Barracks in 1937, joined 71 other boys in his intake, made up of two squads of 36. One squad was of musicians, the other of trade apprentices: 8 clerks and 28 armament artificers.

We were called boys in those days regardless of whether we were clerks, artificers, mechanics or trumpeters, and the set-up in the RASC was that the Boys Company was part of the No 2 Training Company. Our programme was for the initial training as soldiers for the first three months. This meant a cross country run every morning before breakfast, followed by square bashing, PT, classes for the second class certificate of education—map reading, military history and, that famous subject, interior economy. This period I found boring because it was a repeat of everything I had done at school. The only [relief from this boredom] was that the drill sergeant frequently lost his voice and every time this happened I had to drill the squad. At still less than 15, I felt as big as my boots drilling a squad on the main square at Buller Barracks. Not until we had our passing out parade were we allowed to get on with our technical training.[5]

The apprentice training programme begun on a large scale in 1924 was evidently a huge success because by 1937, at which time there was still a shortage of specialist soldier-tradesmen, it was decided to build three additional schools based on the Chepstow model. One each was planned for Arborfield, near Reading, Chatham and Jersey (in the Channel Islands). Each was planned to accommodate 1,000 boys at any one time, to produce tradesmen for the RAOC, RE and RASC, respectively. Even a cursory survey of boy soldier strength in 1939, taking account of the apprentice schools operated exclusively for A/Ts, the Infantry, Artillery, Signals, Ordnance, Engineers, Service, Pay and Armoured corps, would indicate a total strength of something in excess of 12,000, a very conservative estimate. It is surprising that the actual figures are not available in any condensed form from military records for the period. Nevertheless, on the basis of the facts I have given, the 12,000 figure estimated seems reasonable.

The bare record of units, the speciality trades for which they catered, and discussion of the needs apprentice training satisfied cannot begin to give an intimate picture of this new type of boy soldier. Measure of the success, achievement, discipline, happiness and satisfaction obtained from the way of life these young boys chose can only be gained from those who enlisted during the early period of the army's apprentice training scheme.

Generally, from the 20 or more respondents who fall into the A/T category for the period 1930–50, it is evident that the majority were well satisfied with their experience. Two, however, expressed dissatisfaction. Rodney Travers-Griffin, who was at the Chepstow School from 1946 to 1949, has unhappy memories and thought it a waste of time. The other, Major Charles G. Ashdown, a still-serving soldier when this was written, wrote a qualified criticism of his service at Arborfield during the war years.

The training at Arborfield should be divided into two parts, military and technical. The lessons learnt from the military training (that is, basic imprinting) have produced impressions and habits which endure until today. It can therefore be typified as successful. The technical training was not successful. I required a great deal of attention to inspire me in that direction, which was not available at the school. Only later did I become successful and that was when I had matured. In summary, my boy service taught me how to be a good soldier, but didn't make me one until later, and succeeded only in producing a mediocre tradesman.

I realise my assessment of the school may be harsh, and concede that in the middle of an all-out war it was not possible to do much more on the technical side. I speak from considerable experience as a military technical educator, as an instructor and, latterly, as a Training Command executive, and therefore believe my views are justified.[6]

Food and messing, not discipline, remained the single most frequently discussed subject of respondents. Bill Adams, who was at Chepstow in 1937, told how he and his companions wolfed the harvest festival displays in the garrison church each year.

At harvest festival the school church was usually decorated by the married families and local people. All the available space was filled with apples, oranges, bananas and so on, but by the end of the service things looked a sorry mess. Apple cores, orange peel and banana skins were strewn over the floor. I am afraid that many of us were not very religiously inclined at that age.[7]

Peter Butler, one of the 1946 intake at the ATS, Arborfield, wrote of the food at that establishment:

I remember breakfast meals being such charming dishes as porridge, made with water and salt and watered down evaporated milk, being dished out by the cook(!) by the small half ladle, followed by four or five baked beans and a spoonful of almost inedible powdered egg; one slice of stale, dirty and even mouldy bread and half a pat of margarine. In fact, I would say that I never ate worse [food] before or after the ATS. A strong recollection is that of hunger.[8]

Prior to the Second World War and before the introduction of the open-necked battledress, A/Ts were issued with the same clothes and equipment as adult soldiers. The A/T's kit consisted of: two suits of khaki (to be fitted by the regimental tailor at no expense to the Crown), two pairs of boots, one pair of slippers, three pairs of grey socks, a pair of puttees, two sets of long underpants and two pairs of short ones, two vests, a woollen cap comforter which could be used as a scarf or as a container for small items, a suit of overalls, braces; a 'housewife' container to hold darning wool, cotton, needles and spare buttons; a 'holdall' for comb, eating utensils, lather brush, razor (the cut-throat type) and brass button stick; a variety of brushes for hair, clothing, boots and brass cleaning; a service dress peaked cap, a soft cap for fatigue duties; a kitbag made of heavy canvas; a cap badge and shoulder titles. A regimental greatcoat completed the ensemble, but this was considered to be 'public clothing' and not the property of the soldier. Walking-out canes in units had to be bought by the boy soldier out of his own pocket; he was not permitted out of barracks without a cane. A clothing allowance of 15 shillings every three months was intended to replace lost or damaged items, the balance of the amount not used being paid to the apprentice in cash.

For military training in the technical schools the staff was drawn from all units of the army and not simply from the corps to which the A/Ts would eventually be posted. At Arborfield, for example, it was customary for the RSM to be provided by the Brigade of Guards. The NCOs were of no particular regiment or corps. Ex-boys from Arborfield recall NCOs from the South Wales Borderers, the Royal Hampshires, the Royal Armoured Corps, and so on. In this respect, the technical schools were no different from their junior military schools, the Duke of York's and Queen Victoria School, in having members of the military staff who were near or past the regular age for retirement. For this reason such personnel tended to hold their appointments for long periods.

It might be thought that such a mixture of represented units in the schools militated against the development of unit pride and an *esprit de corps*, but far from it. The sense of belonging became apparent immediately a boy enlisted. Peter Jones, who was at Arborfield, expressed himself on that subject quite clearly.

My boyhood was in the barracks at Windsor—my father was Corporal of Horse with the Royal Horse Guards, The Blues. Also, my mother's side of the family were soldiers—foot guards—and my grandfather got himself a DCM during the Boer War, so I suppose it was in my blood to join as soon as I could. My grandfather did endeavour to get me into the Grenadiers as a drummer boy but my father nearly had a heart attack! His boy going into the Foot Guards!!

I went to Arborfield in April 1942 where, together with the January 1942 intake, we were the first lot to become General Service Corps, much to our disgust. As I said, the fresh blood came from the Dukies, QVS and Gordon Boys.* The bulk of the school was then of Ordnance boys from Hillsea. Of course, they wore the Ordnance badge of which we were very envious. They were also allowed to wear the REME badge when the Corps was formed in October 1942.

I always remember feeling I was left out when arriving at the gates of Arborfield. I suppose we were uniform conscious because of the war, but although there were quite a few of us barrack kids who got together, we thought that the boys already in uniform—khaki shorts, tunic and forage cap with red piping for the Dukies if I remember, cut-away tunics and glengarries for the QVs, and cut-away tunics and trews for the Gordon boys—were at an obvious advantage. The pecking order had already begun.[9]

Two interesting observations from this account are worth noting. First, the compulsion for boys to follow their soldier fathers in a military career is evident; second, the streaming of boys from the military schools into trades training marks a shift in army policy about this time. For almost 200 years these children of the military schools had been guided into musical careers, and we can state unequivocally that they formed the core of military music in the British Army. The need for tradesmen and technicians changed the emphasis completely and this, in a technological world, proved to be of immense value to these sons of soldiers. However, far more skilled tradesmen were required by the army than the military schools could provide, so it cannot be said that they formed the core of the technical corps as they had of military music.

What of discipline and punishment? Corporal punishment was not the way to discipline apprentice tradesmen, so we find that 'jankers' was the most

*The Gordon Boys were orphans of a civilian-funded paramilitary institution and not, therefore, on the same footing as children of the military schools.

prevalent punishment given. In exceptional cases the authorities despatched offenders to the glasshouse, as Peter Jones reports.

> I think the life was hard, the food bad and the discipline pretty harsh in the first couple of years. We really were at the mercy of the individual 'old sweat' and some had rigid methods. To get on defaulters under the evil eye of Harry Hodgekiss (sic)—the Cheshire Regiment, and Provost Sergeant—was quite something and getting off jankers was something else. There were many cases of injury obtained whilst on jankers. The ultimate deterrent for us of course was Fort Darlan, the glasshouse. When boys came back from there they had changed for sure.
> Dishonourable discharges were pretty grim affairs—one of the boys of my company went. Besides the derision from the rest of us, the collarless shirt, beltless trousers and old boots made him look the part of a criminal or at best a tramp. Quite humiliating I imagine.[10]

Charles Ashdown candidly reported on his own experience at Arborfield when he wrote:

> I was continuously in trouble during boy service. I did a total of 55 days jankers. I was well known to Sergeant Hotchkiss and his staff. My main trouble was a considerable inability to conform to the rather petty routine of the school which brought me regularly before my OC and the Commandant. Since I am very stubborn by nature, but also have a high IQ, these disparate elements of my character warred within me, until determined counselling by a Sergeant Taffy Evans of SWB convinced me of the basic stupidity of my behaviour. Because of his intervention, and a so-called fresh start, I did not have any further serious trouble in the last year at the school. I would therefore say that the discipline was fair, firm and inexorable, and based primarily on instilling the military ethic.[11]

If punishments awarded were no more severe than defaulter parades, they were given more freely. Peter Butler says:

> I remember some 150 boys plus (15 per cent of the school), who had been confined to barracks—the janker wallahs we called them—having to chip ice off the main road running through camp; it was a pretty cold and miserable task, particularly as the only implement allowed was your jack knife.[12]

Mild as such punishments were compared with those inflicted in the far-off days of boy service, the apprentices were not short of imagination and enterprise with which to plague those set in authority over them. In 1940 the Provost Sergeant of Beachley Camp, Chepstow, had the unfortunate name of Wit. It was the common practice of the older boys there to instruct the newcomers to report to Sergeant Dimwit in the guardroom, which was never amusing to that august person. Reported Tony Dutton of the ATS, Chepstow:

Another target of our humour was the padre, who was not generally liked and rather stupid. He always insisted on being saluted regardless of how far away a boy might be. I can remember one summer evening when he was seen pushing his bicycle through the company lines while balancing a load of books. He was spotted early in his journey, so at five second intervals just about every boy in the company came around the corner and threw him a very smart salute. As he always returned a good salute, for each boy he had to stop, hold the bike and balance the books with one hand and salute with the other. It took him a long time to travel that 300 yards and I don't think he ever suspected that his leg was being pulled.[13]

If boys had their wily tricks the old soldiers, the NCOs responsible for their military training, had theirs. Dutton recalls how he and four companions were outwitted.

Boys were not allowed to smoke or drink, but most of us did within the limits of our two shillings per week. With a party of boys I responded to the challenge to 'have a drink'.

Only one of us had ever been in a pub before so we followed this experienced man about town to an off-the-beat pub where, with our collars undone and caps pushed back in tough soldier style, we swaggered to the bar behind our leader and waited for him to tell us what to order.

'Pint of mild,' he shouts, and we all say 'the same as him.' Our drinks were no sooner lined up than, to our horror, the door behind the bar swung open and there stood our 6 foot 2 inches platoon sergeant who in one breath shouted: 'Put those drinks down. Caps on straight, get those collars done up, stand to attention. You're all on a charge.'

From being six-foot men we shrank back into five-foot boys and in ten seconds flat were out of the pub and on our way back to camp, leaving our sergeant with the whole evening before him to drink at his leisure the five untouched pints.[14]

If the life led by A/Ts lacked the excitement and dash of that of their fellow boy soldiers, the buglers and drummers, they were at least being provided with skills of lasting worth. The introduction of apprentice training of the type offered at Chepstow meant that a soldier-tradesman would be well equipped at the end of his military service to compete on an equal footing with his civilian counterpart in the workforce. It is true that the same reasoning applied to the tailors, bootmakers, masons and bricklayers of an earlier era, but postwar Britain had been transformed into a highly technological society. There was a need for army trade training and the related technical qualifications to be brought into line with the mainstream of national life and those who directed the army's technical arms were not slow to appreciate this fact.

The army had always adjusted itself to changing times. Sometimes it was slow to do so, with conservative disregard for critics who would force the pace. On the other hand, it had often taken the lead in the past. This was certainly the case with education, hygiene and physical training programmes. The introduction of certificates of education tied into promotion had been a great incentive to young soldiers, for this gave them a head start over those who enlisted at the normal adult service age of 18. By the 1950s, however, it was clearly evident that the army had long since lost its commanding position in the field of education. For instance, there was no provision for higher education, even though the army had as great a need for university graduates as did other institutions of national life.

It is seen as no coincidence that drastic revisions in the training programme were imminent by the late 1940s. The military schools excepted, it was not considered the army's responsibility to report a young soldier's progress in technical proficiency, education or any other sphere to anyone but the youth's superiors. This attitude changed, for around 1950 the commanding officers and technical instructors of boys' units began reporting to parents on their sons' progress. The reports were simple but comprehensive, and took on the character of end-of-term school reports.

WO II John Moon, who joined the RASC in 1949 when he was 15, sent in his end-of-term reports, which were issued three times a year at the end of the Easter, summer and winter terms. They covered five academic subjects (maths, English, history, geography and map reading); military training; physical training; proficiency at sports; and carried a personal report from the OC of the Boys Company. The OC wrote on John Moon's first end-of-term report: 'I am extremely pleased with his progress and he certainly has tried hard. I am very hopeful of his future and feel he will justify every confidence.'[15] The OC's hopes were realised.

Obtaining the permission of parents or guardians to thrash a boy for misbehaviour was of fairly recent origin in the late 1940s, although one respondent said that this permission was sought in his unit (Boys Mounted Squadron, Royal Artillery) in the late 1930s. The submission of progress reports was a new departure, an indication that the military authorities were no longer content to be a law unto themselves in the care and training of their young charges.

It can be seen that things had altered considerably since the turn of the century. They were to change very much more over the next few years because the army was to enlist boy soldiers on a scale never before equalled, not even during the period of the Napoleonic Wars. Indeed, within a few years the boy soldier strength increased to 25 per cent of the total strength of the peacetime army, and for an exceedingly sound reason.

CHAPTER XVII
THE MORE THINGS CHANGE . . .

A DOCUMENT OF considerable importance with regard to the future care and training of boy soldiers was issued in April 1955. This was the *Report of the Committee on the Organisation and Administration of Boys' Units in the Army*, which came to be known as the *Miller Report* after the officer who headed the inquiry, Lieutenant-General Sir Euan A. Miller. It was as frank and candid as that written by School Inspector Moseley following his visit to the Royal Military Asylum in 1846. The main difference between the two reports was that the Miller Committee found living conditions of positive luxury as compared with those with which Moseley had been confronted more than a hundred years earlier.

The Miller Committee was given the following terms of reference:

To investigate the organization (including staffing) and administration of those units of the Army which have been set up to train enlisted boys and to report whether such units best meet, under present day conditions, the Army's requirements for enlisted boys, bearing in mind that the object is to provide long service regular NCOs for the Army.[1]

There were eleven major centres for training underage soldiers at that time. These included four apprentices' schools and six squadrons, companies or regiments for the RAC, RA, RE, R. Signals, RASC and RAOC. The eleventh unit was a Boys' Infantry Battalion at Plymouth. This last unit was a significant addition to the total number of training depots for young soldiers because, in its enthusiasm to provide itself with skilled tradesmen over the previous 25 years, the army had neglected the infantry. There had been no interruption of the enlistment of young musicians for military bands, but the inference of the neglect was that the infantry could make do with adult recruits. The need to train junior soldiers for positions of leadership in this branch of the Service was shown by the postwar creation of the Boys' Infantry Battalion.

Among the recommendations of the Miller Committee were a more stringent selection system to raise the standard of entry; improved facilities; a unit strength of about 800 (meaning that some units would need to be expanded and others decreased); acceptance of the principle that boys' units be 'conducted more as schools than military units'; and a more selective appointment of the officer, warrant officer and NCO staff. The extent to which these recommendations were accepted and implemented will be discussed, but it is first worth quoting the following passage from the Committee's report.

> In addition, we have had the benefit of paying an interesting visit to the Duke of York's Royal Military School at Dover, where we were able to discuss with the Commandant and his staff many relevant and comparable problems.[2]

What this meant, in effect, was that although the Committee was primarily concerned with corps and regimental units it did not neglect the military schools. To some extent the Duke of York's served as a model and prompted the Miller Committee to recommend that the units be 'conducted more as schools than military units'. This was because the previous year (1954) had marked the culmination of a fiercely debated campaign to bring about reforms in the military schools system. (The authors of the Miller Report saw fit to refer to the excellent accommodation provided at the Duke of York's for its pupils.) Let us first deal with these reforms, for they, too, are part of the changing pattern of boy soldier service as perceived in this history.

General Sir Archibald Nye, one-time Chief of the Imperial General Staff, was also a leading member of the Board of Governors of the school and it was he who led the campaign for reform. Nye had been a pupil of the school at the time it moved from Chelsea to its present premises at Dover. He had unhappy memories of his years there and once in a position to make changes he did so—but not without strong opposition from the well-organised and active Old Boys' Association of the school. Until the early 1950s the curriculum and interior economy of the institution had been distinctly military in character and Nye was determined to change this emphasis to bring the operation of the Duke of York's more into line with the English public schools (private schools in North America) and to alter its curriculum to conform to the education standards of the state.

To the extent that military affairs are aired in public, Nye took the issue beyond the doors of the boardroom after his views had been accepted, but when his opposition was still refusing to accept a *fait accompli*. Writing to the *Royal United Services Institution Journal* in July 1954, in reply to an article published in the May 1954 issue, he expressed his own views.

> I have recently read an article in the [RUSI] Journal [May 1954] written by a Lieutenant-Colonel R. Evans of the Duke of York's Royal Military School from which it is evident that this officer, who purports to write with some

authority, is unaware of the background of events in recent years . . . which affected a fundamental re-organization of the School.

I was at the School from 1905 to 1914 and it seems relevant to record my impressions of the School during that time because the action which was taken in recent years springs directly from my experiences.

The outstanding impression is that the School was organized on predominantly military lines. The people who really mattered were the Commandant, the Adjutant, the Regimental Sergeant-Major, the Bandmaster, the Drum-Major, the PT Instructor and the Company Sergeant-Majors of the various companies. Considerable time was devoted to drill, band and drum practice, physical training and such like military subjects; and the military atmosphere pervaded the School.[3]

He went on to discuss the officers and NCOs of his day: a Colonel Norris, a 'short fat man with a fine fighting record in West Africa, foul-mouthed both to his staff and to his wife and utterly unsuited for the job'; a Colonel Nugent of the Irish Guards with the 'severe limitations' typical of the guardsmen of the era; and subordinate staff drawn from the old regular army and having the good and bad qualities of those days.

The General confessed that he had only once in his career departed from his self-imposed inflexible rule of not actively seeking appointments. This was when he suggested that he might become a specially-appointed Commissioner to the Duke of York's, to bring about much-needed change. He was successful and overnight the school was transformed. Off came the khaki uniforms, the studded boots, the chevrons of boy soldier rank and insignia of military organisation, and on went the grey flannel trousers and blue school blazers. The Commandant was replaced by a headmaster, the Adjutant by a bursar, and the Company Sergeant-Majors by housemasters. Boys still paraded at the weekends, in newly-issued blue uniforms and dashing blue berets bearing the school regimental cap badge, so some aspects of the former regimen remained, but the miltary influence was greatly subdued in favour of a public school atmosphere.

Fred Barry, who was at the school from 1948 until 1956 and who later enlisted in the Royal Military Police, noted the change, especially in the freedom given formerly to (sergeant) prefects to administer corporal punishment, but curtailed by the reforms.

When I joined the school, prefects were allowed to administer the cane, but this changed during my time. Prefects could still punish boys in other ways.[4]

When the Miller Committee visited the premises in 1955, it saw acres of playing fields, neat red-brick buildings with contrasting white windows, curving roads resting gently on the eye, and trimmed grass verges. Here was what could be done with planning and effort and the Committee thought that similar facilities should be provided for all boys' units.

That the changes recommended by the Committee were brought about is evident from the correspondence of men who served as boys during the following years. Some changes came more slowly than others, but the adult staff began to treat their young charges with more concern, improved facilities were provided, and greater emphasis was placed on organised sports and outdoor activities. Adventure training, for example, was unheard of befvore 1955, but is now considered an important part of junior soldier training.

If the adult staff could be influenced by the change in policy to show a more humane regard for young soldiers, there was still the continuing problem of how to tame the boy NCOs. Inadequately coached, they could become martinets who terrorised their fellows. How boys adjusted themselves to some sort of pecking order in the larger units is a recurring theme in the letters of more recent ex-boy soldiers. WO II Richard A. James, now serving with the Royal Scots Dragoon Guards, began his service at the age of 15 in 1959. Of the terror caused by some of the boy NCOs, he wrote:

It wasn't discipline, it was fear, not of the regular sergeants, but of the boy NCOs. For the first 3 months I had a sealed letter in my locker, asking my mother for £20 to purchase my discharge and twice I walked along the road to the post bunk to post it. Each time, at the last moment, pride forced me to turn round. How could I go back home and say I couldn't take the discipline after telling everyone how good the new life was going to be?

Inspections were endless and any infringement of the rules was punished by extra work. The thing I couldn't understand was the mental cruelty that went on. Boys in the army 3 months longer than you treated you like a second-class citizen.[5]

James moved with others to Chepstow in a major reorganisation of the apprentice schools in 1961. The bullying there, he said, was worse than at Harrogate (his former station) and that's when he decided to make a stand.

This was not received as a popular idea, but after three months I was promoted to sergeant and was able to exercise more power. I believe you can be strict without demeaning those under your command.

'It's all different now and maybe rightly so,' James concluded. One wonders if it is. Recruits of the late 1950s are now the army's old sweats with children of their own. These children, in turn, have become the boy soldiers of today and the army, we find, is more selective than it ever was. WO I David Wiggins of the 1st Wessex Regiment enlisted in the Infantry Junior Leaders Battalion in 1959 at the age of 15. Of the type of boy recruited during his time, he wrote:

It is interesting to note that many of my companions came from cities and large towns. Many had brushed with the police and most, according to them, had experienced some sort of sexual activity and numerous fights (punch-ups). I must admit that in hindsight these boys were far more mature for their age than I, a boy from the out-back of Berkshire, known to them as a Swede. These boys were the ones who came to the fore more readily than most. I have heard of many who made the grade later on in their service. My point is that the Army in 1959 was prepared to accept junior soldiers with what could be called a grey background; it is doubtful if they would in 1982.

I was one of two English boys after I was transferred to B Company, the rest being Welsh. (B Company provided recruits for the Welsh Brigade, the Light Infantry Brigade, the Mercian Brigade, and the Regiments of York-shire and the Fusiliers.) The Welsh boys were completely different in their outlook, extremely humorous and ready to accept me at once. Many of them I still see today; I always have a thick head the next day.[6]

On the other side of the coin there was the adult staff, the officers and instructors. WO I Tom Taylor was instructor at the Apprentice School at Arborfield. In providing a picture of apprentice training during the 1950s, he confirmed what Wiggins had to say about the type of recruit.

Boys, or junior leaders as they became known after about 1956 or so, differed greatly from adult recruits or adult soldiers. I was appointed to the post of CSM REME Enlisted Boys Company in 1954. In those days many of these young fellows were problem kids who were pushed into the service to get them out of the way, or to save somebody the task of sorting out their problems. They didn't have police records (they wouldn't have been enlisted), but were probably a bit wild and too much for mum and dad to handle.

We certainly didn't treat them as children; neither did we wrap them in cotton wool, but we did keep a very careful eye on them in view of the fact that during a term we were virtually their parents. I was affectionately known as 'Dad', but behind my back, of course.

The staff of these junior establishments were normally selected fairly carefully, with the accent on athletic ability, good service record, patience and, above all, they had to be volunteers. The latter did sometimes cause a problem as on at least one occasion a rather peculiar type slipped through the net and had to be removed in very short order; very unusual occurrence.

It was rarely necessary to work on the question of regimental pride. After their first term as recruits this always appeared, at least in my experience, to come so naturally to the boys that at times it was a little overpowering.

In the question of being 'little devils', I can only say they were normally healthy boys. Always game for mischief, but usually of a harmless nature. An unlocked kitchen door was considered fair game and a barrack room feast of sausages could only lead to a shortage of breakfast next day.

The system underwent changes after my retirement in 1961, as many probably as took place to improve the system before this time. The upheaval caused by the suicide of an RE enlisted boy in, I think, '56 or '57 I well remember. He had been subjected to some rather rough discipline, dealt out by his fellows. One thing that horrified me . . . was the amount of control left in the hands of boy NCOs. This led to some bullying and quite a bit of unhappiness, but in those days it was considered a fairly hard school. I discovered afterwards, during a seminar at the School of Education at Beaconsfield, that the life was nowhere near as hard as that considered normal at some of the well-known public schools.

We quickly changed the system and kept a very careful watch to ensure that barrack room courts and the like were not held. The boys had a very rigid code as far as personal hygiene was concerned and would, if allowed, deal with these things themselves in a somewhat unkind way with cold scrubbings, etc.

I must say that at the period in question, the 1950s, I did not agree with the system whereby a boy of 15 years was expected to contract to serve with the colours until the age of 25. I was sure that a lot of the young men regretted their decision or, in so many cases, that of their parents to sign away a large chunk of their lives. Many had absolutely no idea of what they were letting themselves in for. On the plus side, a young man determined to make a career of the Army entered his adult service with a 1st Class certificate of education, a good regimental background, many military skills, and full of old soldier's tricks of the trade.[7]

By 1960 junior soldiers, as they are now known, were permitted to leave barracks in civilian clothes, subject to official approval. David Wiggins explained the procedure:

At the start of each term, every company had a civilian clothes inspection when your proposed attire for the next three months was checked. Items of clothing approved were entered on to your civilian clothes pass. Then, presenting yourself to the guard room for walking out, you produced your clothes pass . . . to ensure that your dress conformed to the listed items. I can remember many being sent back to change their socks.[8]

What about the 1960s and 1970s? With the coming of the controversial raising of the school-leaving age to 16, the army was forced to increase the minimum age for enlistment to junior soldier training to 16 years. The adult staff found itself committed to spending an increasing part of the day with its young charges—a far cry from the time of John Holland when boy soldiers lived with the men in tents, cooked their own food, and cleaned their eating utensils in sand and salt water by the seashore.

Yet another change was the institution of a more careful selection system by which entrants were graded as apprentices, junior leaders or junior soldiers.

Robert Kennelly, an RAOC junior soldier at the age of 15 (1962 intake), considered himself and his companions at Blackdown at the very bottom of the boy soldier heap. Apprentices and junior leaders were regarded as superior entrants, even among the young recruits themselves. Nevertheless, upon arriving at Dettingen Barracks to begin training, Kennelly's intake was reminded that they would be the future NCOs and WOs of the army.

Absence without leave was common in his time, he said.

> Boys got homesick or missed their girl friends so they just took off. They usually went home. The Army then sent the police for them and that was enough for them to report back to camp on their own. That was not only better than having an escort, but cheaper. Prisoners had to pay the escort's train fare and living allowance from their own pockets. I know; it happened to me.[9]

This is yet another indication that times were changing, when young soldiers were being put on trust to return to camp. Discipline, though still firm, was more relaxed. WO II Alan Carroll (RAOC, 1963 intake) reported:

> Discipline . . . became stricter when we joined our permanent platoons and came under the command of boy NCOs and WOs who ran every aspect of platoon life. It was a hard, active regime, but not brutal. The odd kick, cuff or punch, both by boy and regular NCOs was accepted with a sort of perverse pride that 'we could take it'. We were treated with a mixture of mild aloofness and amused contempt by the regular soldier to whom we were known by the universally-accepted term of 'a fucking rat'.[10]

The underage recruits still indulged in horseplay which, psychologically, varied little from that practised by pre-1939 Dukies who used to roll their victims off company block roofs clamped inside a dustbin or condemned 'prisoners' to the electric chair (an upturned laundry basket in which another boy was concealed) and shocked him with the aid of a darning needle thrust through the wicker into his behind. Sergeant Geoffrey Carter (Jnr Leaders Battalion RA, 1967 intake) described a variation of the electric chair treatment.

> At the Junior Leaders Regiment there was no bullying, but I witnessed so-called horseplay. One such act was to hold a recruit's face against the wall, remove his shirt, and let him watch you plug in an electric iron. He was then told that once it was hot it would be placed on his back. By this time the recruit was terrified. The iron was then unplugged and held a few inches from his back to let him feel the heat. Then, at the last moment, a cold mess tin was slapped on his back.[11]

The 1970s saw the rise of the troubles in Northern Ireland and the army found that not a few Irish youths, enlisted for junior soldier training, later put this to use in the service of the IRA. Philip McCullough (RAOC, 1962 intake), who later joined the 16th Para Workshop unit, was one such entrant. In 1966, by then on his adult service, he stole two pounds of plastic explosive in Northern Ireland and demolished a post office letter box, for which he served an 18-month prison term. (He recently turned up in Adelaide, Australia, as a guest of the Australian-Irish Friendship Society, but was quickly returned to Northern Ireland by Australian immigration as an undesirable.)

By 1972, when Sergeant Rhett Corcoran of the 3rd Anglian Regiment enlisted, the changes advocated by the *Miller Report* were clearly well established. Absence without leave came to be regarded more as truancy (a sure indication of the more relaxed atmosphere), members of the staff spent more time in the company of the boys, and more attention was being paid by the authorities to the training of boy NCOs to ensure that they did not abuse their authority. Boys who were unable to take to the life or were found to be in some other way unsuitable were free to leave the service. This was perhaps a reflection of the times, of rising unemployment and, as a consequence, greater selectivity on the part of the military authorities. Wrote Corcoran:

> The first few weeks were bloody hard and the numbers fell off considerably. Of course, boy service is based on the school term system. Our first leave was at Christmas. During your leave your parents received a report exactly as they would when you were at school, except that your report was not based on PT, drill, sport, education and weapon training.[12]

The changes that have taken place in the training of young soldiers since the end of the Second World War are imperceptible when viewed from year to year and can only be seen clearly in retrospect. Similarly, the most recent changes, and those now taking place, will not be seen in clear perspective for another twenty years. Nevertheless, it is certain that changes in the service and treatment of boy soldiers since the end of the Second World War have been profound. The net effect has been to make a military career attractive for boy soldiers as never before. A survey of the recruiting statistics for the period 1968–1978 indicates clearly the results of the post-war conditions of service. Furthermore, a number of interesting observations can be made from the figures given in the following table.

Recruiting Statistics 1968–1978

Year	Total New Recruits	Young Soldiers (YS) & Juniors (Jnrs)	YS, Jnrs & Adults Under 18
1968	17,125	7,991	9,684
1969	20,709	9,449	11,469
1970	21,872	9,890	11,860
1971	29,354	13,722	15,983
1972	27,434	14,346	16,464

1973	15,245	6,596	8,125
1974	21,023	10,890	12,636
1975	25,682	13,684	15,796
1976	23,154	12,911	14,708
1977	18,423	9,620	12,044
1978	22,169	12,929	15,009
Totals	242,190	122,028	143,778

The first thing that becomes apparent when considering these recruiting statistics is that very few recruits over the age of 18 years were accepted for service during the period 1968–1978. In fact the average yearly intake of recruits aged 18 years and over was 1317. This figure represents slightly over eight per cent of the total recruits for the ten-year period.

A young soldier is defined as one less than seventeen and a half years of age on enlistment and this, therefore, by the definition given at the beginning of this work, qualifies a Young Soldier as a boy soldier. Further, the difference between the last two columns represents the annual intake of recruits who were aged 17.5 to 18 years of age. Strictly speaking, by the original definition, this group too was composed of boy soldiers on enlistment. The number in this category for the ten-year period is 21,750 which is higher than the over-18 recruits by some 8000. For the purpose of the calculations which follow, however, recruits in this category are ignored. The statistics are striking enough without them.

Considering, then, the first two columns of recruits, the annual intake of boy soldiers is well over half the total figure for each year. In 1978, for example, boy recruits represent 58 per cent of the total recruits for that year. Similarly, the total boy recruits for the period 1968–1978 is calculated at 78 per cent of the total.

On enlistment recruits sign to serve a 22-year engagement, committing themselves initially for periods of 3, 6 or 9 years' colour service with the possibility of longer service if both they and the military authorities are willing. Colour service for all recruits is measured from the age of 18 or the recruit's age on entry, whichever is later. Based on the sampling of respondents who answered the questionaire prepared for this study, the average service as full-time soldiers (usually termed 'colour service') spent by boy soldiers once they began their man service at age 18, was ten years.

Ignoring the effect of attrition for such reasons as medical discharge, unsuitability and mortality, it is now possible to make those observations to which we earlier referred concerning the practise of boy soldier recruitment in the British Army; but first we should take note of the total strength of the present-day Army. Including trainees, NCOs and officers, the size of the Army ranges from 150,000 to 160,000. If we reduce this figure, however, by the number of the officer and senior NCO core, which has been given as 30,000, we are left with a total strength of about 130,000. Of this figure some 75,000 are ex-boys (although they may no longer be young) and up to 14,000 (possibly more) will still be under-age soldiers; this last figure being the combined young soldier, junior soldier and apprentice soldier elements. From this it follows that the total strength of the 130,000 includes 89,000 serving boy soldiers and ex-boy soldiers combined. This is a large component and one is curious to know why, for it represents 68 per cent of the army's total strength – excluding the commissioned officers and senior NCOs, of course.

During a tour of a cross-section of junior entry units in 1980, I was able to interview many officers and NCOs of unit training staffs. Brigadier J. R. Smith, OBE, Chief Education Officer of the United Kingdom Land Forces (UKLF), in reply to a question as to why this large junior army exists (by which is meant the combined total of under-age soldiers) said, 'To recruit; for the good of the army and, thirdly, for the future NCOs.' Cost, he said, was an important consideration, and the malleability of young recruits in preparing them for a military life was another. Yet cost and malleability are not the only criteria. There is a preference for young recruits over adults for the benefits obtained when it comes to thoroughly grounding a soldier in the required technical skills.

One training officer expressed it another way. He said, 'Military weaponry is sophisticated. It is easier to train young recruits in the operation and main-tenance of high technology systems than adults who, by the age of 18, are more set in their ways.'

In this respect, the British and Australian armed forces (Australia also has a well-developed apprentice training scheme) have an advantage over other armies. Youths, carefully selected and screened for intelligence and technical aptitude, whether for an infantry or technical role, are better able to adjust to the technology they are to use and maintain than the adult recruit.

There is evidence to suggest that ex-boys have an advantage over adult recruits when it comes to promotion. For example, the statistics for promotion to the junior NCO ranks of one regiment were given as follows.

| | Age on Promotion | |
	L/Cpl	Cpl
Ex-Apprentice	21.7	24.9
Ex-Junior Leader	21.0	25.5
Ex-Adult Recruit	24.5	27.2

The machines of war, like the machines of production in modern society, become more and more automated; yet, no matter how sophisticated they do become, with memory banks, computer control chips, and other electronic gadgetry, they still need men to operate and maintain them, which brings us back to technical training and military discipline.

The long bows which won the day at Crecy and Agincourt were handled by men hard-trained at the butts, and well-disciplined to obey. A bowman who loosed a premature arrow might have had his legs thwacked by the Captain of

Archers, but no serious harm was done. A similar breach of discipline in a modern army could have dire consequences, so the need for training and discipline, far from diminishing since the days of bow and arrow warfare, has increased immeasurably. Indeed, the more complex the equipment the greater the need for teamwork. For this reason it is more necessary than ever to train soldiers from an early age. Raw courage has always been reckoned an important quality in the soldier's psychological make-up, but it is not enough. Training, education and discipline are what make the modern soldier professional. As long as these qualities are needed there will be a demand for boy soldiers.

As a footnote and endpiece to this history of boy soldiers, it is worth mentioning the occurrence of the Falkland Islands conflict in which the army played a leading role – not forgetting the Royal Navy, the Merchant Navy, the Royal Air Force and support services. Numerous were the reports of journalists on the scene concerning the extreme youth of those engaged. While there is no record, as yet, of boy soldiers taking an active role as they did in British military conflicts up to the Second World War, we may be certain from the statistics dealt with earlier that a good number, and probably half, were ex-boy soldiers.

In response to an enquiry as to the ex-boy soldier element of the Falkland Expeditionary Force, the Ministry of Defence regretted that it was not possible to provide such information because of the work involved. Perhaps some diligent researcher at a future date will be able to glean this information from the official records. In the meantime, from other sources, it is known that at least one ex-Duke of York's boy was killed in the conflict and that others took part in the fighting. Lance-Corporal Paul Lighfoot of the Royal Signals, who was in the Duke of York's in the mid-seventies, died in the helicopter crash in which 21 men of the SAS lost their lives. Two others, Sergeant Terry Anderson of the 1/7 Gurkhas and Cadet Jeremy MacAnley with the Fleet Auxiliary on the RFA Resource, are known to have taken part.

It is perhaps fitting that this history of boy soldiers should be closed with a reference to the oldest military school unit of the British Army, the Duke of York's Royal Military School (formerly the Royal Military Asylum, it will be recalled) which has provided a steady stream of boy soldier recruits for the army since the institution was established in 1803, for of them it may be truly said that they are the Sons of the Brave.

APPENDIX A

PRO DOCUMENT WO 43/796 749

Confidential report issued by the Privy Council
Office, dated 7th April 1846 and addressed to

The Right Honourable
The Lords of the Committee of
Council on Education

My Lords

In pursuance of your Lordships instructions conveyed to me by the Secretary of the Committee of Council on Education, I have visited the Royal Military Asylum at Chelsea and instituted an enquiry into the 'extent of the instruction and the degree of religious and moral training afforded by the institution'.

I enclose for your information a copy of the regulations for its establishment and government.

The building is erected on land which is held under a lease of which 33 years remain unexpired from Lord Cadogan. It contains in its central portion eight principal rooms each of which is 86 feet long and 34 feet wide, four of them being on the ground floor on either side of the vestibule and four others above. Five of these rooms are used as refectories, one as a music room and one for exercise in gymnastics. The four remaining rooms situated on the ground floor serve the purpose of school rooms. They are lofty apartments having a double row of windows and admitting of a thorough ventilation. The wings of the building, five stories in height, including the attics, are occupied by the dormitories of the boys of which there are four in each story together with apartments for a School Sergeant. Each dormitory is 34 ft 9 in long, 19 ft wide and 9 ft 9 in high and is intended to contain 24 boys two sleeping in each bed.

The ventilation of each dormitory is provided for by a grating communicating with the external air on a level with the floor and by ventilators in the ceiling the space between which and the floor of the dormitory above communicates with the external air.

The Chapel stands detached at some distance from the principal structure. A ready access supplied to it from the May grounds.

The building supplied accommodation for the residence of 1200 children by a regulation made in the year 1820. The number is however limited to 330. 330 were resident at the time of my inspection of which number 17 were sick.

Of 310 boys whom I examined

47 were in their 14th year
43   13th ,,
46   12th ,,
43   11th ,,
36   10th ,,
34   9th ,,
31   8th ,,
30   7th ,,

They are children born in wedlock of soldiers in actual service in whose selection preference is given

1st   To orphans
2nd   To children whose fathers have been killed in battle or have died in foreign service
3rd   To children who have lost their mothers and whose fathers are absent on duty abroad
4th   To those whose fathers are ordered on foreign service

Where these claims for preference do not obtain the regimental character of the parent forms the principal ground of accommodation. To diffuse the benefits of the institution as widely as possible the number of children of the last mentioned class admitted from each regiment is limited to four.

I am informed however that soldiers whose regiments are quartered at a distance manifest very little desire to secure the benefits of the Institution for their children and that although forms of petition are transmitted from time to time to the Commanding Officers, the number of appointments allotted to each regiment is not in many instances filled up.

The children are admitted between the ages of 5 and 10 years and discharged at the age of 14.

The average time of their residence in the asylum is five years.

To orphans the option of a trade or a regiment is offered on their discharge.

To boys not being orphans who are disqualified from entering the army on their discharge, a trade is offered.

A premium of £10 is paid with each boy bound to a trade and a further sum of £5 given as an award at the expiration of his apprenticeship if the Master to whom he is bound certifies to his good character.

With a boy who is fit for the Army but who prefers a trade no premium is paid.

In the case of a boy who under these circumstances is discharged to his friends, inquiry is first made as to their ability to maintain him and if they are unable to do so he is advised to let the institution provide for him.

Four days holidays are allowed at Christmas, Easter and Whitsuntide. The average number of boys whose friends avail themselves of this opportunity of taking them home is 170.

The officers of the Institution are

The Commandant	Col Brown
Chaplain	Rev G. Clark
Adjutant & Secretary	Capt Siborne
Quartermaster	Capt Byrne

| Surgeon | I. Lawrence |
| Assistant Surgeon | T. Hartwell |

The assistant officers and servants of the Institution are, the Serjeant Major of Instruction, Six school Serjeants, Two Trade Serjeants, One Serjeant Porter, Two Pioneer Corporals, a Drum Major, 22 Nurses and assistant Nurses.

The Commandant exercises a general superintendence and control over the interior economy of the Institution.

All the officer assistants and servants are subject to his orders and he is responsible for their conduct.

The Chaplain is responsible for the religious instruction of the Children and exercises a general supervision over their education.

The Adjutant and Quartermaster is charged with the administration of the discipline.

The task of instruction in secular knowledge devolves upon the School Serjeants.

The Children attend divine service in the Chapel twice on Sunday and on Monday morning and Friday morning.

On the afternoon of Sunday they are catechised by the Chaplain and he assembles the first fifty boys on two other evenings in the week for religious instruction.

Prayers are read in the dormitories and in the School rooms morning and evening.

The discipline is maintained under the direction of the Commandant and the Adjutant by the School Serjeants.

These men carry canes and are permitted to use them in respect to what are considered minor offences. Offences of a graver character are punished by flogging, by confinement in a cage or a black hole, by carrying a log chained to the person or by the drill.

The punishment of flogging is not inflicted except by the authority of the Commandant and in his presence.

A register of the punishments so inflicted has been kept since the appointment of Col Brown to that office.

I find by reference to this register that in the month which terminated with the 6th of April, 10 floggings of 12 stripes each were inflicted and 2 of 24 stripes and that in the preceding month of February there were inflicted 17 floggings each of 12 stripes.

It will afford your Lordship an opportunity to estimate that state of the discipline of which these facts afford the evidence if I inform you of the number of similar punishments inflicted in a twelvemonth in the Greenwich Schools.

I find that in the Lower School at Greenwich composed of 400 boys there were inflicted in the year 1844 only 21 such punishments and that in the whole School comprising the Nautical Upper and Lower Schools and containing 800 boys there were inflicted in that year 51 floggings. So that as many floggings were inflicted on 350 boys at Chelsea in the six weeks terminating with the 6th April last as upon the 400 boys of the Lower School at Greenwich in a whole twelvemonth. Or taking the whole of the Greenwich Schools, the number of floggings inflicted on 800 boys in a year is one fourth only of the number inflicted in the same time on 350 boys at Chelsea.

The punishments of the drill and the log are those most frequently resorted to. Six boys are on an average daily under the punishment of the drill.

From the 25th of March to the 29th of September the boys rise by beat of drum at 6 o'clock and from the 29th of September to the 25th of March at 7 o'clock.

They are allowed one hour to clean their shoes and to wash. A division of one third then devotes an hour to gymnastic exercises and the rest are occupied in domestic labours pumping water, carrying coals.

They breakfast at 8 o'clock in Summer and 9 o'clock in Winter. At 9 in Summer and at 10 in Winter they commence their studies and continue then until 12.

At 1 o'clock they dine.

From 2 until 4 in Summer and from 3 to 5 in Winter they devote again to the labours of the School.

At 7 o'clock in Summer and 6 o'clock in Winter they sup.

They retire to the dormitories at 6¼ o'clock in Winter and are locked up until 7 o'clock the next morning.

Diet Table Royal Military Asylum for one Child

Days	Breakfast	Dinner	Supper
Sunday	Milk potage Milk 1/6 of a quart Oatmeal 1/6 of a pd Bread 1/18 of a 4 lb loaf	Beef 8 ounces Potatoes 12 ounces Bread 1/18 of a 4 lb loaf Beer ½ pint	Bread 1/18 of a 4 lb loaf Cheese 1½ ounces Beer ½ pint
Monday	Ditto	Pudding suet 1½ ounces Flour 6 ounces Potatoes 8 ounces Beer ½ pint	Bread 1/18 of a 4 lb loaf Milk ½ a pint
Tuesday	Ditto	Ditto as for Sunday	Ditto as for Sunday
Wednesday	Ditto	Soup peas ½ a gill Potatoes 12 ounces Bread 1/18 of a 4 lb loaf Beer ½ a pint	Bread 1/18 of a 4 lb loaf Milk ½ a pint
Thursday	Ditto	Ditto as for Sunday	Ditto as for Sunday
Friday	Ditto	Ditto as for Monday	Ditto as for Monday
Saturday	Ditto	Mutton 8 oz & Potatoes 12 oz stewed Bread 1/18 of a 4 lb loaf Beer ½ pint	Ditto as for Sunday

NB The meat is estimated as taken from the butcher including bone. A proportion of the very small children on 6 ounces of meat.

I have ascertained from the above table the quantity of each article of food allowed *per week* to each boy and I have placed beside it in the following table the quantity of the same article of food allowed *per week* to a boy in the Greenwich Schools.

Diet per Week for each Child

	Royal Military Asylum, Chelsea		Royal Naval School, Greenwich	
	lb	oz	lb	oz
Bread and flour	4	15 5/9	7	11
Meat (incl suet)	2	3	2	16½
Potatoes	4	12	3	8
Oatmeal	0	7	0	0
Cheese	0	6	0	0
Sugar	0	0	0	3½
Cocoa	0	0	0	3½
Milk	3 5/6 pints		4 3/8 pints	
Beer	6½ pints		3½ pints	

The boys of the Greenwich Schools thus appear to be allowed 43½ more ounces of bread a week than those at Chelsea—being more than half as much again and 13½ more ounces of meat being one third more.

The average number of boys at one time in the Infirmary is at Chelsea out of 350 boys from 20 to 25. At Greenwich out of 800 boys it is (taken in respect to the whole of last year) 19. One boy died last year at Greenwich and six at Chelsea (and 3 the year before).

This disproportion in the number of cases of sickness and death in the two Institutions receives perhaps in some degree its explanation in the fact that of the boys at Chelsea 170 are under the age of 11 years whereas none are under that age at Greenwich.

Scofula [sic]* has been mentioned to me as among the most prevalent diseases at Chelsea and the children are described as remarkably subject to chilblains.

The task of instructing the children in all secular knowledge is intrusted to the School Serjeants. They have also the entire charge of them out of School hours.

Three of these men before they filled their present office were *Privates* in the Army—three others were non-commissioned officers. In respect to their qualifications for the responsible duty of instructing youth I have no other means of forming an opinion than that which is supplied me by the gross ignorance of the boys under their charge and by the information which the Chaplain has obligingly communicated to me in respect to them.

I learn from Mr Clark that they can read but know nothing of the 'stops'—that 'they can also write and know a little of arithmetic, but that the four first rules are as much as ever they can do' and that 'if they had been placed in a row before me and asked the same questions which I had addressed to the Children they would have been found equally unable to answer them'.

At the head of these six School Serjeants is the Serjeant Major of instruction, to whose qualifications for the duties with which he is entrusted I believe all that I have said of his subordinates to be equally applicable.

---

*Scrofula: a tuberculous disease of lymph nodes and of bone, with slowly suppurating abscesses.

A statement of the daily routine of the instruction of the boys has been put into my hands of which the following is a copy.

Table of the employment of a Class of boys in the Royal Military Asylum

	Morning	Afternoon
Monday	Work	Work
Tuesday	Read	Writing or ciphering
Wednesday	Work	Work
Thursday	Read	Writing or ciphering
Friday	Work	Work ¼ holiday
Saturday	Read	½ holiday

From this document I gather that the secular instruction of these boys is limited to reading, writing and arithmetic; and that being formed into two principal divisions they pass alternate days in the School rooms and the work shops.

No other trades are taught to them but tailoring and shoemaking and their labours in the workshops are limited to the work of the institution all of which is done by them. Many labourers however connected with the household department devolve upon the boys and I have reason to believe that the School business is greatly interrupted by them not only are the boys but the Serjeants also, frequently called from the School room to assist in the kitchen and the laundry. To such an extent indeed are their services required in the laundry that they would require the *constant* attendance of not less than eight of the boys there.

Music is taught from 10 o'clock in the morning until 12 to 70 boys of whom 40 compose the band and 30 are Drummers and Fifers. These boys go to school—every afternoon, being exempted from attendance in the Workshops. Whilst the other boys are discharged at 14 years of age these remain until they are 15.

There is no other drill—except for punishment—than a roll call of one quarter of an hour before each meal, when the boys are marched round in slow and quick time.

I found in these Schools none of the apparatus of instruction which I am accustomed to meet with in elementary Schools. There are neither black boards nor easels nor maps nor globes nor any other of the expedients for lightening the labours of the teacher, and aiding the intelligence of the scholar with which my eye had become familiar.

A lending library has been provided for the use of the boys. It contains 263 volumes generally of entertaining reading. Each boy in his 12th, 13th or 14th year is allowed the use of one of these books every other week so that on the alternate weeks he is without a book. The library contains no book which is not small enough to go into a boy's pocket, because he is allowed no box or locker or other place than his pocket in which he can deposit it with safety. The following is a list of the books used in the School rooms.

> Bible
> Prayer Book
> Church Catechism
> Walls' Short Catechism
> Bible Exercises
> Mrs Trimmer's Spelling Book
> Mrs Trimmer's Teacher's Assistant
> Manners of the Jews
> Mrs Markham's History of England

I do not find the subjects of instruction otherwise specified in the 'regulations' for the government of the Asylum, than by the following paragraph in that Section which prescribes the duties of the Serjeant Major of Instruction 'he shall cause them to proceed to the School business of reading, writing and the four first rules of arithmetic or such other employments as may qualify them for the duties of a soldier or for other subordinate stations in life.' Practically the secular Instruction of the children is limited to Reading, Writing and Arithmetic.

READING

I have examined individually 310 boys in reading. Of the remaining number of 20 boys 17 were in the infirmary.

I find that of those, 47 in number, who are in their 14th and 15th years and who have been resident on an average from 5 to 6 years, 10 only can read with tolerable ease and correctness in the Fourth Book of Lessons of the Commissioners of National Education in Ireland.* 25 could read the Epistles but could not read the Fourth Lesson Book. 12 could not read with ease and correctness in the Epistles but could read the Gospels.

Of those boys who being in their 13th year had been resident an average period of 4 years 8 could read in the 4th Book, 8 could read with tolerable ease and correctness in the Epistles but could not read in the 4th Book. 27 could read in the Gospels but not in the Epistles.

Of those 46 in number who being in their 12th year have been resident an average period of 3 years, 20 can read pretty well in the Epistles and 26 cannot. 17 can read with ease and correctness in the Gospels, 26 cannot.

36 in their 10th year resident and average period of 1 year. 7 can read in the Gospels, 27 cannot.

34 in the 9th year. 7 can read in the Gospels, 27 cannot.

31 in their 8th year. 13 read the Gospels fairly, 18 cannot.

30 from 6 to 8 years of age. 5 read easy lessons, 18 are beginning to read, 7 are in letters and monosyllables.

Thus it appears that out of the whole number of 310 boys whom I examined; 18—being 6 per cent—read tolerably well in the 4th Book; 77—being 25 per cent—in the Epistles; 118—being 38 per cent—in the Gospels.

Your Lordship will be enabled to estimate that degree of proficiency of which this statement affords the evidence by a comparison with the results attained in the Lower School at Greenwich composed of the Sons of Common Sailors as this School is of the Sons of Common Soldiers.

I find then, in respect to 265 boys who compose the three lowest classes of that School—many of whom entered the Institution without being able to read at all, none of whom have been resident more than 3 years and the great majority less than 2 years—that 111 read in the 5th Book, 52 read in the 4th Book.

In the first class composed of 120 boys none of whom have been resident more than 3½ years and a great majority less than 3 years *all* read the 5th Book.

Thus it appears that at Greenwich out of 400 boys 19/20ths of whom have been resident less than 3 years 283—being 71 per cent—can read the 4th Book, whilst at Chelsea out of 350 boys, nearly one half of whom have been resident *more* than 3 years and many more than 5 years, 18 only—being 6 per cent—can read the same Book.

WRITING AND SPELLING

That I might judge of the ability of the boys to write and to spell I caused those who were in their 12, 13th and 14th years to write respectively the three following paragraphs upon paper (by dictation).

By the Boys in their 14th year

'Besides those who work for their living some at a higher and some at a lower, there are others who do not live by their labour at all, but are rich enough to subsist upon what they or their fathers have laid up. There are many of them rich men indeed who do hold laborious offices as Magistrates and Members of Parliament—But this is at their own choice: they do not labour for their subsistence but live on their property.'

By those in their 13th year

'Some animals that feed upon fruits, which are to be found only at one time of the year, fill their holes with several sorts of plants which enable them to be concealed during the hard frosts of winter contented with their prison, since it affords them plenty and protection.'

By those in their 12th year

'The answer to this question in the Catechism "What desirest thou of God in this Prayer?" '

From the penmanship of these exercises which I enclose for your inspection I think myself mistified in expressing an opinion that no boy in the School can be considered to write a fair hand.

To afford your Lordship however the opportunity of forming a judgement on this matter by comparison I have caused 60 boys of the first class in the Lower School at Greenwich to write from dictation the same paragraph which was written by those boys of the Royal Asylum who are in their 14th year. I enclose those Exercises of the Greenwich boys. Their average time of residence is two years and 3 months—They will serve for a comparison of the spelling of the two Schools as well as the writing.

The average number of errors in spelling which the boys in their 14th year have made in writing out the paragraph which was read to them is 15 and no boy has written it with less than 4 errors. Many of them have not however written out the whole paragraph.

The Exercises of the boys of the 12th and 13th years are scarcely worse than those of the boys of the 14th year. I have indeed been struck with the remarkable uniformity in the attainments or, to speak candidly, the ignorance of these 3 classes of boys thus a year in advance of one another. It seems to show that when a certain stage is reached their education stands still, and that when a corresponding period in the history of the mind is attained it requires other food for its growth than is here ministered to it.

The boys of the Greenwich School in addition to the paragraph written by the boys of the Asylum have written that which follows it in the Book from which it was taken. Whilst the latter, who have been resident an average period of 4 years, in writing the single paragraph have made on an average 15 mistakes in spelling. Many of the former have written the two paragraphs without any error, and their average number of errors in writing them does not appear to exceed 3 or 4. They have been resident an average period of 2¼ years.

ARITHMETIC

To test the skill of the Boys of the Asylum in arithmetic I proposed to those in their 13th and 14th years the following sums.

1. Each line in a Book contains 45 letters, each page 27 lines, and there are 378 pages in the Book. How many letters are there in the Book
2. Find the cost of 6 tons of iron at 9s 4½ for 1 cwt 9qr.

The first of these sums was worked correctly by five boys in their 14th year. None of them was however able to explain the way in which he had worked it. No boy in the School could work the second sum.

I feel it would be a great injustice to the boys in their Greenwich School to institute any comparison between their skill in Arithmetic and that of the boys of the Military Asylum.

Summary in respect to the Technical Branches of Inspection

Looking at this School simply with reference to their technical instruction in reading, writing and arithmetic which according to the tenor of 'the regulations' is perhaps all that was contemplated in its Institution—I am of opinion that in the whole of my experience now extensive in the inspection of elementary Schools, I have visited none so little deserving of commendation; taking into my view that the State stands in the place of a *Parent* to the greater number of the children who compose it, that these children remain in it a period amply sufficient for the accomplishment of the highest purposes of Education, that it is maintained under public expense and may claim in those senses the character of a model on which the public education of the Country should be formed, I hesitate to give expression to the opinions I entertain in respect to it.

Looking at the class of persons from which the Chaplain is required to select his teacher, I consider that it would be unjust however to attribute its inefficiency to him.

I find a sufficient explanation of it in the 'regulations' under which the School is conducted and particularly in that regulation which limits the instruction to reading, writing and the first four rules of arithmetic. I have always observed that where little is aimed at in an elementary school that little is ill done. Where nothing but the technical branches of instruction in reading, writing and arithmetic are taught, there the children read badly, write ill and know but little of arithmetic—but that where a higher standard of instruction is taught and other elements of instruction are included in the course than these, *there* these lower branches are more perfectly taught. However anomalous this may appear it admits of an explanation and I can speak of it as a fact of which my experience supplies me with ample proof in many other schools and in those at Greenwich.

I believe therefore that whilst the total disqualification of the School Sergeants for the office of Instruction is one cause of the bad reading, writing and cyphering of the boys of the Military Asylum, another is that their Instruction is limited to those subjects.

A remarkable deficiency in general knowledge and intelligence is observable amongst the children. I have rarely pursued an official enquiry with sentiments of so much pain as that which I have thought it my duty to institute into the advantages these children have enjoyed in respect to the cultivation of that faculty which distinguishes them as intelligent beings, the capacity proper to their years to reflect, to reason and to understand.

I have found them entirely incapable of comprehending the lesson book, out of which

I caused them to read or, I believe, any portion of it. They cannot answer the simplest questions as to the meaning of the words which compose it; they do not possess that collateral knowledge which is necessary to the intelligence of its subject matter nor, had all these resources been at their command, would they I am convinced have been found to possess the power so far to fix their judgement as to collect from the greater number of its sentences the ideas they are intended to convey.

In reading, they make a measured pause after every word as in marching they stop after every step. In their manner of reading no reference whatever to the connection of the words is apparent or to the sense. No ray of intelligence lights up their faces as they read nor do they give any other sign of interest in what they read. I have taken no notes of the answers I received from them to questions suggested by the lessons they were reading. The following occur however to my recollection. As samples they will convey a more favorable impression than would have been derived from listening to the whole. Not any of these in their 14th year (some of them being band-boys were probably in their 15th year) could tell what was meant by the 'British Empire' and none of them who 'the immediate successor of David was' although they all knew perfectly well that the next King to David was Solomon. Some of them know a little of English History, but of the simplest Elements of Geography they are utterly ignorant and they know nothing of English Grammar—elements of instruction which are now common to almost every parish school in the Kingdom.

Something more is necessary for the Education of these children than for those of an ordinary school.
It is obvious that something more is required for the education of these children than for those of an ordinary school to bring them even to the *same* degree of intelligence. Admitted at a tender age, not allowed to pass the gates of the Asylum except for 4 days at 3 different times in the year and at least half of them orphans or friendless children for whom this privilege is never sought, the State takes upon itself in respect to them the entire responsibilities of a parent. Their case does not find a parallel in that of the child of an ordinary elementary school. That child by daily contact of its mind with the minds of its parents has at least some of the faculties of intelligence roused into constant activity and often greatly sharpened by that struggle with the physical elements of existence in which it is necessary that every member of the household should take a part. The parents too going daily into the world cannot fail to bring back with them some elements of general knowledge and diffuse it throughout the family. But it is not so with these children. From the moment they pass the walls of the Asylum every avenue to the external world closes upon them and all the knowledge they acquire must come to them through their teachers or not at all. To limit their instruction to reading, writing and arithmetic is thus to leave them with far less than half those means of education which other poor children possess. To supply to them through their teachers, nothing to reflect and to reason upon and to understand is to leave their powers of reflection, of reason and intelligence to stagnate.

To deprive a child of its freedom from an early age, to shut out from it the light of the sun, to minister to it insufficient element for the support of its body—by a process like this to check its physical development and dwarf its stature—would be an offence cognizable I believe by the laws.

It is only in this way that I can convey to you my sense of the injustice which has been done these children in debarring them almost from their infancy from every element of instruction proper to the growth of their intellectual life.

RELIGIOUS EDUCATION

Nothing appeared to me more worthy of observation than the extent to which the religious instruction of the children was impaired by the deficiency of their general intelligence.

I have rarely heard children questioned in religious knowledge with so much clearness and judgement as by Mr Clark, and as I listened to his examination it was impossible not to feel how redeeming a feature in the course of instruction of this place were the lessons of piety and virtue which these poor boys have so long been accustomed to receive from his lips. I can well understand that his admonitions have been carefully measured up and that when they recall in after life the period of their childhood to them too often alas—otherwise without a friend—the recollection of him is associated with all they have learned to love and to venerate.

Still it was impossible not to be struck with the remarkable character of simplicity which he was compelled to give to the questions he addressed to boys of 13 and 14 years of age and the difficulty which he experienced in eliciting from them any answer which required the slightest independant exercise of the judgement or intelligence. With respect to the principal facts of Scripture history they are well informed but I have found them imperfectly acquainted with the Catechism. In the existing stock of their secular instructions I believe indeed that it would be impossible to make them comprehend it.

I have been requested by your Lordship to report to you upon the extent of instruction and upon the degree of moral and religious *training* which the Institution affords. As to all that concerns the instruction Religious and Secular, I have now completed the task with which you have honoured me.

The question of the religious and moral training of the children is one on which I have a great difficulty in expressing an opinion. It is scarcely to be judged of except with other opportunities of estimating it than have been afforded to me.

So far as the personal influence of the Chaplain, so venerable for his years and his character, is concerned, nothing can be more favourable than the circumstances of religious and moral training in which the children are placed.

In respect to the School Serjeants with whom they are brought in contact far more intimately and more continually than with any other class of persons connected with the Institution, I have learned nothing unfavourable nor anything on the other hand to distinguish them favourably from the like number of non-commissioned officers and privates of good character who might be selected for another service.

I have no reason to suppose that the example of these men operates in any respect unfavorably for the highest interests of the children. Looking upon them in the light of agents in the religious and moral training of children I see in them however no fitness nor any qualifications proper to a moral action on the minds of the children nor are these likely in my opinion to be found in men of their class. So far as the amount of punishment inflicted may be supposed to afford an evidence of the moral and religious training of the institution I draw from it an unfavourable conclusion and I am desirous to call your Lordships attention particularly to one regulation the tendency of which is I conceive in this respect most prejudicial. It is that by which these boys many of them in their 14th and 15th years are locked up without light in their dormitories from 6½ o'clock in the evening in Winter until 7 the next morning.

A paper has been placed in my hands in which are recorded the characters of those soldiers at present serving in the Army who have been educated in this School. I am informed however that the characters here referred to are the *military* characters of the men and that no other element of the moral character than sobriety is usually included under the military characters so recorded.

In concluding the estimate I have been led to form of this School—an estimate far more unfavourable than that which I have ever recorded of any other—I am desirous to call your Lordships attention to the fact that the period during which the boys reside (an average period of five years) is amply sufficient for the full accomplishment of all those great purposes of religious influence and secular instruction which appear to me to have devolved upon the State, when in receiving these children—many of whom are orphans almost from their infancy—to look upon itself the whole responsibility of a parent in respect to them.

I am desirous to convey to your Lordships the sense I entertain of the courtesy and kindness which I have experienced from the Commandant, the Chaplain and the other officers of the Institution in answering the enquiries of which I have now recorded the results.

They have promoted the objects of my Inspection by every means in their power and answered the questions I have addressed them with the greatest candour.

> I have the honour to be,
> my Lords,
> Your Lordships' Most Obedient Servant
> (Signed) Henry Moseley

APPENDIX B

The following article was written by the Rev. G. R. Gleig for the journal *Edinburgh Review* and was published in April 1852, under the heading 'National Education No. 95'.

Some time in the summer of 1846, two gentlemen met on the deck of a river steam-boat, which was plying its usual course from the Nine Elms Pier to Hungerford Market. One was the late Lord Ashburton, better known to the monied and political world as Mr. Alexander Baring; the other was the Rev. G. R. Gleig, now Chaplain-General of Her Majesty's Forces, and Inspector General of Military Schools. There had occurred not long previously some modifications in Sir Robert Peel's Government, by which the present Lord Ashburton, then Mr. B. Baring, was transferred from the Board of Control to the Pay Office. The two passengers by the steam-boat touched many other topics of conversation upon this event, when Lord Ashburton remarked, that this son, though he could not refuse the advancement which had been pressed upon him, was little pleased with his change of office; because as Secretary to the Board of Control, he had been always engaged in important affairs of State, whereas at the Pay Office there was only routine business to attend to, and not very much of that. 'Does Mr. Baring really desire to undertake a great and a difficult work?' 'Certainly', was the answer, 'provided it be a useful one'. 'A useful work', and a great one too, even if it do not prove, as we anticipate that it will, the forerunner of another greater than itself, was immediately suggested.

Whatever may be thought of the military talents and statesmanlike opinions of the late Duke of York, nobody can deny that he was a kind-hearted and amiable man. He did great things for the army during his reign as commander-in-chief; and has a right to the merit of having established, as a place of refuge for the orphans of soldiers, the Royal Military Asylum at Chelsea. It was intended to be a home for these children, in every sense of the word, till they should attain the age of fourteen, when the boys were either to be apprenticed out to trades, or enlisted—while, for the girls, situations should be found as domestic servants, or in factories. But, besides clothing, feeding, and otherwise taking care of them, it was determined to educate both classes after the most approved fashion: and Dr. Bell, being then in the height of his popularity, organised the school, and watched over it anxiously. Finally, the desire to educate grew with what it fed on. No sooner were the Asylum children taught to repeat by rote so many words in the hour without understanding them, than His Royal Highness determined to extend a similar boon to the children of soldiers actually serving; and one or more non-commissioned officers from each corps being transferred to Chelsea, learned there all that Dr. Bell undertook to teach and sent back again to communicate the results of their training to their regiments.

Time passed, and year by year, the Commissioners of the Asylum entered in their minute book, records of the flourishing state of the institution. The masters and mistresses were described as attentive and able; the general discipline was mild; the children were healthy, happy, and of good report; the system, as regarded both nurture and education, was perfect. It is true, that on the female side of the house, things occasionally went wrong. Comparatively few of the girls reared there turned out well; indeed, the sore became at last so malignant, that the Commissioners quietly resolved among themselves to receive no more female children into the place. But boys continued to be admitted, though in progressively diminishing numbers, down to the period of which we now write; and there could be no doubt, taking the minute-book as an authority, that their lot was in every respect an enviable one.

There are people in the world who have an awkward trick of distrusting even official documents. The teachers in the Asylum were known to be discharged sergeants, who frequented the low public-houses that abound in that locality, and whose manner of expressing themselves in common conversation was not such as to create a very lively impression of their aptitude to communicate to others either literary tastes or urbanity of manners. A glance within the rails, likewise, exhibited a set of poor, thin, wanfaced, spiritless looking children, many of whom had their heads covered with black silk caps—a sure token of disease—while not a few wandered about dragging heavy logs which were fastened with chains to their ankles. Such outward and visible signs did not very accurately correspond with the inward and spiritual grace of which the Commissioners boasted; and doubts of the reality of the latter multiplied themselves. How far these were or were not well-founded, will best appear from the following narrative, which we are enabled to give on the very best authority.

A few days after the conversation in the steam-boat, noticed above, Mr. Baring, then Paymaster-General of the Forces, called upon Mr. Gleig, and the two gentlemen proceeded together to the Asylum. No announcement having been made of their intention to visit the place, they found it in what may be called its every-day dress. It was school hour, yet to and fro numbers of boys were passing—along the walks and about the corridors, some laden with baskets of coals, some carrying filthier utensils, some bearing provisions, some sweeping out the colonnade in front of the building. A large wheel was then used for the purpose of raising water, by the process of the forcing-pump, from certain underground tanks to the top of the house. Three or four unfortunate boys were at work upon this wheel, straining beyond their strength, and in constant risk, should they lose their hold, of having their limbs broken; while others, in the kitchen, seemed to be kept to the tether by the not very euphoneous oratory of the cook, and an occasional box on the ears. Our visitors, after noticing these things, penetrated through the door-way, and were greeted by sounds of the strangest and most discordant kind. The hoarse harsh voices of men rose, occasionally, above the hubbub of children, both being from time to time drowned in the crash of many ill-tuned instruments. Then would come the sound of a smart blow, followed by a shriek; and succeeded by what startled and shocked as much as either, a brief but profound silence. This was not a very promising commencement of their proper business, but it did not deter the visitors from going through with it. They mounted the stairs, opened the schoolroom door, and became witnesses to a scene which neither of them, we should think, is likely to forget in a hurry. The schoolroom was a huge hall, measuring perhaps sixty or eighty feet in length by thirty in breadth. Two enormous fireplaces, so constructed as to consume an immense quantity of fuel without diffusing any proportionate amount of heat, testified to the good intentions of the architect, however little they might vouch for his skill. In other respects the fitting up was meagre enough. A single platform, whither, when the writing lesson came on, the children by classes were supposed to repair, occupied about twenty feet in the middle of the room. All the rest was void, except where chairs stood for the accommodation of the masters; and cages for the punishment of the boys. For in addition to the cane, which these sergeant-masters appear to have used very freely, they had at their command four instruments of torture, in the shape of iron cages, each occupying a corner of the room. Observe, that these cages were so constructed, as to render it impossible for the little prisoners to stand upright; who were nevertheless required to turn a heavy handle continually; and whose diligence or its opposite was marked by a process, which if they did not see it, they never failed to feel.

The visitors, if painfully surprised at the ornamental arrangements of this place of study, were still more amazed by beholding its machinery at work. Four or five groups of boys were gathered round as many sergeant-masters, some bawling out sounds, which were not words, though they intended to represent them; some roaring forth arithmetical tables; some repeating the Church catechism at the top of their voices; some conversing and all shuffling and struggling, among themselves. There was no order, no regularity, no attention; indeed, the latter would have been impossible, inasmuch, as in the very heart of the classes was one, more numerous than the rest, which seemed to be taking lessons on the fiddle. It was altogether one of the strangest, and in spite of other and more bitter feelings, the most ludicrous scenes, which school examiners were probably ever called upon to witness. As to the acquirements of these poor lads, their proficiency proved on examination to be exactly such as might have been expected. They had learned nothing. They could not read, they could not write, they could not cipher, they could not spell. They did not know whether Great Britain was an island, or how, if divided from France at all, the two nations were separated. 'We can't help it, Sir', said one of the sergeant-schoolmasters, when appealed to on the subject of his school. 'We never learned these things ourselves. How can we pretend to teach them?' The Paymaster-General of the Forces had seen enough. He repaired at once to the War Office, over which Mr. Sidney Herbert then presided, and Mr. Gleig being called in as amicus curiae, the work of reform began.

The work of reform is not easy of accomplishment under any circumstances. A proposal to remodel the Asylum amounted, in the present instance, to a vote of censure on Commissioners, commandant, chaplain, doctor—on everybody, in short, who had heretofore been charged with the management of that institution. It was resisted, of course, both openly and covertly; but it was carried. In like manner, a project of annexing to the boys' school a normal or training institution for regimental schoolmasters raised a storm in the camp. The Horse Guards became seriously alarmed; the army astounded. What had soldiers to do with book-learning? They did not want people who could read and write—such were nuisances in the ranks. Mischief enough had been done by the abolition of corporal punishment. If the schoolmaster were brought into cantonments or garrisons, there would be an end of military discipline in a year. The liberal-minded and thoughtful men, who had taken up a wise project, listened patiently to all these remonstrances, and over-ruled them. The Asylum was remodelled. There was appended to it a training institution for regimental schoolmasters; and the experience of five years has exposed fully, and to the conviction we believe of all parties, the groundlessness of the alarm with which the undertaking was at the outset contemplated. Not only has discipline not been relaxed in the army, it has been braced up. Crime is less frequent than it used to be; men's manners are softened, their very language taking a different tone, in exact proportion to the progress of education among them. And we are happy to say that to be educated has grown into a fashion. So at least we collect from the evidence of Mr. Fox Maule, the able and indefatigable successor of Mr. Sidney Herbert at the War Office, before the late Committee on Military Expenditures, by which this important subject was very fully investigated.

'Do you find', asks Sir James Graham, 'that where schoolmasters (meaning school-masters trained at Chelsea) have been sent, there is a willingness on the part of the men to avail themselves of the advantages of going to school?'—'To such an extent that the schoolmasters complain that they are overworked, and have no time to themselves; that they cannot overtake the demands made upon them for instruction. The men come to the school in such numbers, and with such a desire for instruction, that we have been obliged, in some instances, to grant the school-master an assistant, for the purpose of overtaking the demands upon him'.

'Then, from your experience, as far as it has gone, your opinion is, that when each regiment shall have had the appointed establishment of instructors, the soldiers generally will avail themselves of that advantage, and that the system of instruction will be complete throughout the British Army?'—'I am certain that when the system shall be thoroughly spread over the whole army, there will not be a body of better instructed men in any service in the world than in the British Army'.

'With your knowledge of the British Army, have you a confident belief that that instruction will tend to the easy maintenance of discipline without severity?'—'I am quite certain it will; and what is more, I am quite sure of this, that with the limited enlistment bill, whereby a man can enter the service at eighteen, and, if he pleases, leave it at twenty-eight, he may enter it with all the ignorance that is to be found, either in the towns or in the most ignorant rural districts of England, but he will have an opportunity, of which I believe he will avail himself, (from the great length of time a soldier has on his hands) of making himself a thoroughly well-educated man, fit to find his way in the world, in any capacity'.

'What is the quality of the instruction provided?'—'The quality of the instruction is very high. In the first place, it is rudimental for children, and after those rudiments it goes on to history, sacred and of all other descriptions, geography, geometry, arith-metic, mathematics, as high up as algebra, and even into higher branches. It conveys instruction in mensuration and fortification [sic]. Those who are capable of being instructed in a short time are instructed at the Military Asylum, to a certain extent, in drawing.'

'You have sent forth twenty-three masters from the Normal School; have those masters, when sent forth, undergone a strict examination in every branch of knowledge which they are to teach?'—'They have undergone a strict examination in every branch of knowledge; they are all fit, and they are certified to me by the master of the school, and by the Inspector-General of schools, not only as being perfectly acquainted with all those branches, but as being perfectly competent to teach all those branches'.

So much for the opinion of one who is as competent as most persons to judge of the probable effects, in a moral point of view of education in the Army. Let us see next what is said upon the subject by gentlemen actually in command of corps, and belonging, as such to a class, among whom 'the fear of change' wrought, as might have been expected, no small tribulation at the outset of the measure.

Mr. Mills to the Secretary of War, 'Can you state the number of scholars educated in the garrison and regimental schools?'—'That is not a question I can answer at present; but with reference to that subject I should wish to state shortly in what condition those schools are at present, and I think it a statement which will be very interesting to the Committee. The Training or Normal School in the Royal Military Asylum, Chelsea, was opened in the spring of 1847, with thirty civilian students. In the spring of 1849 five trained masters went out; one to the depot for recruits to the Guards, at Croydon, one to Weedon, one to Preston, one to Plymouth, and one to Horfield, near Bristol; all as garrison schoolmasters. In the autumn of 1849, a second batch of seven went out, and were attached to the 13th Regiment at Belfast, the 14th at Newport, the 21st at Edinburgh, the 30th at Manchester, the 40th at Dublin, the 52nd at Preston, and the 93rd at Stirling. In the winter of 1849, a third batch of six went out to the 4th regiment at Portsmouth, the 48th at Dublin, the 57th at Enniskillen, the 1st battalion of the 71st at Naas, the 92nd at Clonmel, and the 12th Lancers at Cork, respectively. Besides these, trained masters have been appointed to the 19th regiment in Canada, the 72nd at Trinidad, and to the 84th and 87th in India. Serjeant Barnes, trained at Chelsea, was removed from the 12th Lancers discharged, and re-enlisted under the new system, and settled at Balincolig. Wherever a trained master goes, the number of adults attending school increases rapidly. Take, as instance, the 12th, 21st, 28th, 39th and the 40th regiments, where the adult scholars have advanced from a very small figure to 108, 150, 128, 153, 180, and 171, respectively. Several school-rooms have been erected, and existing buildings have been adapted to school purposes, in sixteen different stations. As we go on supplying the different stations with convenient places of study, the system will more develop its excellences. The same books and implements are used in all the schools. With reference to the good effects likely to be produced in the ranks from the general adoption of the system, I beg leave to read an extract of a letter from Lieutenant Colonel Browne of the 21st Fusiliers'.

Mr. Hume: 'Of what date is it?'—'I have not got the date, but it is very lately; it is since he received a schoolmaster from the training school. He says, "The schoolmaster is behaving admirably; and the new system of education has already had a visible effect on the regiment in many ways. Many men have been able to fit themselves for promotion, who were previously unable to do so; others have learned to read and write, and have found occupation for time which used to be spent in public houses. It is very popular, and next to the good conduct warrant, is, I think, the greatest boon the army has received since I entered it. Experience has convinced me, that crime diminishes in proportion as men have rational occupation and comfort in their quarters. We have had very few defaulters during the past month, and in six days, none; which is very unusual in a place like Edinburgh, and is, I think, to be attributed to the school, and the occupations attendant on it." '—'What force has Colonel Browne?'—'I think the force of the regiment is about 700 men.'

'In the same strain we have letters from Lieutenant Colonel Stuart of the 13th, from Lieutenant Colonel Magennis of the 27th, Lieutenant Colonel Patton of the 12th, from Lieutenant Colonel Stretton of the 40th, and from Lieutenant Colonel Spark of the 93rd.'

Mr. Maule gave his evidence and quoted his authorities, so long ago as February 1850. Many additional masters have since gone out from Chelsea, and the reports of their proceedings and of the results attendant on them, do not, as we are given to understand, vary from the preceding. No doubt in regiments, as well as in civil life, much must depend upon the care that is taken of such institutions by those in authority. If commanding and other officers either discountenance the schools, or, which is quite as injurious, treat them with neglect, it would be absurd to expect that they should flourish. But instances of this sort are, we believe, rare; and hence the success of the system, so far as it has been carried, seems to be complete. We must look a little more closely than we have as yet done into the constitution of these schools, and their consequent fitness for the classes of persons among whom they have been established.

The British Army is composed of men taken, generally, from the lower orders of society. With few exceptions our recruits are composed of agricultural labourers and operatives out of work; to whom may be added a small sprinkling of tapsters, clerks, scriveners, serving men, and broken down young gentlemen. They come to us from all parts of England, Scotland and Ireland, and profess as many forms of Christianity as are to be found among the five and twenty millions of human beings which together make up the sum of the population of the United Kingdom. After four or five years' service a large proportion of them marry, and their children are of course brought up in the religious opinions of their parents. So that, upon the whole, you could not find gathered together in any one place, a more perfect epitome of religious England, Scotland and Ireland than in a regiment of the line. Indeed, if there be any difference between the religious condition of a regiment and that of a civil community of similar magnitude, the bias is against the regiment. There is a larger proportion of Roman Catholics in our service than you will find anywhere out of Ireland; indeed, the balance of numbers may be said upon the whole to agree very nearly with that presented by the population of the three kingdoms; about one fourth of our soldiers are Romanists, and of the remaining three-fourths, one, if not more, belongs in part to the Church of Scotland, and in part to other denominations not in conformity with the Church of England.

The business of the school—we mean of the children's school—opens every morning in barracks at a quarter before nine o'clock with prayer. This may occupy, perhaps, five minutes, after which the trained master reads to his scholars, collected together, a portion of Scripture, and explains it in its grammatical and historical bearing; deducing from the whole such a lesson in moral and religious truth as it seems to convey. He touches, in so doing, upon no topic of sectarian controversy. He has been trained to speak as the Scriptures speak, without casting about for inferences which lie beneath the surface.

The children assemble at a quarter to 9 o'clock. The Master reads a few verses of Scripture, then Prayers. The Master gives a Bible-lesson to the whole School; at the close of which the children fall off to their classes.

The subjects taught are, besides elementary reading:—

   Scripture History
   England
   Colonies
   India
   Greece
   Rome
   France
   Arithmetic, Slate and Mental
   Geography
   Natural History
   Object lessons
   Grammar: Dictation and Composition
   Writing

   All from Gleig's Series

The school hours for the men necessarily vary according to the demands that duty makes upon their time. Generally speaking, volunteer privates attend from two to four in the afternoon—non-commissioned officers and recruits from four to six, when they are instructed in reading, writing, and arithmetic. But there are extra lessons, especially in the winter evenings, for such as desire to proceed into higher branches, and geography, mathematics, algebra, and fortification are then studied. The same class-books are used in the adult as in the children's school; and the master not unfrequently gives lessons in mechanics, natural history, and such like. Nobody is forced to go to school, and everybody pays for the instruction which he himself receives. There is, indeed, a graduated scale, which exacts more from the sergeant than from the corporal, more from the corporal than from the private, and more from the private than from his son or daughter; but everybody pays—the sergeant eight pence, the corporal six pence, the private soldier four pence, per month. On the same principle the children pay according to the numbers from each family admitted into school: one child four pence, two children sixpence, three children, and all above three, eight pence monthly.

What is there to prevent the adaptation of this system, modified of course, in its details, to the acknowledged wants of a nation composed, like its army, of persons professing many creeds, yet all alike willing to be taught, provided their favourite opinions be dealt with tenderly? Popular prejudice, we shall be told, which, taking the name of popular opinion, would drive from his place any minister who should have the hardihood to take the lead in such an enterprise, or even openly to approve of it. We wish that some minister would pluck up heart to dare the adventure. We are confident that it would prove, like many others, far more perilous in appearance than in reality.

APPENDIX C

The following questionnaire was sent to ex-boy soldiers who responded to the many appeals in international journals and military publications. Many happy, sad, stupid and hilarious things were the experiences of ex-brats during their boy service. The total experience has barely been tapped. Perhaps readers have experiences as striking as some of those recorded in this book. You can take part in the growing record by writing to me, Art W. Cockerill, c/o Martin Secker & Warburg Ltd, 54 Poland Street, London WiV 3DF.

Name: Date of birth:
Year & age service began: Unit:
Length of service: Rank (present or attained):
Students of Military Schools: Year joined:
School: Trade:
House/Div/Company: Current address:

Respondents are asked to answer these questions in detail:

1   Was boy soldiering a worthwhile experience? Yes or no; say why.
2   Would you describe your boy soldier life as harsh or cruel?
3   Describe the discipline in force in your day. Were you ever flogged, birched or caned? If so, why? What about barrack law?
4   Were you ever a witness to a drumming out parade? If so, provide details.
5   What were the circumstances of your enlistment into boy service?
6   Were you following a family tradition? Was your father or were brothers boy soldiers? What can you say of the soldier history?
7   What anecdotes have you of boy soldiering?

NOTES

Introduction

1 McKee, Alexander, *Caen*, 1964.
2 McKee, ibid.
3 McKee, ibid.
4 Carter, Thomas, *Curiosities of War*, 1860.

Chapter 1: Devils and Demons

1 Fortescue, J. W,, *History of the British Army*, 1910.
2 Hanford, S. A., translation of *Caesar: Conquest of Gaul*, 1951.
3 Markale, Professor J., *Celtic Civilisation*, Paris, 1976.
4 Kinsella, Thomas, translation *The Tain*, 1969.
5 Kinsella, ibid.
6 Kinsella, ibid.
7 Kinsella, ibid.
8 W. R. Paton, translation of Polybius's *The Punic Wars*, Cambridge, 1960.
9 Warner, Rex, translation of Thucydides' *The Peloponnesian War*, 1954.
10 Plutarch's *Lives* (Life of Alexander).

Chapter 2: Medieval Apprentice Soldiers

1 Ffoulkes, Charles, *Inventory and Survey of the Armouries of the Tower of London*, 1916.
2 Burne, Alfred H., in *The Crécy War*, 1955.
3 Burne, ibid.
4 Burne, ibid.
5 Preston, Prof. Richard A., Duke University.
6 Webb, Henry J., in *Elizabethan Military Science*, 1965.
7 Fortescue, J. W., in *History of the British Army*, 1910.
8 Fortescue, ibid.
9 Prof. Richard A. Preston considers this an unjust view of Elizabeth because, he contends, there is no evidence that she treated discharged soldiers any worse than her predecessors had done. His view will be shared by many.
10 Bradford, Ernle, *The Great Siege*, 1970.
11 My ideas on Shakespeare's lost years are derived from Duff Cooper's *Sergeant Shakespeare*, 1950.
12 Cooper, ibid.
13 Cooper, ibid.
14 Cooper, ibid.

Chapter 3: A New Beginning

1 Markham, Clements R., in *The Fighting Veres*, 1888.
2 Markham, ibid.
3 Munro, Robert, in History of the McKay Regiment.
4 Munro, ibid.
5 Noted from state papers held at the Public Records Office, at Kent. Specific PRO reference unfortunately lost.
6 Fortescue, J. W., *A History of the British Army*, 1910.
7 Fortescue, ibid.
8 Laffin, John, quoted in his *Tommy Atkins*, 1956.

Chapter 4: A Push from Corporal John

1 Fortescue, J. W., in *A History of the British Army*, 1910.
2 Fortescue, ibid.
3 There may be confusion in the minds of some readers between boy officers and boy soldiers. All are boy soldiers, some more privileged than others. I have attempted to distinguish between the two when there is need to avoid lumping them together.
4 Rogers, H. C. B., in *The British Army of the Eighteenth Century*, 1977.
5 I have drawn on the knowledge of Lieutenant-Colonel W. Heard, Curator of the RCMI Museum, Toronto, for this description of early manufacture of the Brown Bess musket. Later manufacture of the weapon in Birmingham is acknowledged.
6 Lieutenant-Colonel W. Heard also provided this description of the manufacture of gunpowder.
7 Lieutenant-Colonel W. Heard, ditto.
8 Fortescue, ibid.
9 Fortescue, ibid.
10 Laffin, John, quoted in *Boys in Battle*.
11 Frey, Professor Sylvia R., in paper 'Courts and Cats' (*Military Affairs Journal*, February 1979).
12 Frey, ibid.
13 Frey, ibid.
14 Barnes, Major R. M., in *Regiments and Uniforms of the British Army*, 1950.
15 Barnes, ibid.

Chapter 5: Scabby Sheep

1 Fortescue, J. W., *History of the British Army*, 1910.
2 Fortescue, ibid.
3 Rogers, H. C. B., in *The British Army of the Eighteenth Century*, 1977.
4 Duncan, F. P., in *History of the Royal Artillery*, 1879.
5 Atkinson, C. T., in *The South Wales Borderers*, 1937.
6 White, A. C. T., in *The History of Army Education, 1643–1963*, 1963.
7 Rogers, ibid.
8 Duncan, ibid.
9 Duncan, ibid.
10 Duncan, ibid.
11 Fortescue, ibid.
12 Forster, Margaret, in *The Rash Adventurer*, 1973.

Chapter 6: Gentlemen from Virginia

1 Craig, Neville B. (editor), in *Memoirs of Major Robert Stobo*, 1854.
2 Craig, ibid.
3 Craig, ibid.
4 Craig, ibid.
5 *History of the Inniskilling Dragoons*, author unknown, circa 1880.
6 Quoted by Laffin, John, in *Boys in Battle*, 1967.
7 Barker, A. J., in *The History of the Yorkshire (East Riding) Regt*, 1971.
8 Gurney, Russell, in *The Northamptonshire Regiment*, 1935.
9 Hawkins, F. and Roberts, D. W., in unpublished ms on the Royal Hibernian Military School (RHMS), Dublin, 1964.
10 Hawkins-Roberts ms ibid.
11 Hawkins-Roberts, ibid.
12 Stark, J. H., quoting the historian Grodon in *The Loyalists of Massachusetts*, Boston, 1910.
13 Washington's Writings, Vol. III.
14 Hawkins-Roberts, ibid.
15 Johnson, ibid.
16 Johnson, ibid.
17 Atkinson, C. T., *History of the South Wales Borderers*, 1937.
18 Quoted in *The Revolution Remembered*, 1980, ed. John C. Dann.
19 In *The Revolution Remembered*.
20 In *The Revolution Remembered*.
21 In *The Revolution Remembered*.
22 Washington's writings. Vol. III.

Chapter 7: Likely Lads

1 Robinson, H. B., in the *Life of Sir T. Picton*, 1836.
2 Fuller, J. F. C., in *Sir John Moore's System of Training*, 1924.
3 Robinson, ibid.
4 Thompson, E. P., in *The Making of the English Working Class*, 1963.
5 Duncan, F. P., in the *History of the Royal Artillery*, 1879.
6 Parker, Rowland, in *The Common Stream*, 1975.
7 Parker, ibid.
8 Thompson, ibid.
9 Hawkins-Roberts ms.
10 White, Lieutenant-Colonel A. C. T., *Tommy Atkins' Children*, 1963.
11 Burns, A., in *The Noble Duke of York*, 1949.
12 Laffin, John, in *Tommy Atkins*, 1956.
13 Fuller, J. F. C., in *British Light Infantry in the Eighteenth Century*, 1925.
14 PRO Doc. WO 3/18.
15 Advertisement quoted in the *Journal* of the Army Historical Research Society.
16 Shipp, John, *Memoirs of the Military Career of John Shipp*, 1843. Shipp quoted a figure of 1,000 boys per regiment. While he quoted three (the 22nd, 34th and 56th Regts of Foot), there were five (the others being the 9th and 16th); 4,000 such boys is therefore a conservative figure.
17 Shipp, ibid.
18 PRO Doc. WO 3/17/325.
19 PRO Doc. WO 1/10/84.
20 PRO Doc. WO 3/19/130.
21 PRO Doc. WO 14/485/76.
22 PRO Doc. WO 4/196/127.

23 PRO Doc. WO 14/485/76.
24 Royal Charter for the Royal Military Asylum, Chelsea.
25 Bryant, Arthur, quoted in *Jackets of Green*, 1972.
26 Bryant, ibid.
27 *Recollections of Rifleman Harris*, edited by H. Curling, 1848.
28 *The Letters of Private Wheeler*, edited by B. H. Liddell-Hart, 1951.
29 *Private Wheeler*, ibid.
30 PRO Doc. WO 1/1119/451.
31 PRO Doc. WO 3/119/304.
32 McNally, Sir Henry, in *The Irish Militia 1793–1816*, 1949.
33 Irish House of Commons, Act 52 Geo. iii, Chap. 29.

Chapter 8: Field Army Brats

1 Williams, H., *The Life of Wellington* (3 vols), circa 1860.
2 Shipp, John, *Memoirs*, 1843.
3 *The Letters of Private Wheeler*, edited by B. H. Liddell-Hart, 1951.
4 McFarlane, John 'Peninsular Private', Society for Army Historical Research *Journal*, Vol. XXXII, 1954.
5 McFarlane, John, *A Bugle of the 71st*, circa 1830.
6 Miller, Sergeant Benjamin, the adventures of, in Vol. VII, AHR *Journal*.
7 Gwynn, Stephen, *A Brotherhood of Heroes*, 1910.
8 McFarlane, ibid.
9 Gurney, Russell, *The Northamptonshire Regiment*, 1935.
10 Carter, Thomas, *Curiosities of War*, 1860.
11 Laffin, John, quoted in *Boys in Battle*, 1967.
12 Napier, Charles, *Battles of the Peninsular*, 1904.
13 Napier, ibid.
14 Reference source mislaid.
15 Carter, ibid.
16 Williams, ibid.
17 Williams, ibid.
18 Albemarle, Lord, *Fifty Years of My Life*, circa 1860.
19 Albemarle, ibid.
20 Albemarle, ibid.

Chapter 9: Sons of the Brave

1 Punishment books 1850–70, DYRMS.
2 Roberts-Hawkins ms on the RHMS.
3 Roberts-Hawkins ms.
4 Roberts-Hawkins ms.
5 Royal Warrant on the RHMS, 1808.
6 Roberts-Hawkins ms.
7 Royal Warrant for Royal Military Asylum (DYRMS), 1901.
8 Commandant's 'Report to the Board of Governors', 1823.
9 Commandant's Letter Books, Royal Military Asylum, 1805–18.
10 Letter addressed to William Merry, Deputy Secretary at War.
11 Commandant's Letter Books, Royal Military Asylum, 1845.
12 PRO Doc. 43/796/749.
13 'National Education' article in *Edinburgh Review* for June 1852.
14 PRO Doc. 43/796/749.
15 Wellington's letter to Sidney Herbert, Secretary at War, June 1846.
16 PRO Doc. WO OS/108290.

17 Roberts-Hawkins ms.
18 Roberts-Hawkins ms.
19 Roberts-Hawkins ms.
20 Punishment books 1852, Royal Military Asylum.
21 Petition *For A Soldier's Son* (application for entry form), 1937.
22 The figures quoted here are computed from the known returns of the Duke of York's, regular returns being made by those units in which ex-boys from the military schools served. Figures for the RHMS are no longer available.

Chapter 10: Badgie Wallahs

1 Related by Lieut-Col W. Heard.
2 Clarke, Colour Sgt J., *Adventures of a Leicestershire Veteran*, 1893.
3 Holland, John, corres.
4 Holland, ibid.
5 Dobbs, Major J. J., corres.
6 MacKenzie-Rogan, Lt-Col J., *Fifty Years of Army Music*, 1929.
7 Bancroft, Staff Sgt N. W., *Recruit to Staff-Sergeant*, Calcutta, 1885.
8 Hodson, Major V., Soc. Army Hist. Research, Vol. VI.
9 Dutton, A., corres.
10 Dutton, ibid.
11 Dobbs, ibid.
12 Whitehouse, Capt. Sidney E., corres.
13 MacKenzie-Rogan, ibid.
14 Shipp, John, *Memoirs*, 1843.
15 Shipp, ibid.
16 Bancroft, ibid.
17 Ryder, Cpl, *Four Years Service in India*, 1853.
18 Fitchett, W. H., *The Tale of the Great Mutiny*, 1901.
19 Fitchett, ibid.
20 Carter, Thomas, *The Curiosities of War*, 1853. However, Carter was apparently in error in reporting Bugler Hawthorne to be aged 16 when he won the VC. Rose E. B. Coombs, Special Collections Officer, Imperial War Museum, reports that Hawthorne was a mature man at the time.
21 Lord Roberts in his memoirs.
22 Fitchett, ibid.
23 Fitchett, ibid.
24 Carter, ibid.
25 Coombs, Rose E. B., corres.
26 MacKenzie-Rogan, ibid.

Chapter 11: High-water Mark

1 DYRMS Chronicles, Vol. II, No. 16.
2 Interview with ex-Dukie.
3 Mayham, Bglr W., letter dated 29 February 1900, DYRMS Chronicles.
4 Harper, Bglr A. J., undated letter, DYRMS Chronicles.
5 Harper, ibid.
6 Davies, Bglr R. J., letter dated 9 February 1900, from Stellenbosch Chronicles.
7 Clayton, Dmr G., undated letter written at Bloemfontein, Chronicles.
8 Item reported in DYRMS Chronicles, Vol. II, No. 13.
9 Furnish, Cpl A. G., undated letter written at Bloemfontein, Chronicles.
10 Clayton, Dmr T., letter dated 25 December 1899, Chronicles.
11 Hammond, Dmr J., letter 15 January 1900, Isle of Wight, Chronicles.

12 Ratcliffe, Dmr W., letter 1 March 1900, De Aar.
13 Macken, Cpl J., letter 29 January 1900, Modder Farm, Chronicles.
14 Wilde, Tptr Frank, undated letter, Chronicles.
15 Wilde, ibid.
16 Craig, Bglr John, letter 11 July 1900, Natal, Chronicles.
17 Craig, ibid.
18 Wilde, ibid.
19 Trump, E. and Yearsley, George A., letter 1 May 1900, Cape Town, Chronicles.
20 The Canadian naturalist, scientist, and author Ernest Thompson Seaton, from whom Baden-Powell derived most of his ideas on scouting, actually started the scouting movement in the 1870s.
21 DYRMS Chronicles, Vol. III, No. 3.

Chapter 12: Johnny Canuck

1   Mayham, Bglr W., letter 29 February 1900, DYRMS Chronicles.
2   Stanley, George F. W., WO Doc. quoted in *Canada's Soldiers*, Toronto, 1960.
3   Stanley, ibid.
4   Squires, W. Austin, *The 104th Regiment of Foot*, New Brunswick, 1962.
5   Capan, Alan R., *Stories of Prince Edward County*, Belleville, 1971.
6   Capan, ibid.
7   Collishaw Papers 1-C 79 Sqdn, Canadian DND.
8   Henley, WO I R. E., corres.
9   Taylor, Allison, *Oral History of Wm. E. Taylor's Life in the Great War*, 1982.
10 Beck, W., corres.
11 Beck, ibid.
12 Malone, Major J. E., corres.
13 Cloutier, Captain C. E., corres.
14 Cloutier, ibid.
15 Farmer, Captain E. W., corres.
16 Farmer, ibid.
17 Fowler, D. E., corres.
18 Roy, Prof. R. E., corres.
19 Doc. S 8891 FD3, Canadian DND Military Records.
20 DCGS (a) letter 3 October 1942 Canadian DND Military Records.
21 Phipps, WO I L., corres.
22 Phipps, ibid.
23 Phipps, ibid.
24 Phipps, ibid.
25 Doc. D. Hist. PN303-63 Canadian DND Military Records.
26 Morgan, WO I R., corres.
27 Morgan, ibid.

Chapter 13: Easy Grace Down Under

1   Cartoon by Booth, *Bulletin*, 23 May 1912.
2   Barrett, Prof. John, *Falling In*, Sydney, 1979.
3   Barrett, ibid.
4   Barrett, ibid.
5   Edwardson, Lt-Col I. H., Royal Australian Army, corres.
6   Barrett, ibid.
7   Thompson, R., corres.

Chapter 14: A4 Soldiers

1   Holland, John, corres.
2   Dall, A. H., corres.
3   Ebdon, Frank, corres.
4   Ebdon, ibid.
5   Watson, Coun. Joseph J., corres.
6   Burgess, Fred, corres.
7   Waters, John M., corres.
8   Corke, Captain Henry, corres.
9   Waters, ibid.
10 Julian, Major Roy, corres.
11 Corke, Major C. E., corres.
12 Benford, Ben, corres.
13 Luckett, Don, corres.
14 Bradley, Capt. John, corres.
15 Thompson, John, corres.
16 Rawlinson, Cyril, corres.
17 Rawlinson, ibid.
18 Dobbs, Major J. J., corres.
19 Luckett, ibid.
20 Bradley, ibid.
21 Morrison, Major Phil., corres.
22 Corke, H., ibid.

Chapter 15: Hard Tack and Discipline

1   Bradley, Capt. John, corres.
2   Davidson, Major W., corres.
3   Dobbs, Major J. J., corres.
4   Luckett, D., corres.
5   Luckett, ibid.
6   Rawlinson, C., corres.
7   Dobbs, ibid.
8   Corke, Captain H., corres.
9   Limbu, Lt R., VC, *My Life Story*, Gurkha Welfare Trusts.
10 Gregory, Lieut-Colonel H. C. S., corres.
11 Holland, John, corres.
12 Corke, ibid.
13 Scholfield, D. S., corres.
14 Davidson, ibid.
15 Burgess, F., corres.
16 Rawlinson, ibid.
17 Hassel, J., interview.
18 Stephens, T. G., corres.
19 Davidson, ibid.
20 Shorter, G., interview.
21 Luckett, ibid.
22 Corke, ibid.
23 Hassel, ibid.
24 Rawlinson, ibid.
25 Davidson, ibid.

Chapter 16: Jack's Lump

1 Reported by Capt. H. Corke, RE.
2 Dutton, E. A., corres.
3 Stephens, T. G., corres.
4 Stephens, ibid.
5 Bradley, Capt. J., corres.
6 Ashdown, Major C. G., corres.
7 Adams, W., corres.
8 Butler, P., corres.
9 Jones, P., corres.
10 Jones, ibid.
11 Ashdown, ibid.
12 Butler, ibid.
13 Dutton, ibid.
14 Dutton, ibid.
15 Moon, WO II J., corres.

Chapter 17: The More Things Change . . .

1 *Miller Report*, 1955.
2 *Miller Report*.
3 Nye, General Sir A., letter, July 1954, in Royal United Services Institution Journal.
4 Barry, F., corres.
5 James, WO II R., corres.
6 Wiggins, WO I D., corres.
7 Taylor, WO I T., corres.
8 Wiggins, ibid.
9 Kennelly, R., corres.
10 Carol, WO II A., corres.
11 Carter, Sgt G., corres.
12 Corcoran, Sgt R., corres.

PRINCIPAL SOURCES

Manuscripts

Canadian Department of National Defence, Historical Records Section, Ottawa,
 Collishaw Papers 1-C79 Squadron. Doc. S8891, D. Hist. PN303-63, and DCGS (A)
 Letter 3 Oct., 1942.
Commandants' Letter Books of Royal Military Asylum, 1805–1845.
Order (Punishment) Books of Royal Military Asylum, 1850–1870.
Royal Warrants (1801 and 1901) of Royal Military Asylum.
Chronicles of the Duke of York's Royal Military School.
Manuscript (unpublished) on Royal Hibernian Military School.
Royal Warrant for Royal Hibernian Military School.
Petition, *For A Soldier's Son*, Duke of York's Royal Military School, 1937.
The Miller Report, 1955.
Ms Oral History of *Wm. E. Taylor's Life in the Great War* by A. Taylor, 1982.
Public Record Office: WO 1/10/84, WO 1/1119/451, WO 3/17/325, WO 3/18, WO
 3/19/130, WO 3/119/304, WO 4/196/127, WO 14/485, WO 43/796/749, OS/108290.

Journals

Journal of the Society for Army Historical Research
The Bulletin (Australia)
Gurkha Welfare Trusts
Military Affairs Journal
Royal United Services Institute Journal
The Edinburgh Review
Stories of Prince Edward County
Journal of the Military History Society of Ireland

Published books

(Unless otherwise noted, works quoted were published in London.)

Albemarle, George Thomas, Earl of: *Fifty Years of My Life*, 1877
Alberts, Robert C.: *The Most Extraordinary Adventure of Major R. Stobo* (Boston), 1965
Alexander, A.: *The Life of Alexander Alexander* (Edinburgh), 1830
Ancell, Samuel in 'A Circumstantial Journal of the Long and Tedious Blockade and
 Siege of Gibraltar from the Twelfth of September 1779 to the Third of February
 1783' quoted by McGuffie, T. H. in *Rank and File*, 1964
Atkinson, C. T.: *Marlborough and the Rise of the British Army* (New York), 1921
Atkinson, C. T.: *The South Wales Borderers, 1689–1937*, 1937
Bancroft, N. W.: *From Recruit to Staff Sergeant* (Calcutta), 1885
Barnard, W. T.: *The Queen's Own Rifles of Canada 1860–1960* (Don Mills, Ontario),
 1960

Barnes, R. M.: *Regiments and Uniforms of the British Army*, 1950

Blakeney, Robert: *A Boy in the Peninsular War*, 1899

Bland, H.: *Treatise of Military Discipline*, 1759

Bradford, Ernle: *The Great Siege*, 1961

Bryant, Arthur: *Jackets of Green*, 1972

Burne, A. H.: *The Noble Duke of York*, 1949

Carter, Thomas: *Curiosities of War*, 1860

Clark, J.: *Adventures of a Leicestershire Veteran* (Leicester), 1893

Cooper, T. M.: *A Practical Guide to the Light Infantry Officer*, 1806

Cope, Sir William H.: *A History of the Rifle Brigade*, 1877

Corbett, A. F.: *Service Through Six Reigns 1891 to 1953*, 1953

Craig, Neville B.: *Memoirs of Major Robert Stobo*, 1854

Darling, Anthony D.: *Red Coat & Brown Bess* (Bloomfield), 1978

Duncan, Francis P.: *History of the Royal Artillery*, 1879

Dupin, Charles: *View of the History and Actual State of the Military Force of Great Britain* (Toronto), 1804

Dupuy, R. Ernest and Dupuy, Trevor N.: *The Encyclopedia of Military History* (New York), 1977

Fitchett, W. H.: *The Tale of the Great Mutiny*, 1901

Forster, Margaret: *The Rash Adventurer*, 1973

Fortescue, J. W.: *A History of the British Army*, 1910

Foughnan, Thomas: *A Soldier's Life*, 1869

Frey, Sylvia R.: 'Courts and Cats', 1979

Fuller, J. F. C.: *Sir John Moore's System of Training*, 1924

Fuller, J. F. C.: *British Light Infantry in the Eighteenth Century*, 1925

Gleig, G. R., Rev.: *The Life of Wellington*, 1907

Glover, Richard: *Peninsula—Preparation* (Cambridge), 1963

Gowing, T.: *Voice from the Ranks*, 1954

Gronow, Captain: *Recollections and Anecdotes*, 1872

Gwynn, Stephen: *A Brotherhood of Heroes*, 1910

Hall, P. E. A.: *The Winged Messenger*, 1981

Harris, John: *The Gallant Six Hundred* (New York), 1973

Harris, Rifleman: *Recollections of Rifleman Harris*, 1848

Hendry, W.: *Events of a Military Life*, 1843

Johnson, David: *Napoleon's Cavalry and Its Leaders*, 1978

Johnston, Arthur: *Myths and Facts of the American Revolution* (Toronto), 1908

Jones, R. V.: *Most Secret War*, 1978

Kinsella, Thomas: *The Tain* (Dublin), 1969

Laffin, John: *Tommy Atkins*, 1956

Laffin, John: *Scotland The Brave*, 1963

Laffin, John: *Boys in Battle*, 1967

Lawford, J. P. and Young, Peter: *Wellington's Masterpiece*, 1972

Liddell Hart, B. H.: *The Letters of Private Wheeler*, 1951

MacKenzie-Rogan, J.: *Fifty Years of Army Music*, 1936

Markale, J.: *Celtic Civilisation* (Paris), 1976

Markham, Clements R.: *The Fighting Veres*, 1888

McFarlane, John: *Peninsular Private*, 1954

McGuffie, T. H.: *Rank and File*, 1964

McNally, Sir Henry: *The Irish Militia 1793–1816*, 1949

Miller, Benjamin: *The Adventures of Sergeant Benjamin Miller 1796–1815*

Morris, Christopher: *The Tudors*, 1955

Morton, Desmond: *Ministers and Generals* (Toronto), 1970

Motley, J. L.: *History of the United Netherlands* (New York) 1861

Moorson, W. S.: *Historical Record of the 52nd Regiment*, 1860

Napier: *Napier's Battles of the Peninsula*, 1904
Naylor, John: *Waterloo*, 1960
O'Donnell, H.: *Historical Records of the 14th Regiment*, 1893
Oman, C. W. C.: *Wellington's Army 1809–1814*, 1913
Palmer, A.: *Frederick The Great*, 1974
Parker, Rowland: *The Common Stream*, 1976
Robinson, H. B.: *Memoirs of Sir T. Picton*, 1836
Rogers, H. C. G.: *The British Army of the Eighteenth Century*, 1977
Ryder: *Four Years Service in India* (Leicester), 1853
Selby, John: *Gentleman's Battle* (New York), 1970
Sherer, J. W.: *Havelock's March on Cawnpore*, 1910
Shipp, John: *Memoirs of the Military Career of John Shipp*, 1843
Shipp, John: *The Path of Glory*, 1969
Squires, W. Austin: *The 104th Regiment of Foot*, 1962
Stanley, George F. W.: *Canada's Soldiers* (Toronto), 1960
Stark, James H.: *The Loyalists of Massachusetts* (Boston), 1910
Thompson, E. P.: *The Making of the English Working Class*, 1963
Thucydides: *The Peloponnesian War*, 1954
Turner, E. S.: *Gallant Gentlemen*, 1956
Webb, Henry J.: *Elizabethan Military Science* (Wisconsin), 1965
Williams, Lieutenant-Colonel: *Life of Wellington*, circa 1860
White, A. C. T.: *The History of Army Education 1643–1963*, 1963
White, A. C. T.: *Tommy Atkins' Children*, 1963
Whitworth, Rev.: *Field Marshall Lord Ligonier* (Oxford), 1958

INDEX